I0729631

CRASH BANG

Pictures from a Punk

For my wife, Wini.
Thank you for encouraging me to do this, and for everything else.

DB Burkeman

As a DJ, I've occasionally been credited (or blamed depending on your point of view) for bringing Jungle to New York and then helping spread the DNB and Rave virus across the US. But before becoming DJ DB, I had another life.

As a kid growing up in London, I was an escapist. First, by disappearing into TV shows and comic books, and then from about 11 or 12, by adding chemical substances into the mix. By the time I was 14, I lived in an egocentric fantasy land. When daydreaming about my future, I saw myself as a rockstar, but considering I was musically talentless, combined with having major social anxiety, watching myself on TV along with the nation on Thursday night's *Top of the Pops* wasn't exactly in the cards. So I came up with the genius idea of being a rockstar photographer. I could still feel important and literally hide behind a sexy camera. So at 16, with absolute delusions of grandeur and against serious parental and teachers' advice, I dropped out of school. I was going to be the next David Bailey, Helmut Newton, or Irving Penn, or even better, a combination of all of them.

My mom, God bless her, reached out to a pair of commercial photographers she knew and cajoled them into giving me an assistant job. Of course, I wasn't happy with my assigned duties, dropping rolls of film off to labs and making cups of tea for their clients. After two weeks, these guys announced they were going on a work trip for 10 days. They left me with the keys to the studio along with very simple instructions about which contact sheets go to which magazine offices on which days. More importantly, they were having the studio floors re-polished and sealed,

and no one was to walk on them until they returned. Naturally, wanting to impress my girlfriend and all her friends, I threw a party. When the photographers returned, they were greeted by a stack of undelivered contact sheets along with several Converse Chuck Taylor footprints hardened into their new floors. Justifiably, these guys wanted to kill me. That story pretty much typifies my teenage self.

By 18, I was trying to get work as a freelance photographer. A pattern had now also emerged where my parents would roll their eyes when I told them I had a job shooting for some band, as it normally ended in me fucking it up somehow and costing my dad money. I had also now graduated from all the so-called soft drugs and was dabbling with narcotics. The interesting thing about Heroin is that it felt like I'd finally found the magic potion. I became calm, focused, and confident. Also, this was 1977 – the Punk scene in London had a junkie faction with a very specific New York-influenced style that I thought was cool as fuck.

I carried my camera with me everywhere, taking photos of friends in the streets as well as bands at night. My all black Olympus OM-2n also served as a fashion accessory, giving me an identity I believed I lacked.

In 1978, my friend Toby and I took a road trip across America. Some of the photos that sat undeveloped until recently are from our stay in New York and an exhilarating, if not turbulent, 10 days in what appeared to be ground zero of LA's punk scene, the Canterbury Apartments aka *The Punk Plaza*. We met several bands living, or possibly squatting there. We were told that

The Canterbury had once been homes to the likes of Frank Sinatra and Marilyn Monroe. Judging by the rancid state of the place, we theorized that Frank and Marilyn had been the names for someone's pet cockroaches. Being English and maybe cute, we were adopted by girls in bands as somewhat of a novelty. One night we were taken to a space (possibly the Masque) where I believe we witnessed The Go-Go's very first show.

During my year in New York in '79, I suspect that a lot of the incredible places I was given access to – parties, backstage areas, staying at the Chelsea Hotel, and the amazing people I met – Sid Vicious, Nico, Johnny Thunders, etc., all happened because of the drugs. It's true to say there were brilliant moments, but within two years of that first blissed-out high, I became just another lying, cheating, stealing, dope-fiend.

Towards the end of the book, some may recognize Kit Lambert – the manager of The Who and music biz legend – in the filthy flat on a couch that, like him, had seen much better days. That photo was possibly the last ever taken of him, as I believe he died a week after my sad portrait.

While punk rock was the most exciting thing to happen in my lifetime, I was too self-centred, or maybe just too high, to be aware of the seismic shift it was causing in so many aspects of culture. Even superficially, within one year, every young person in the UK had chopped off their long hair, thrown out their flares and now pretended they'd never liked Genesis or Yes.

Crash Bang is a time capsule of pictures taken between 1976 and 1982 – the year I finally got clean and also gave up the delusion that I could be a successful photographer. Without the dope, I was never going to have the self-confidence to be intimate enough with people to make it work.

After my family spent five years terrified, not knowing whether I was going to survive another accidental or deliberate OD, they could finally sleep at night. They were also relieved I was putting my rockstar photographer idea to bed, hoping I might make a more normal nine-to-five type life for myself. I'm not sure rave DJ was exactly what they had in mind.

After my mom died a few years ago, I went back to London and cleared out my old bedroom. I found a bag of 35mm rolls of film I'd never developed. The truth is, getting high was more of a priority than seeing what I'd shot, so any disposable income I had went towards self-medicating. Most of the images in this book I'd not seen since clicking that shutter 40-odd years ago.

I'm proud of the photos and excited that they are finally getting real exposure, though I do feel like a lot were simply right place/right time. They also really needed a talented designer like Sammie Purulak to make them presentable. I was just a punk with a camera.

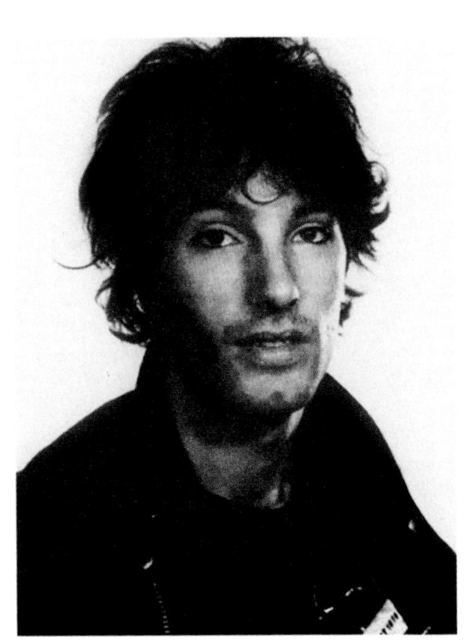

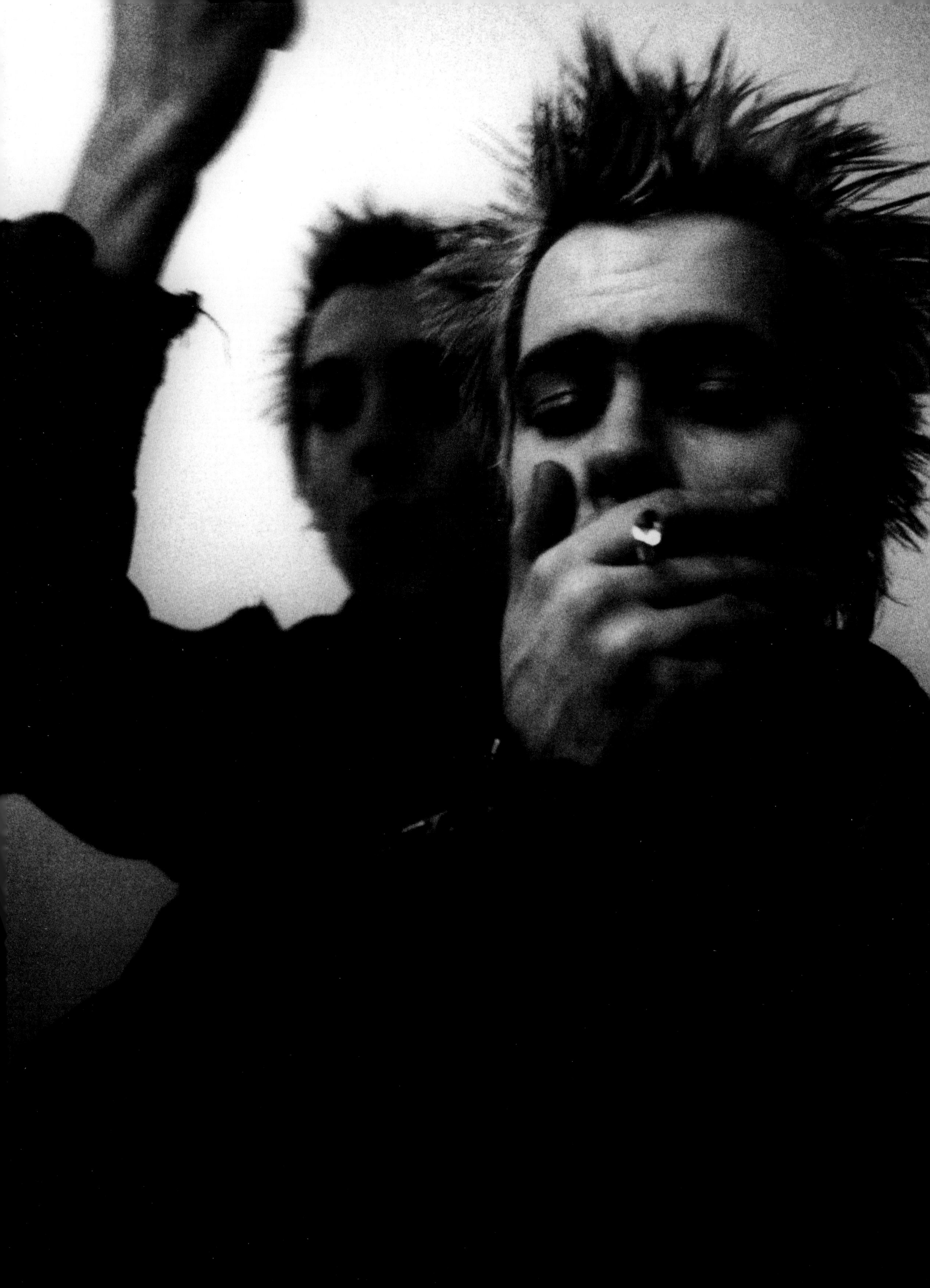

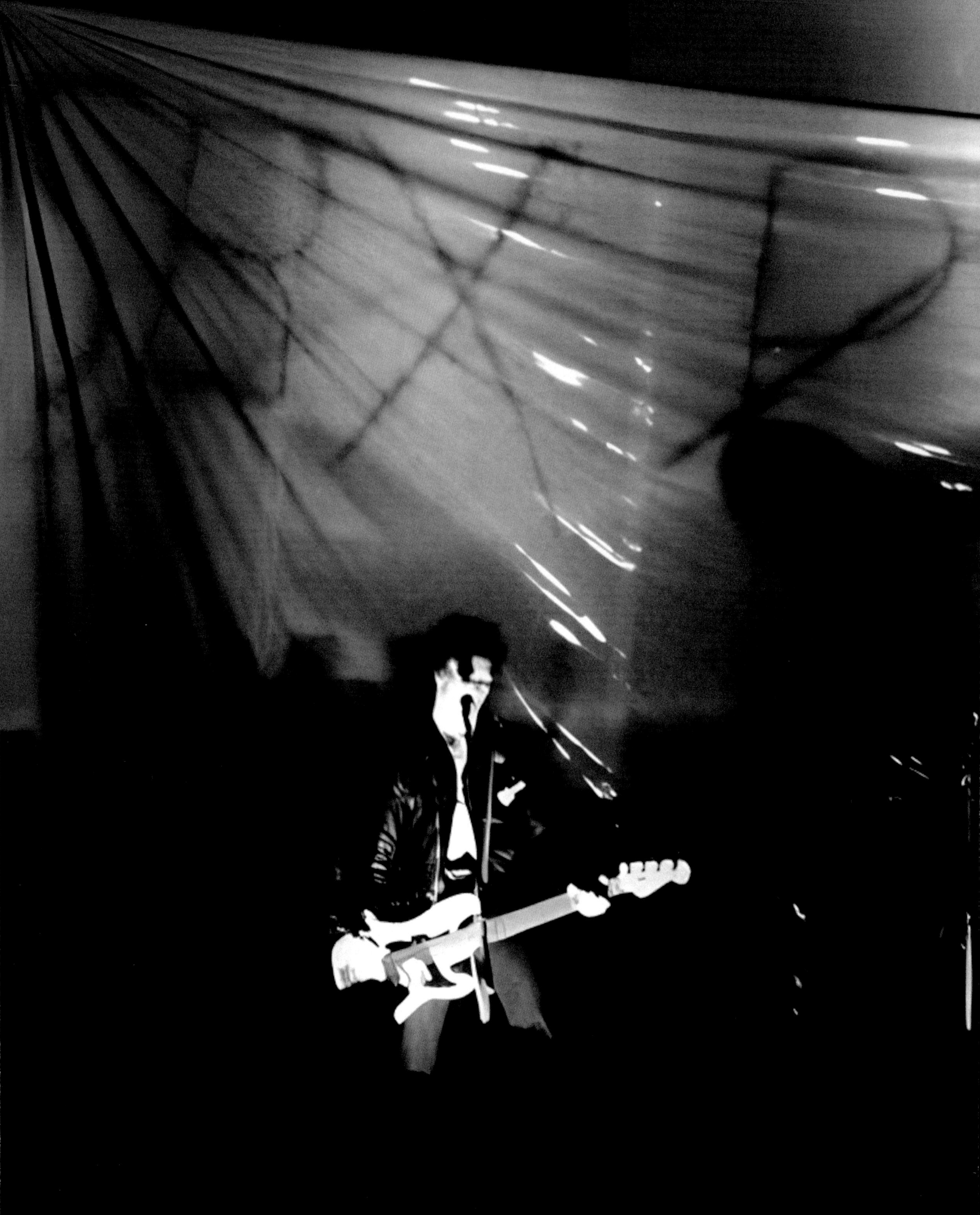

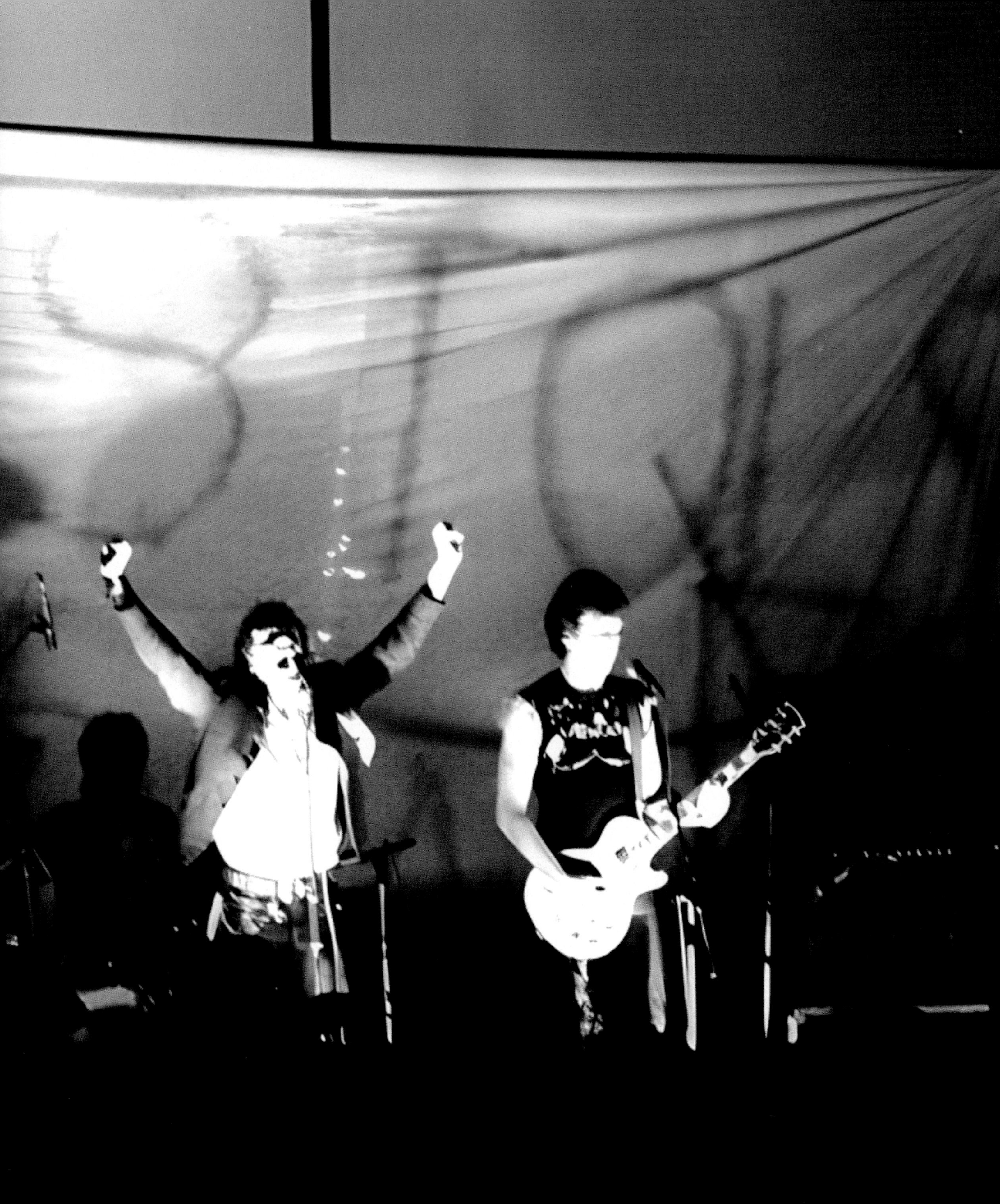

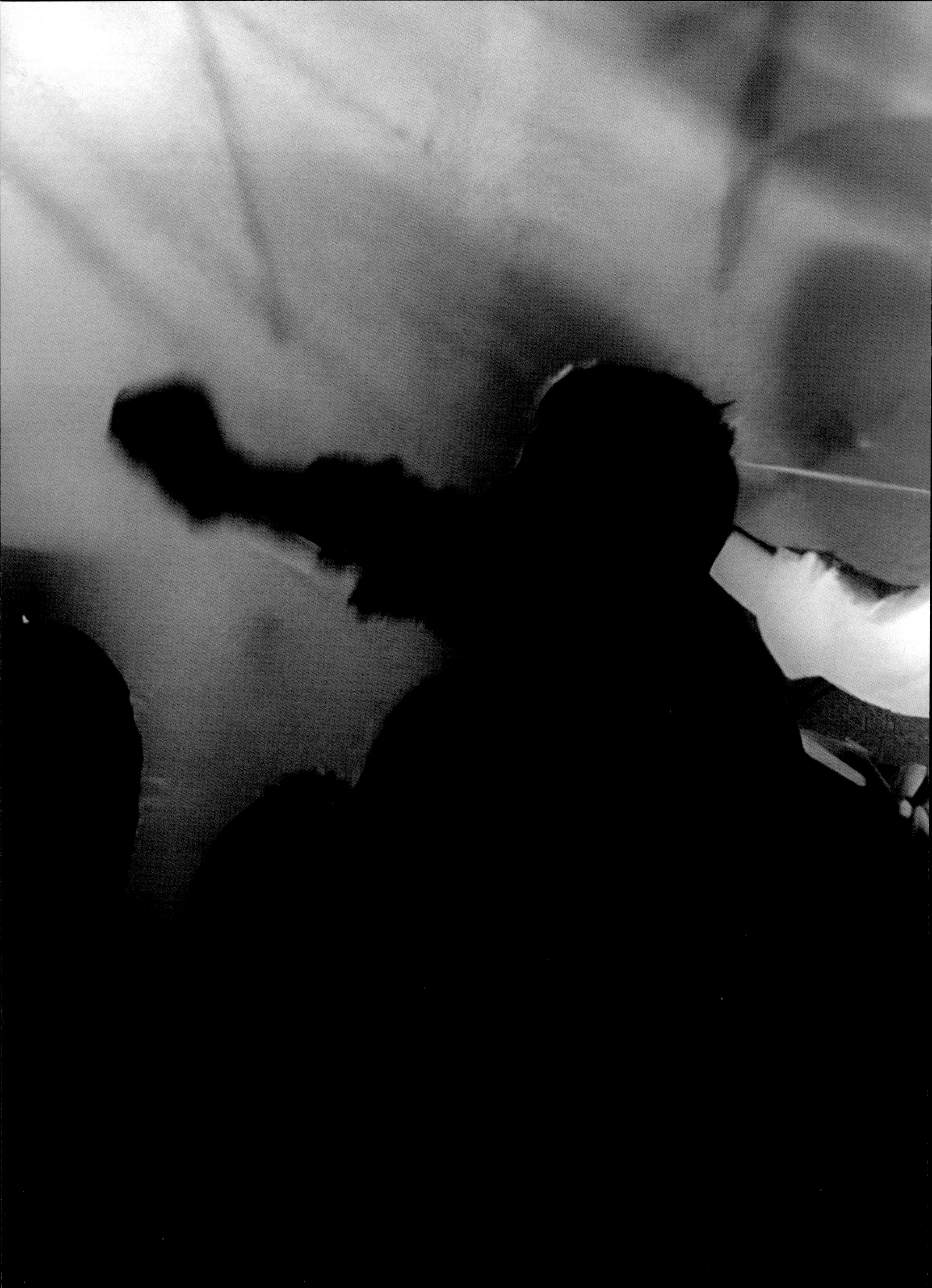

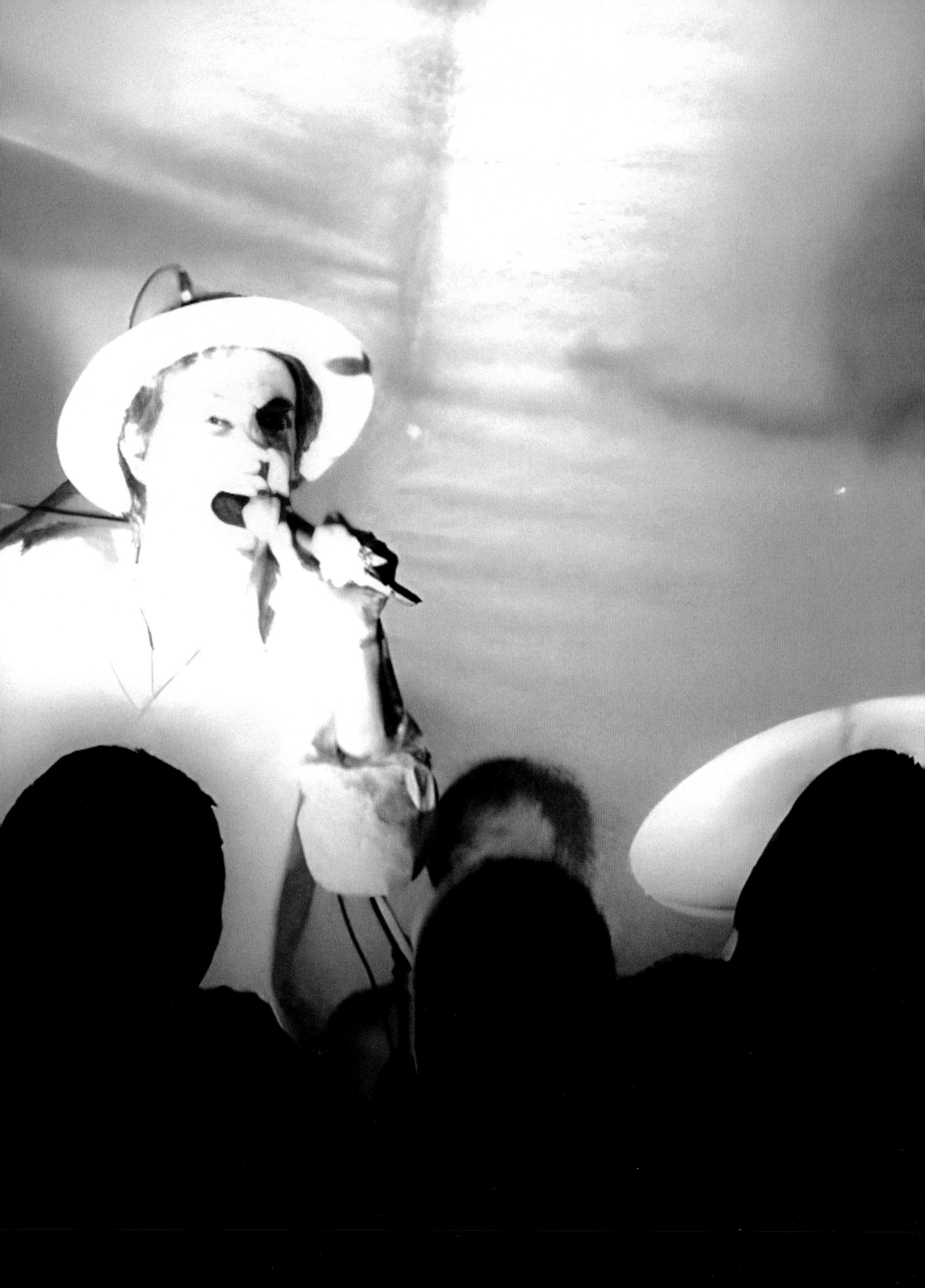

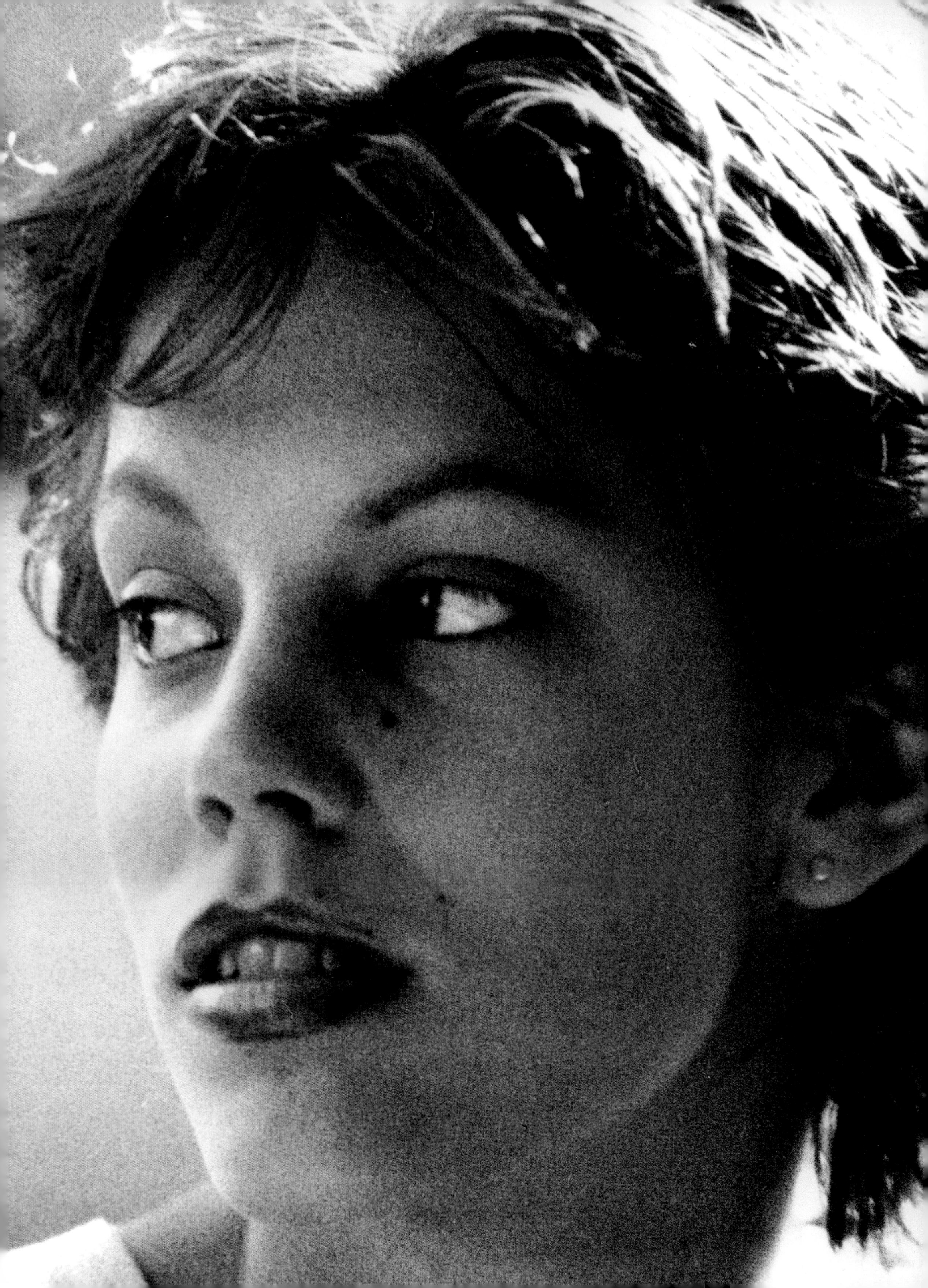

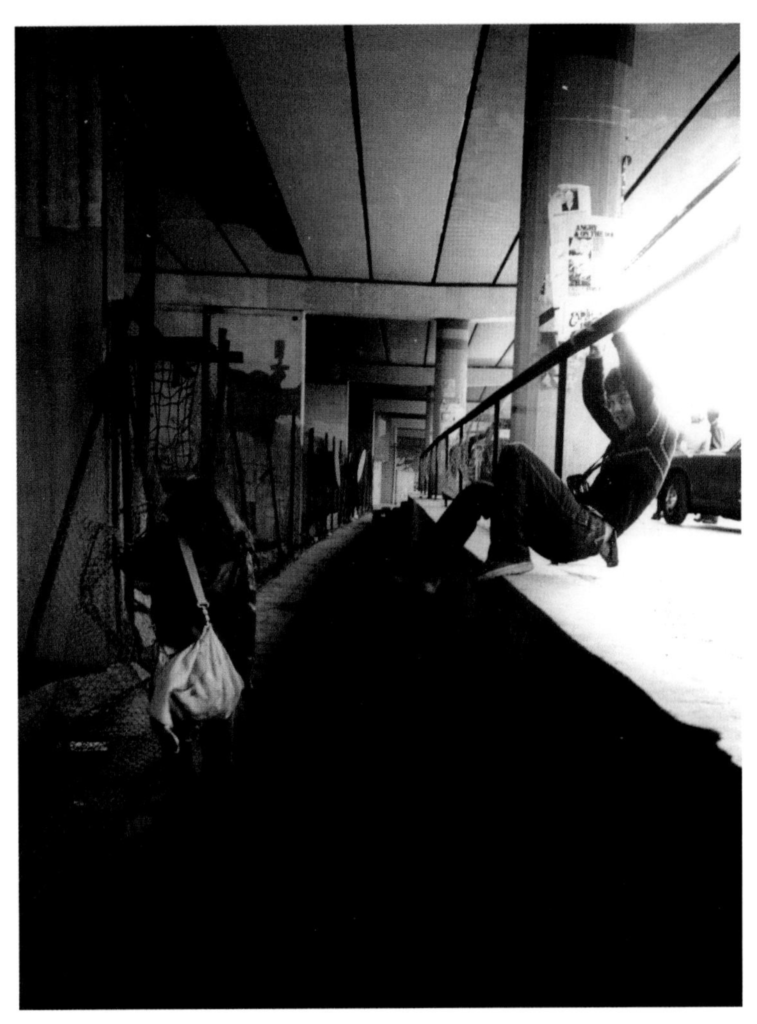

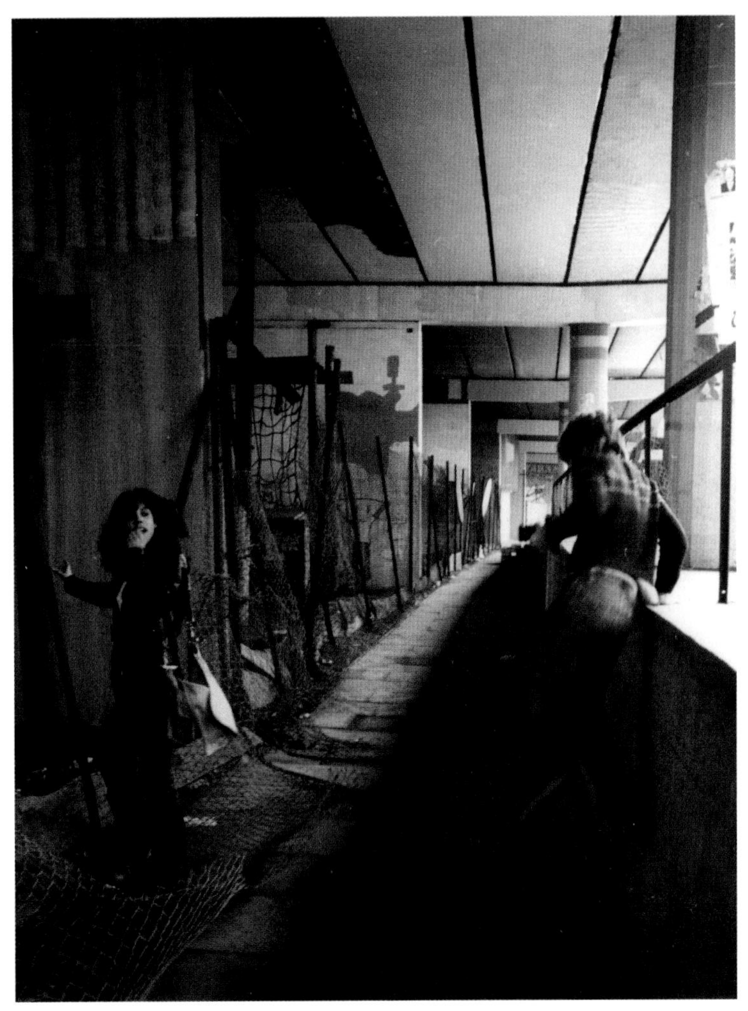

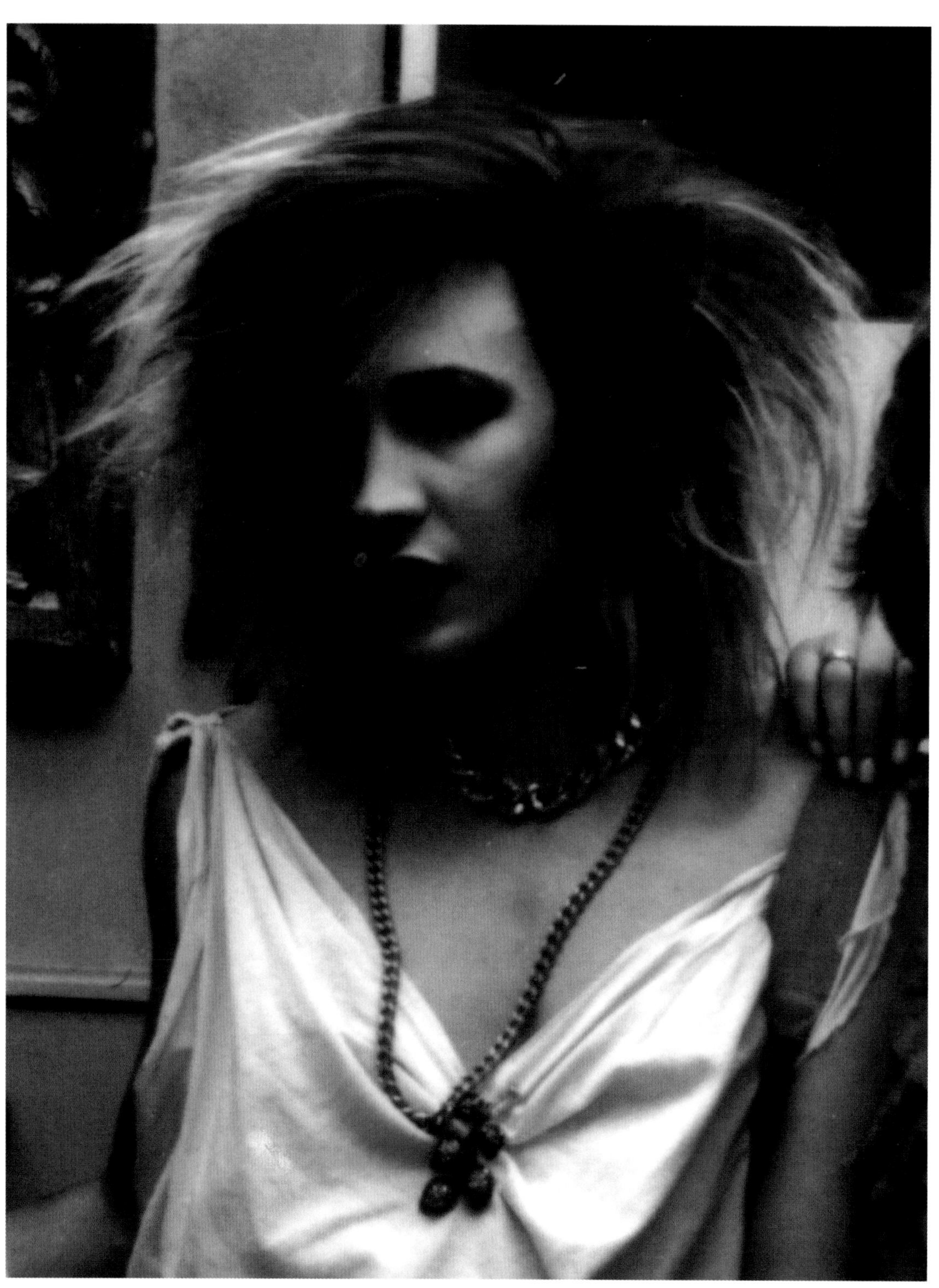

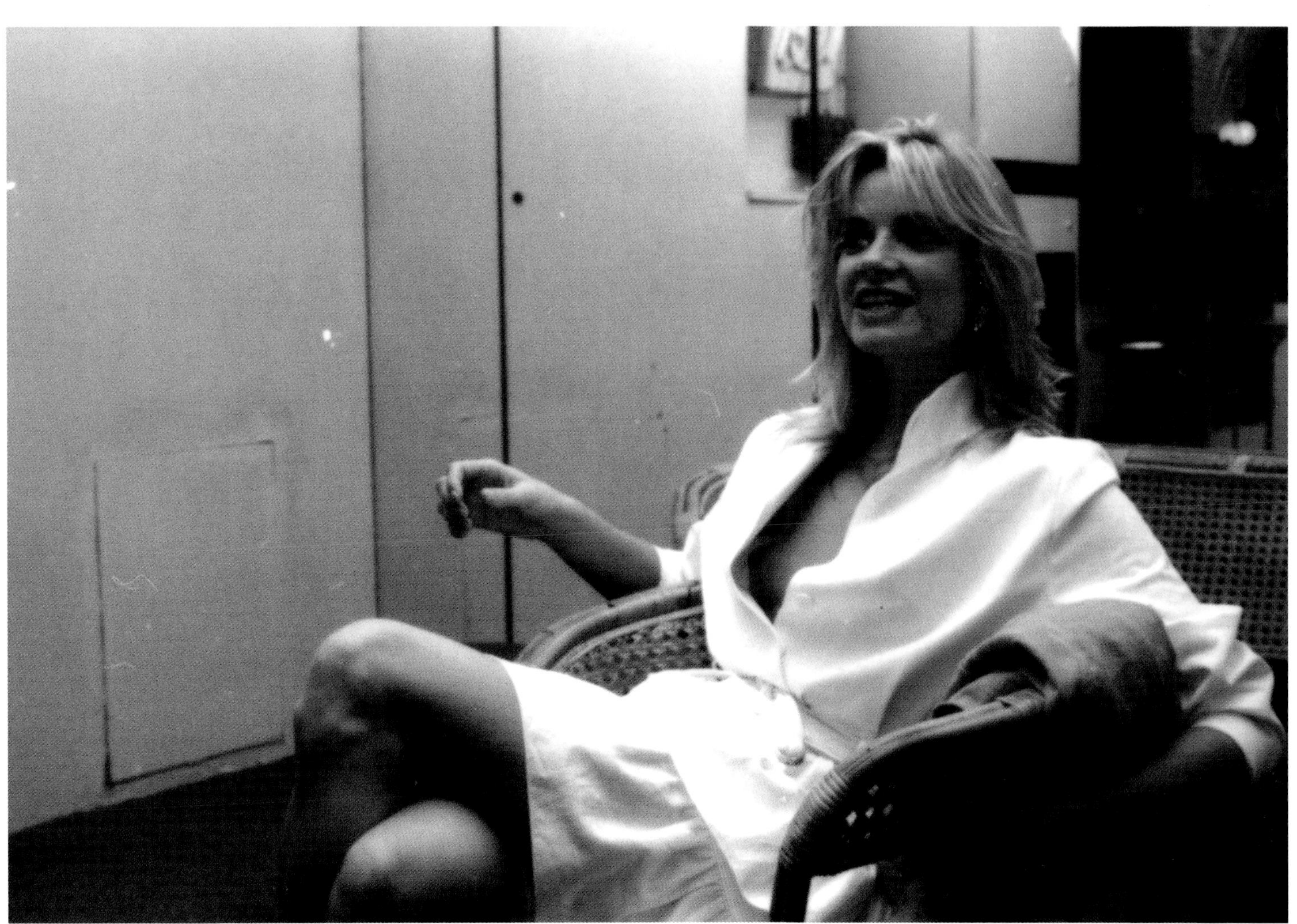

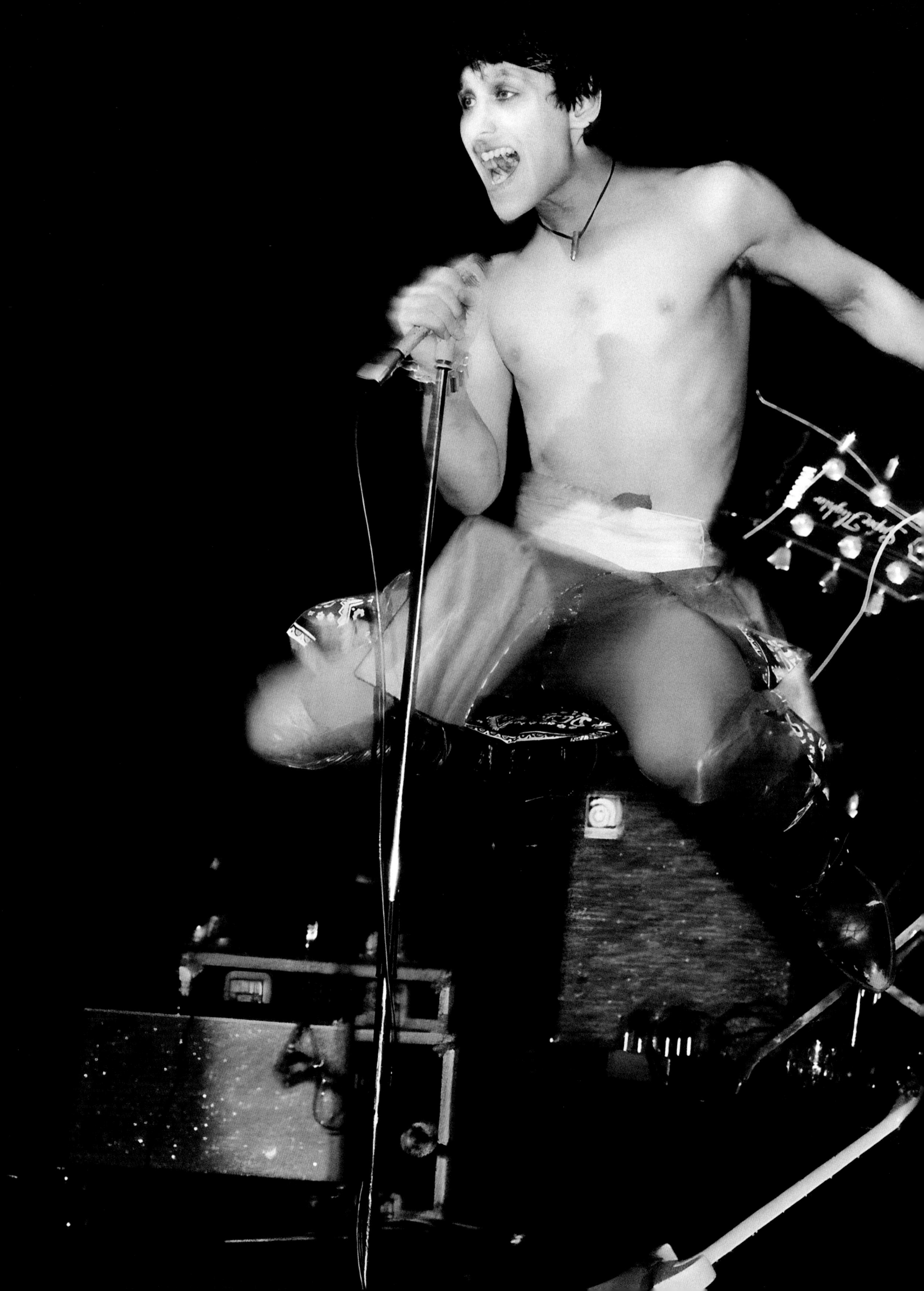

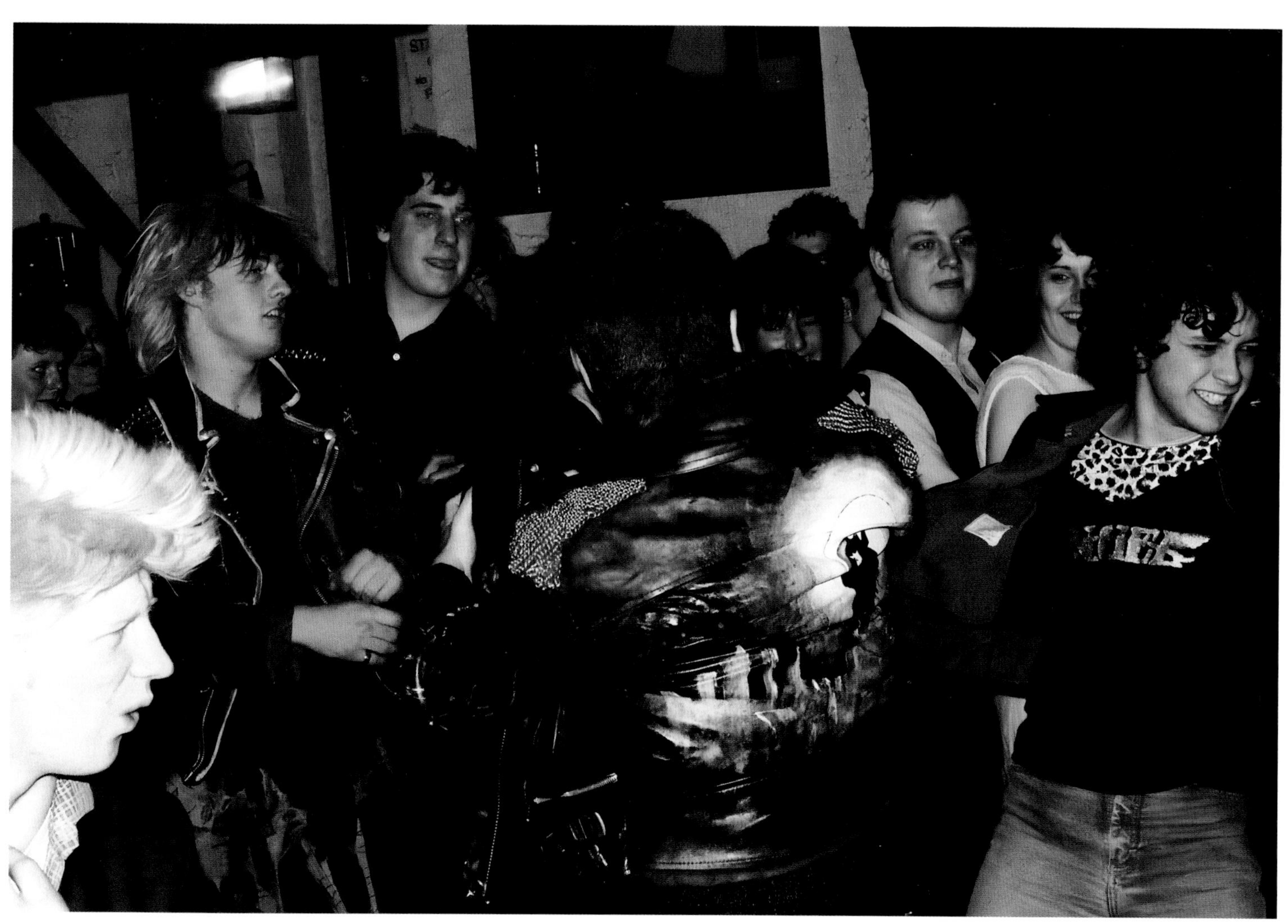

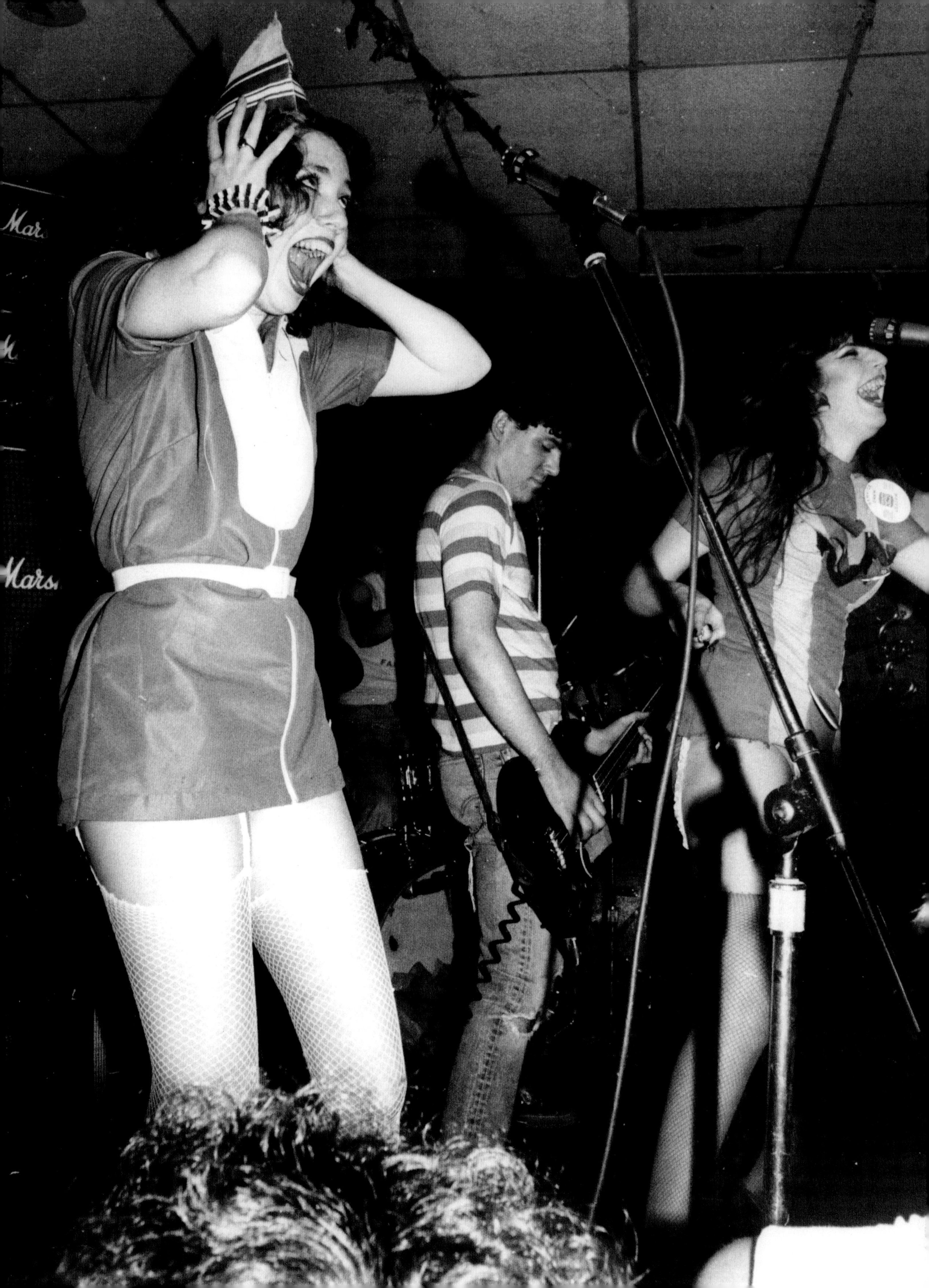

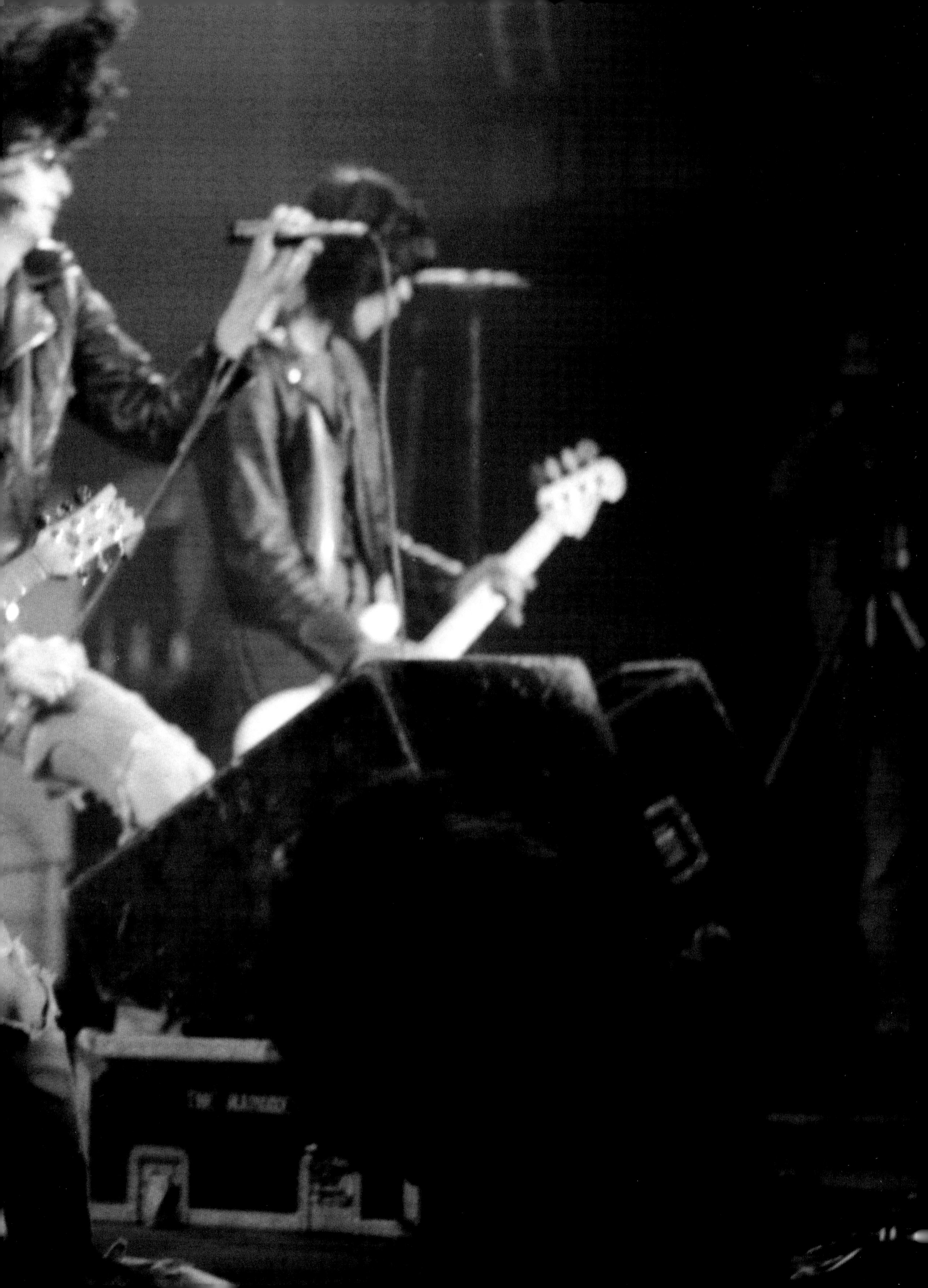

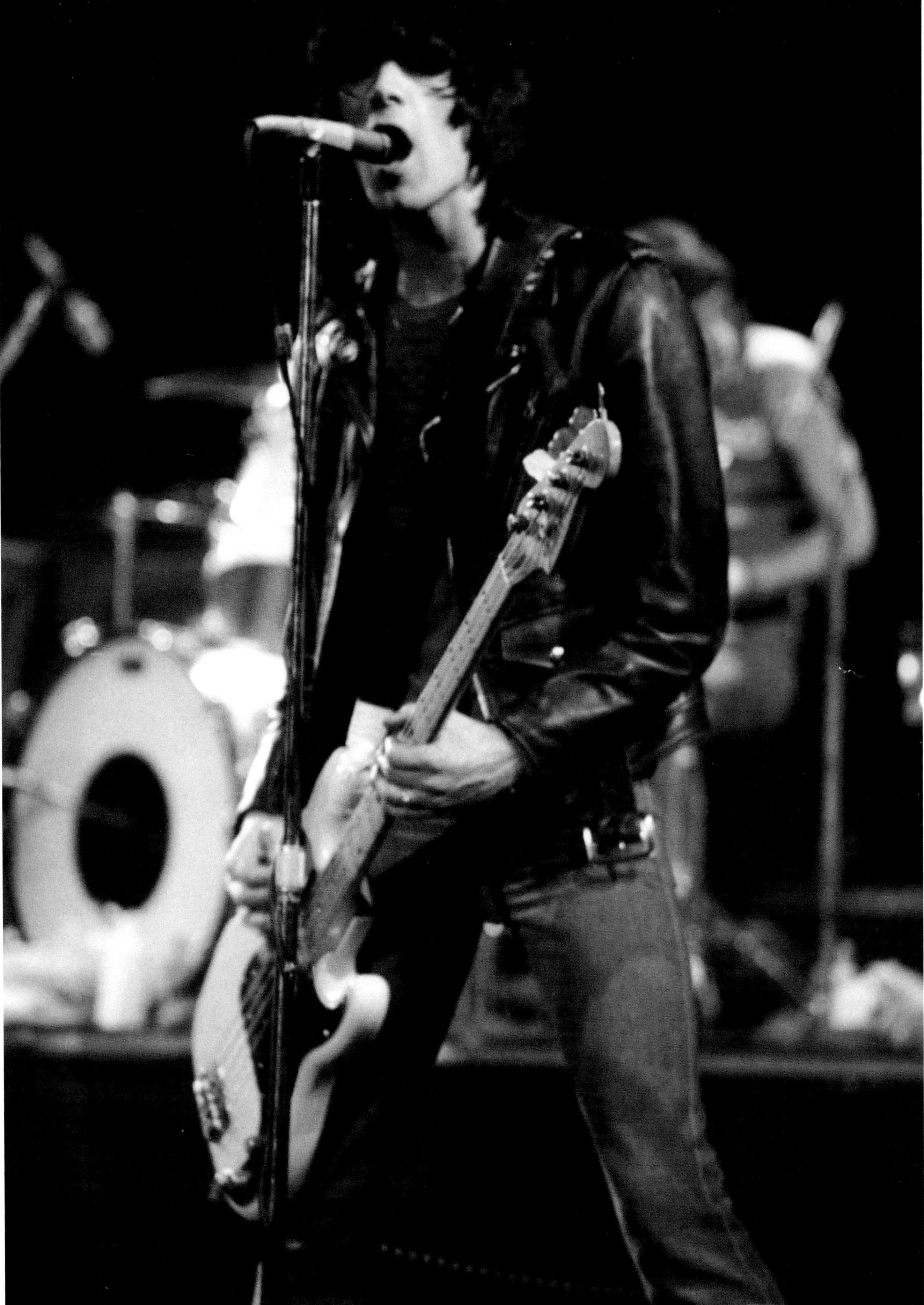

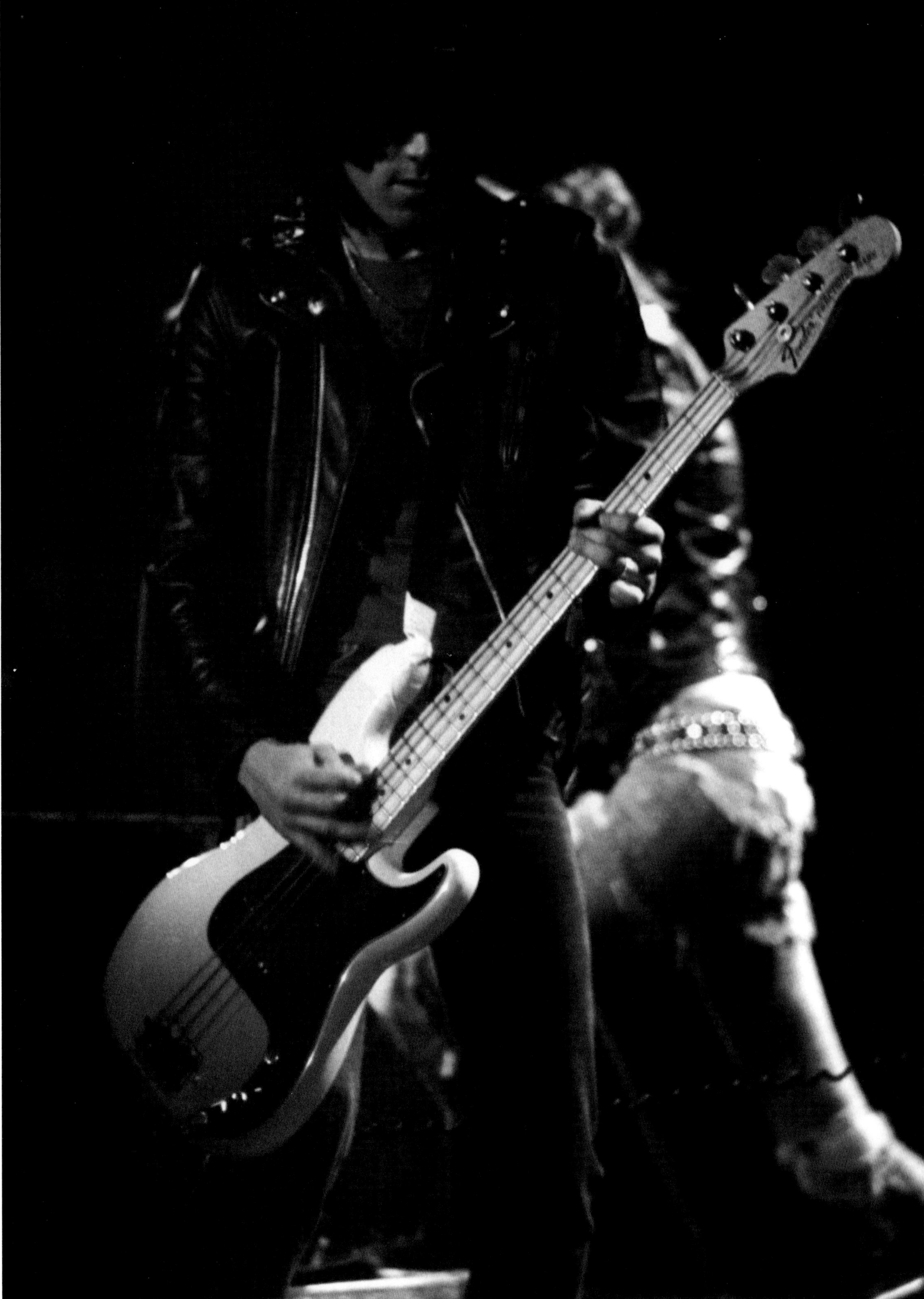

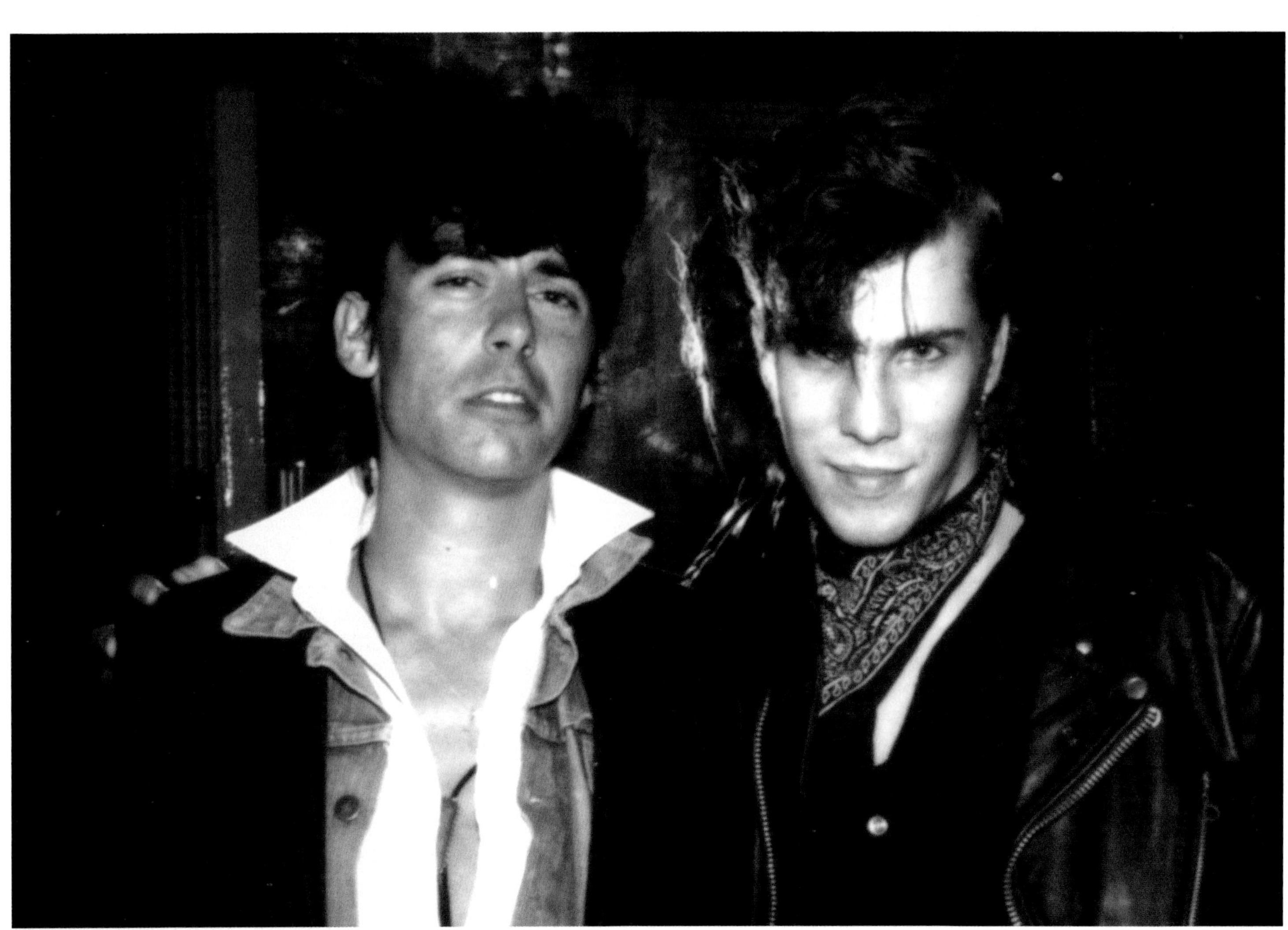

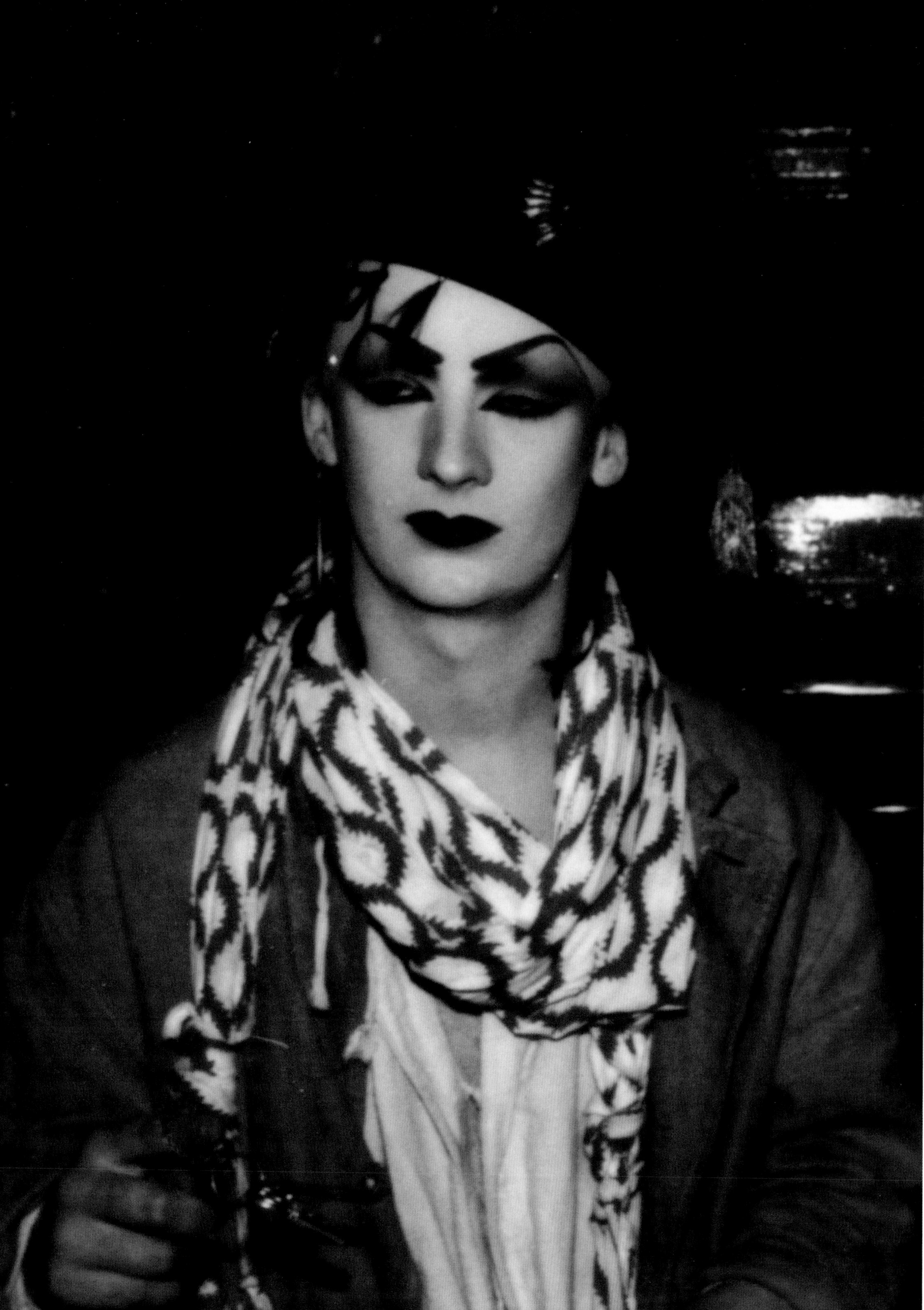

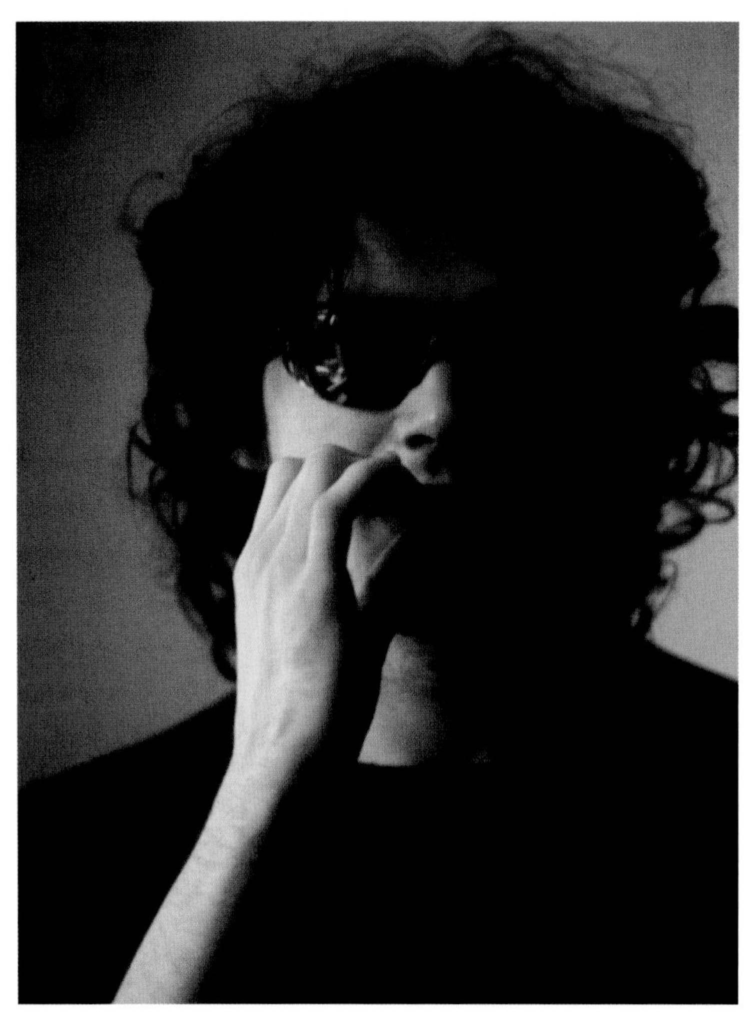

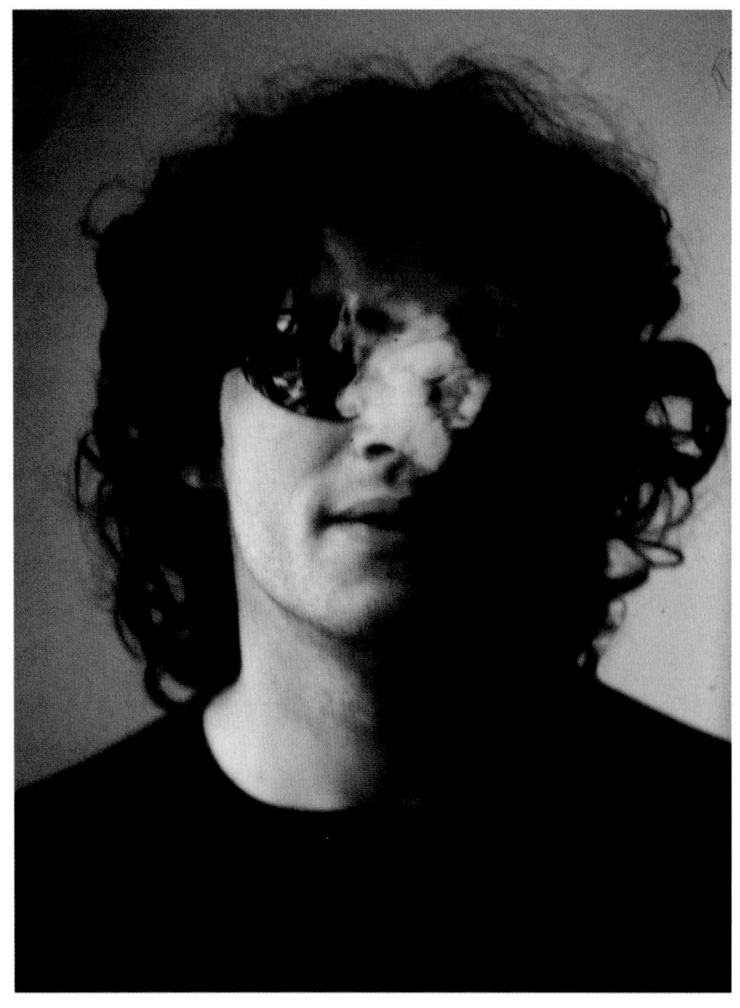

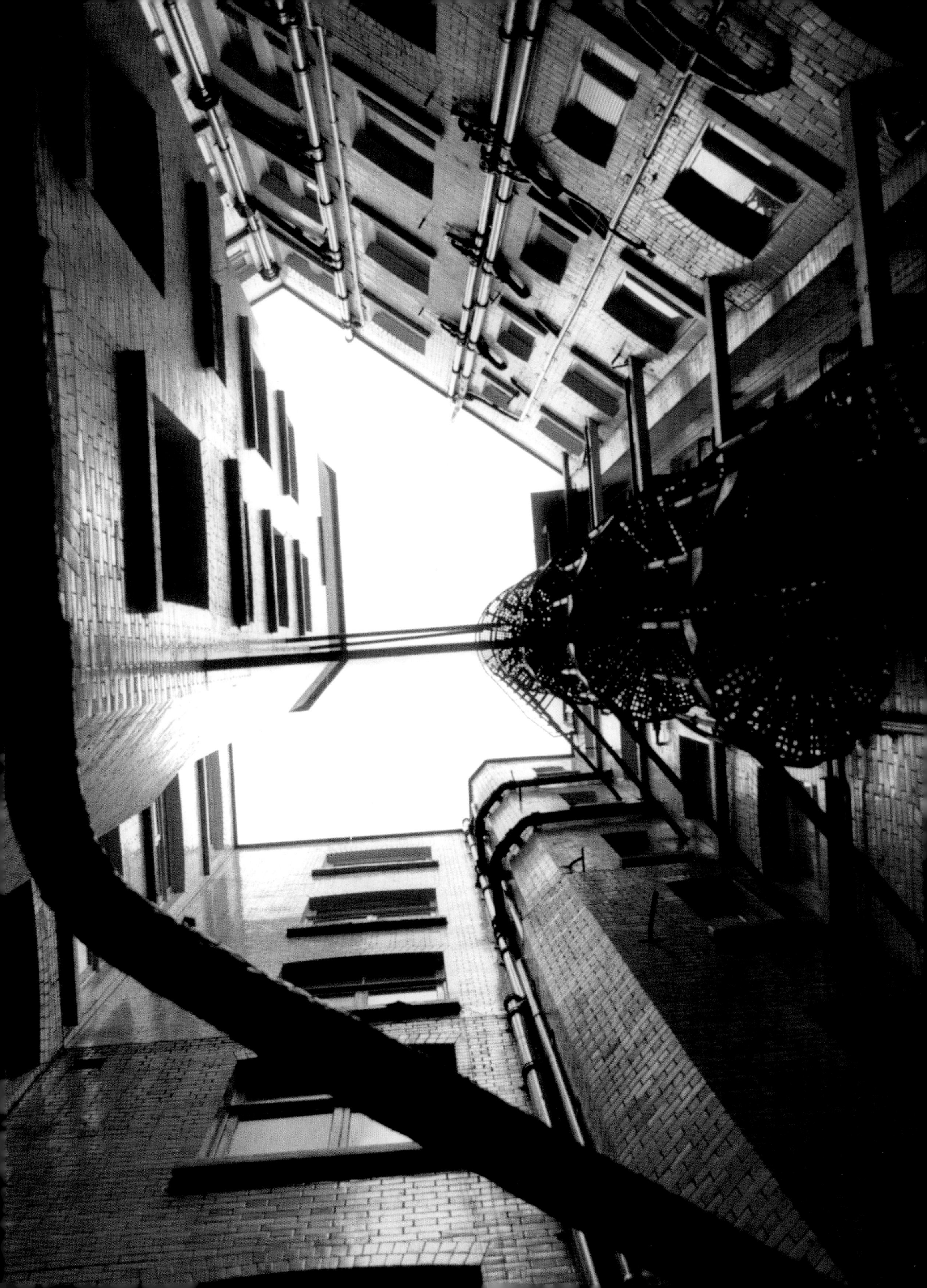

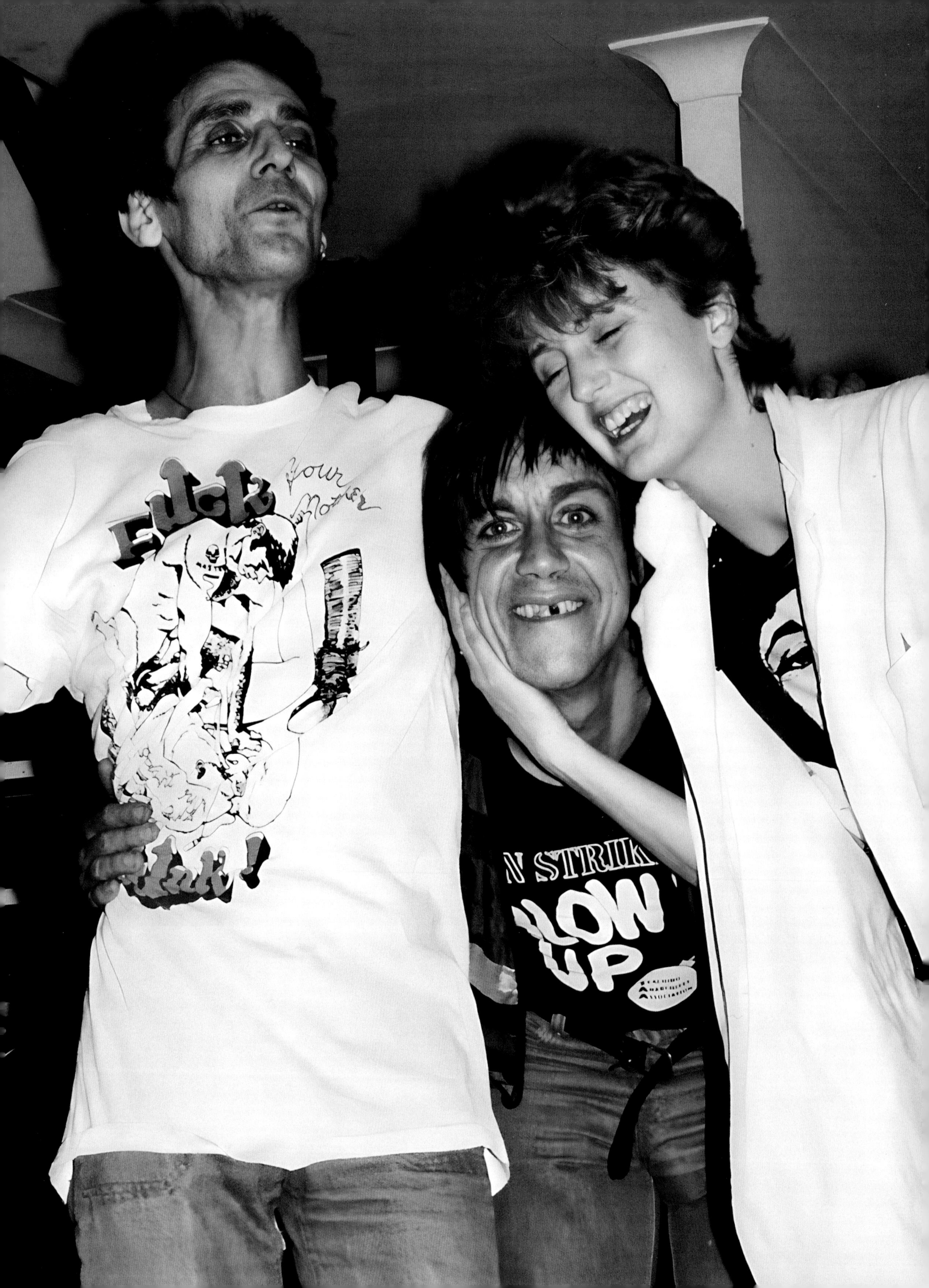
FUCk
Your Mother
Shit !
N STRIIK
LOW
UP

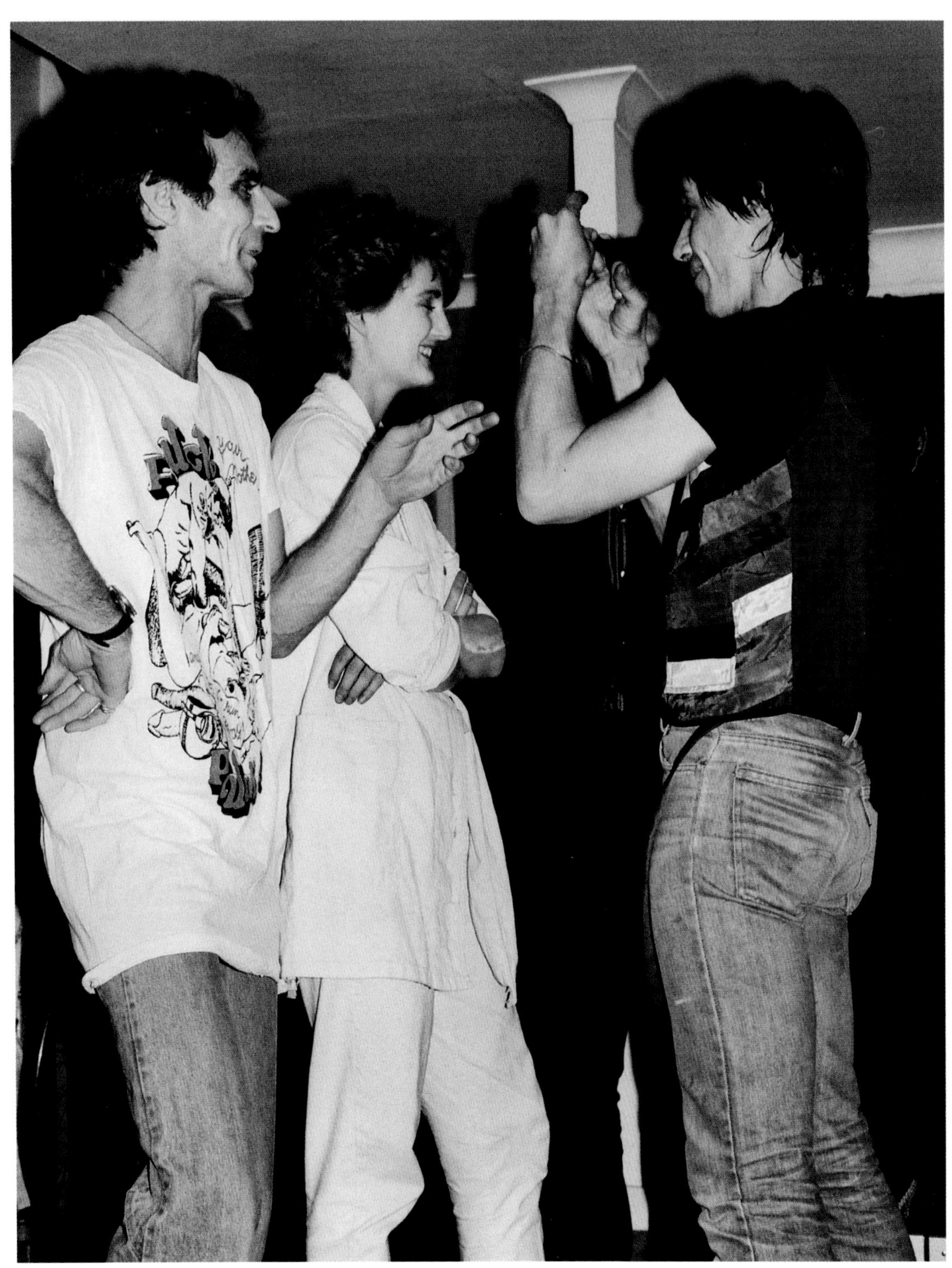

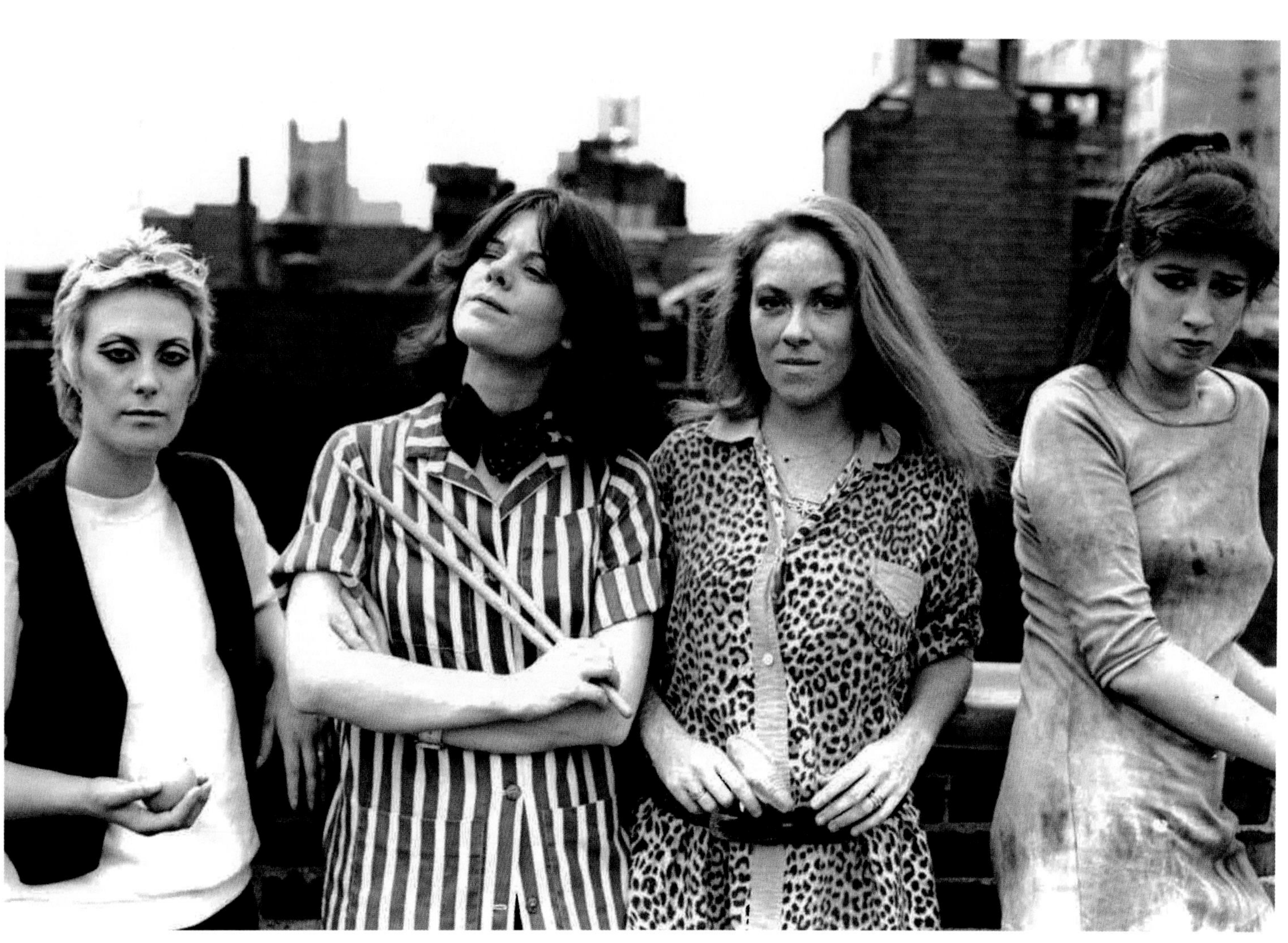

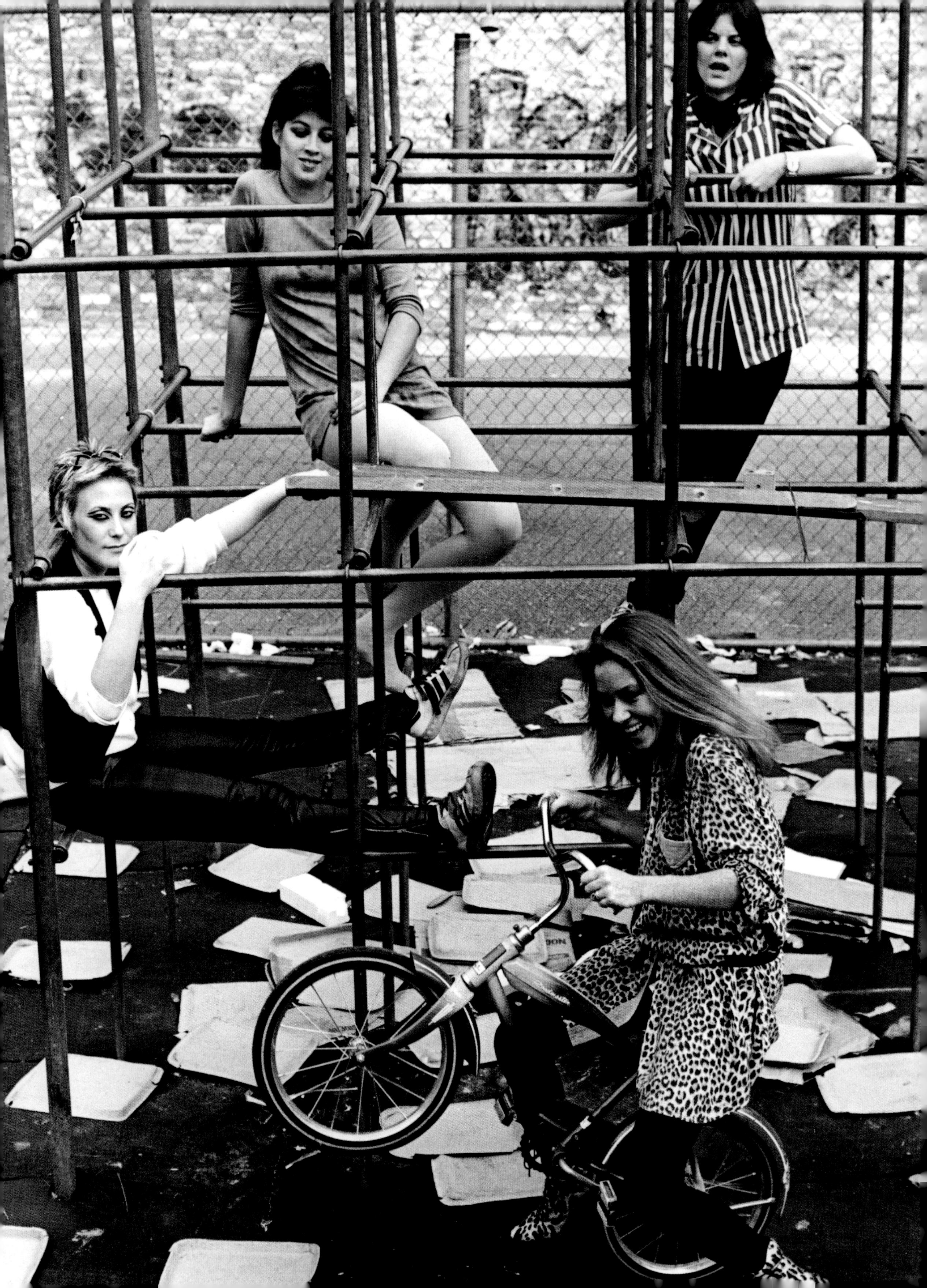

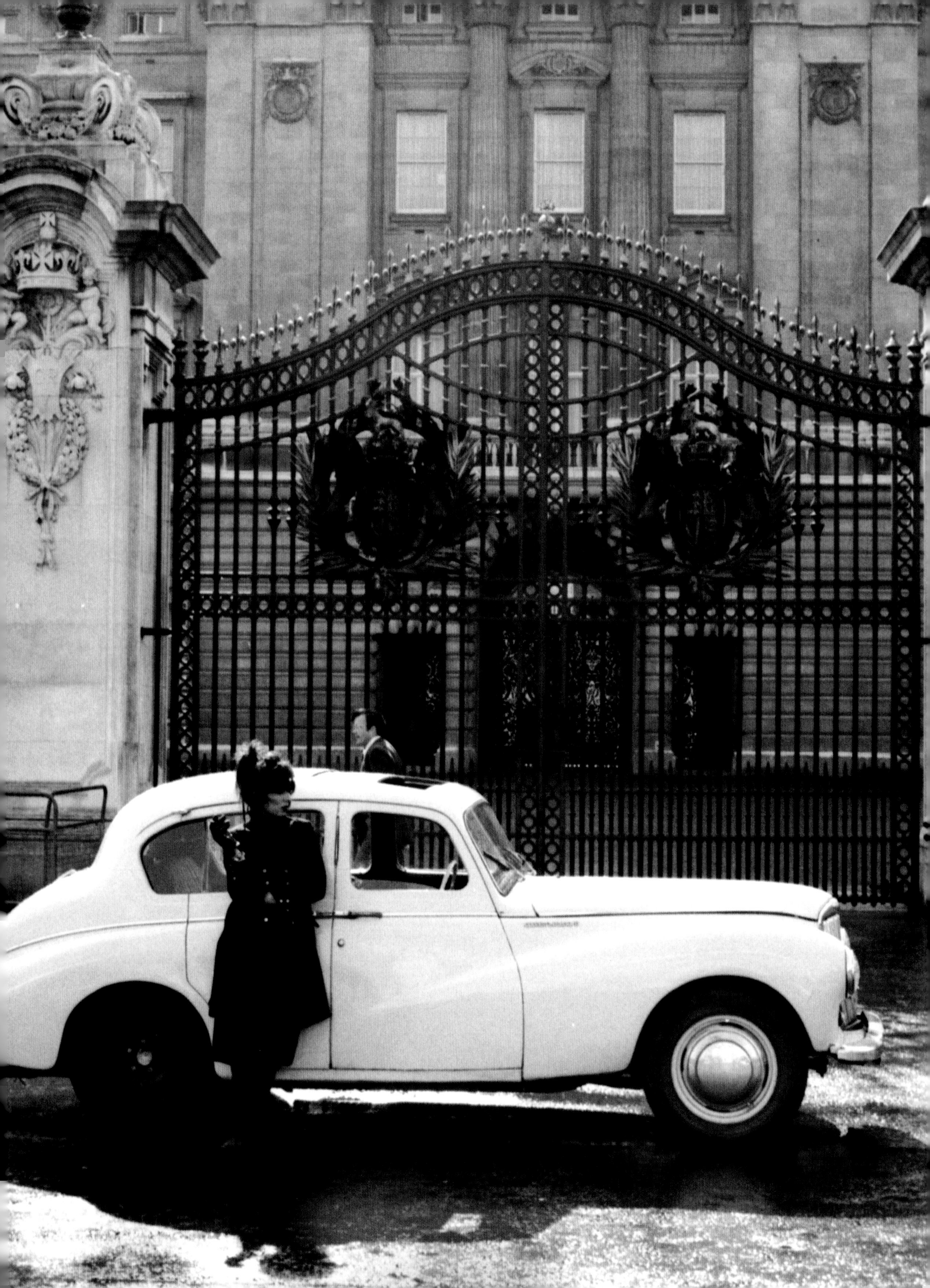

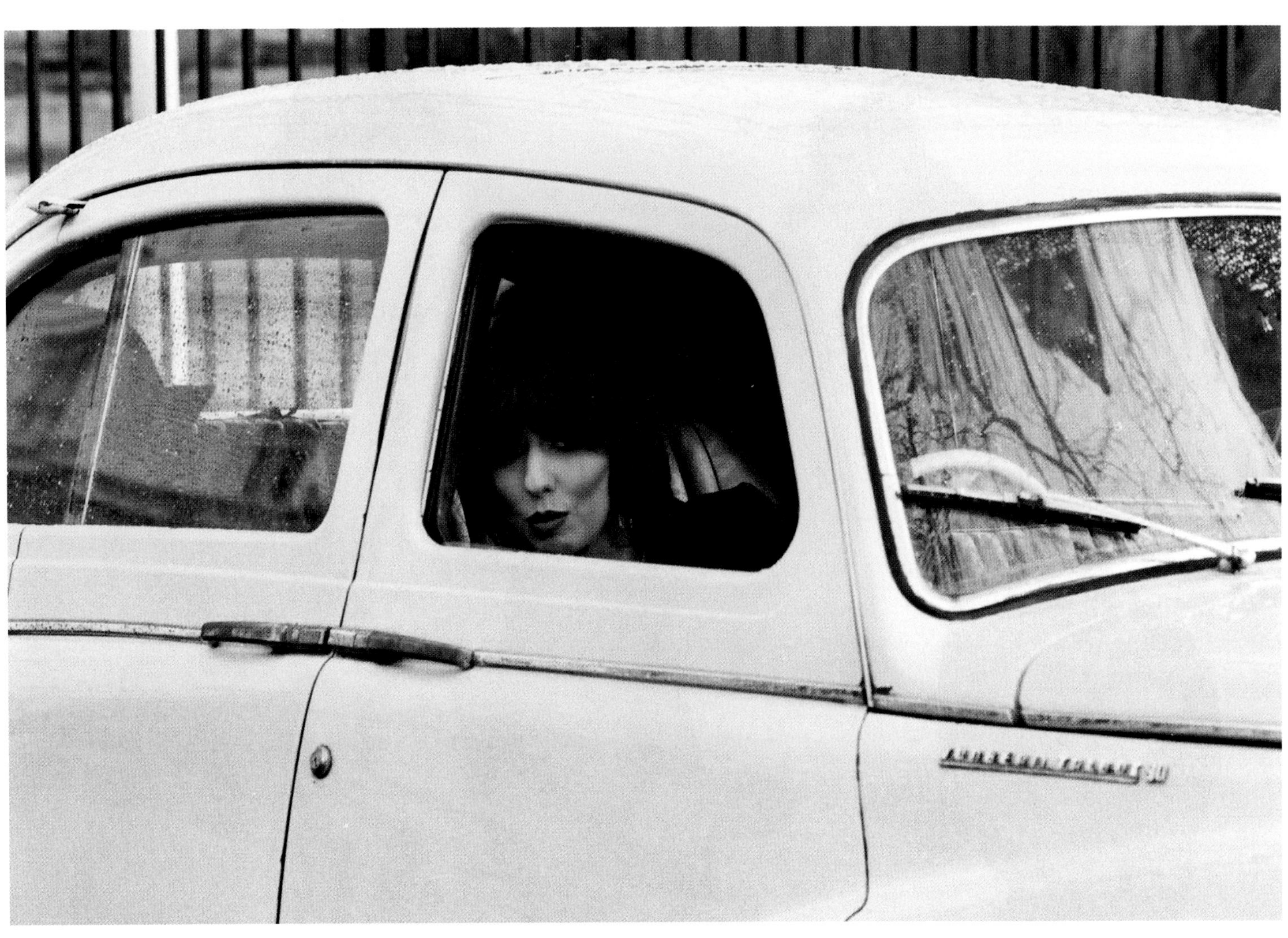

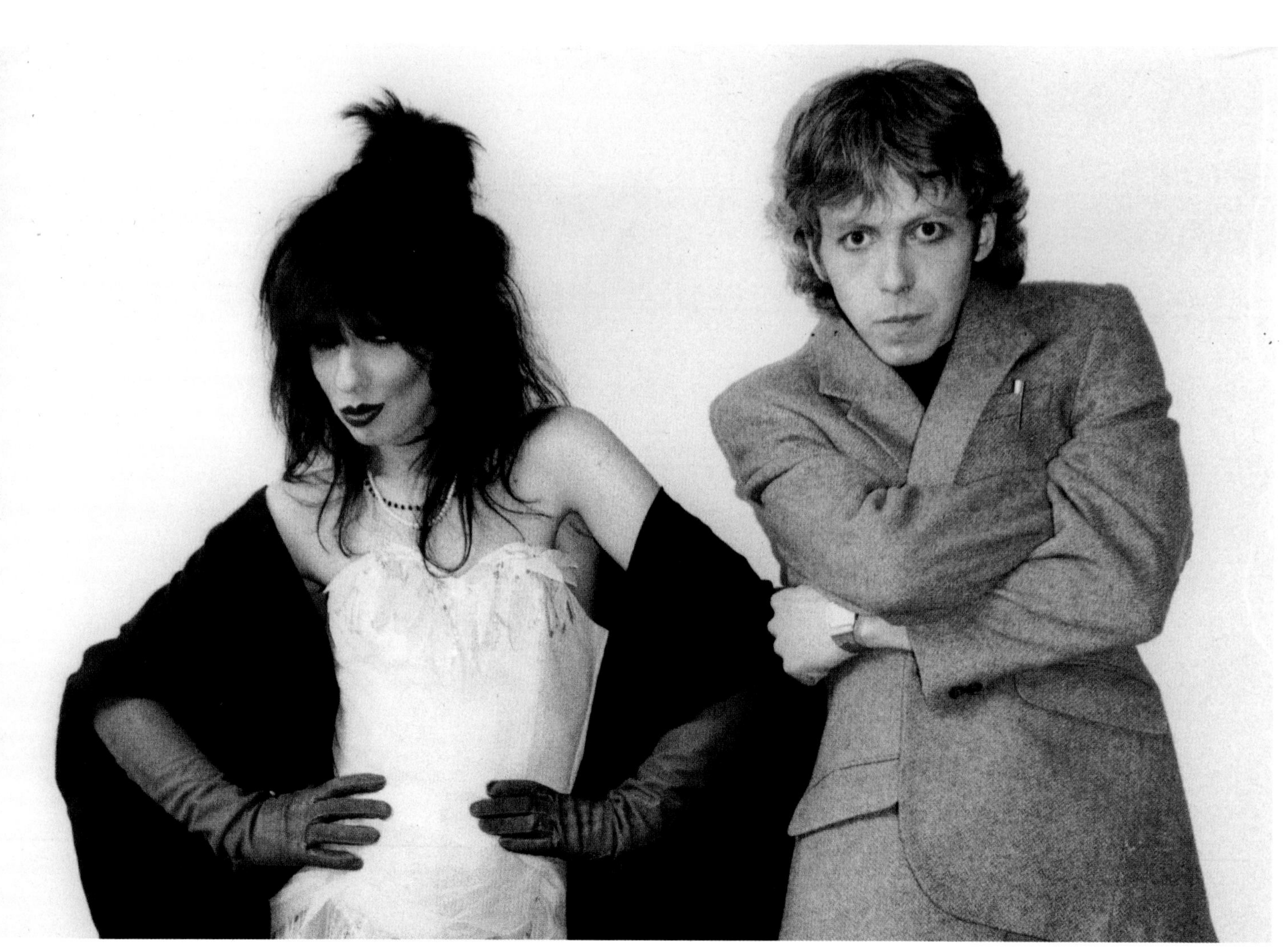

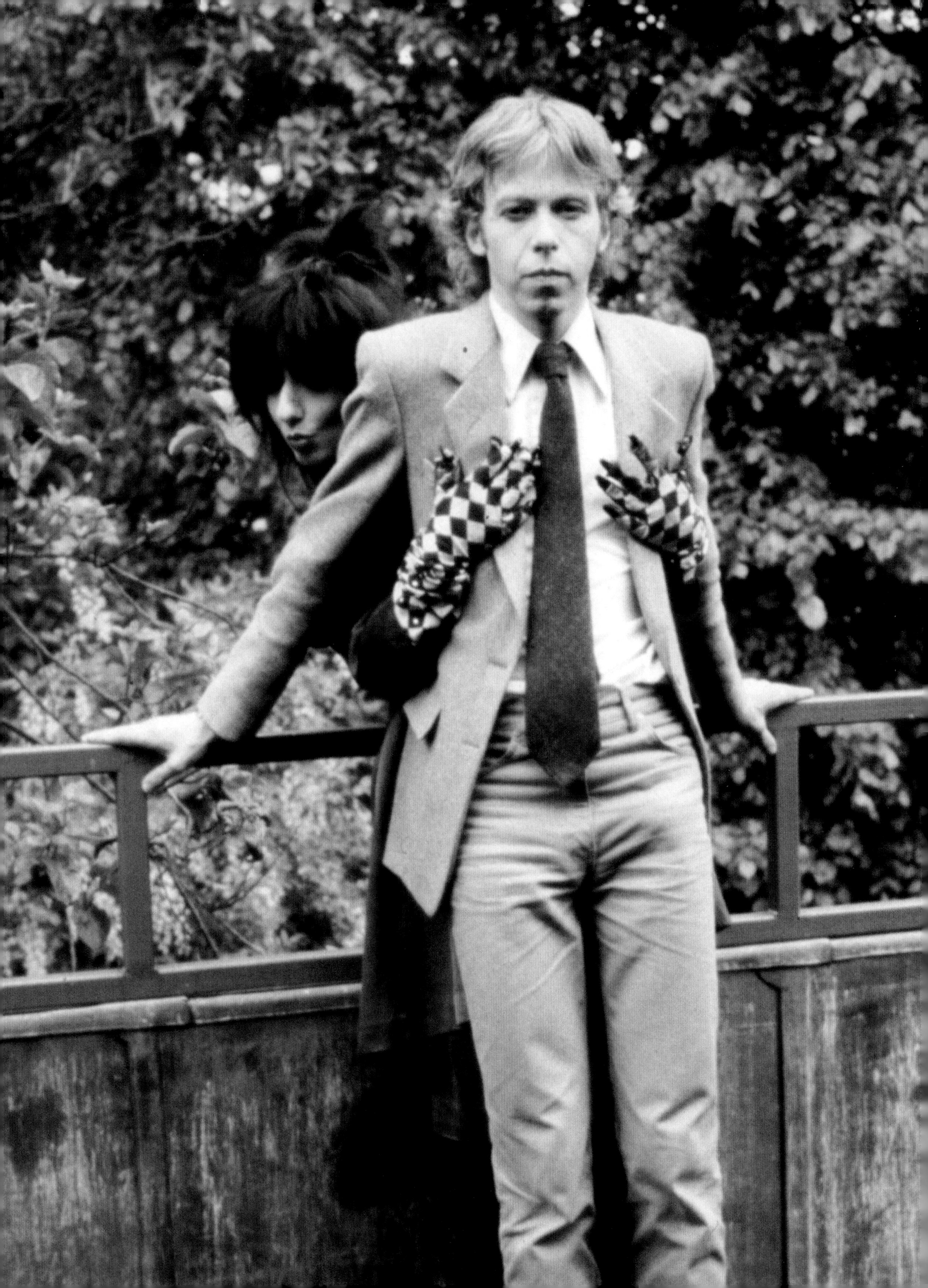

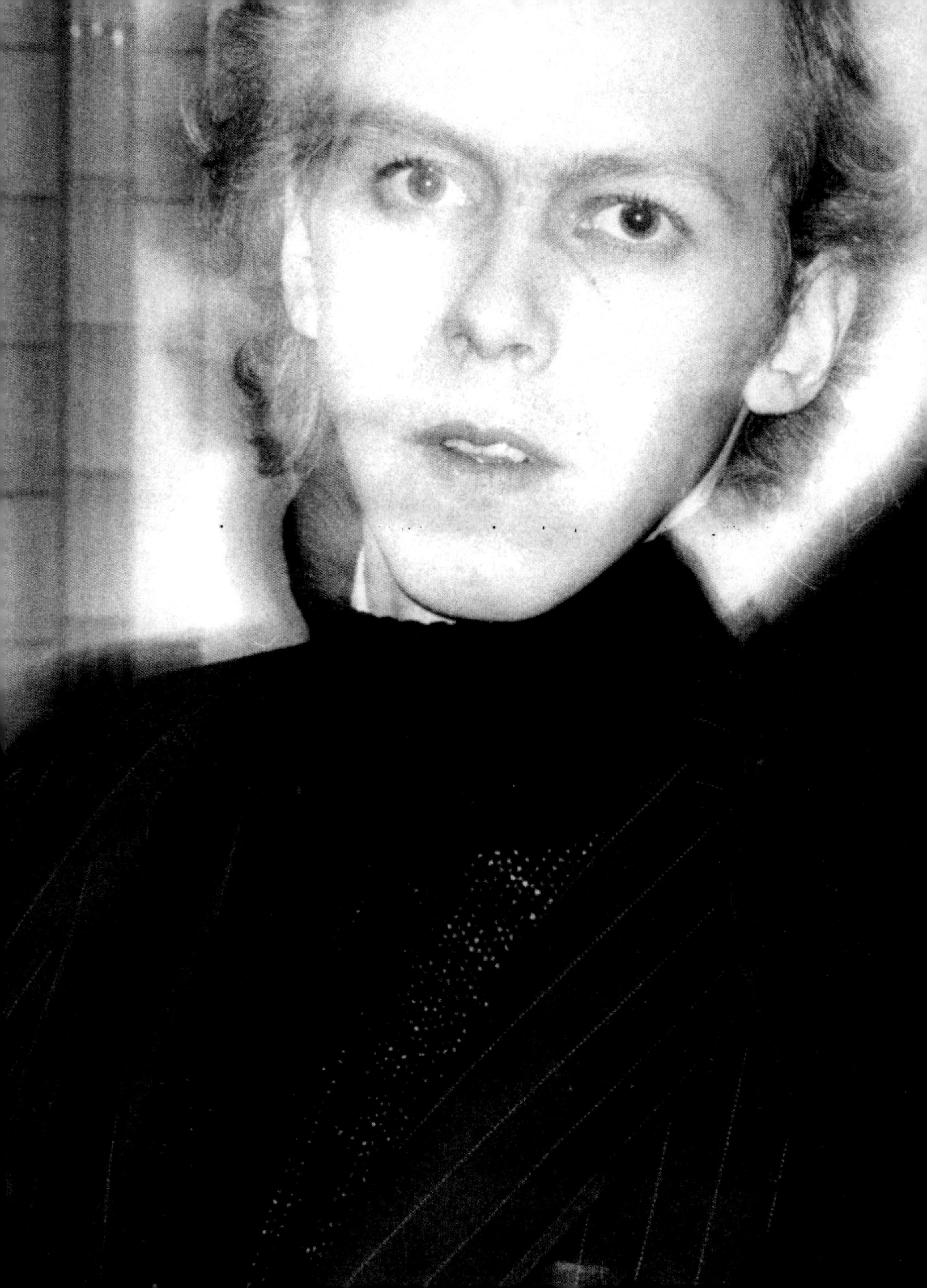

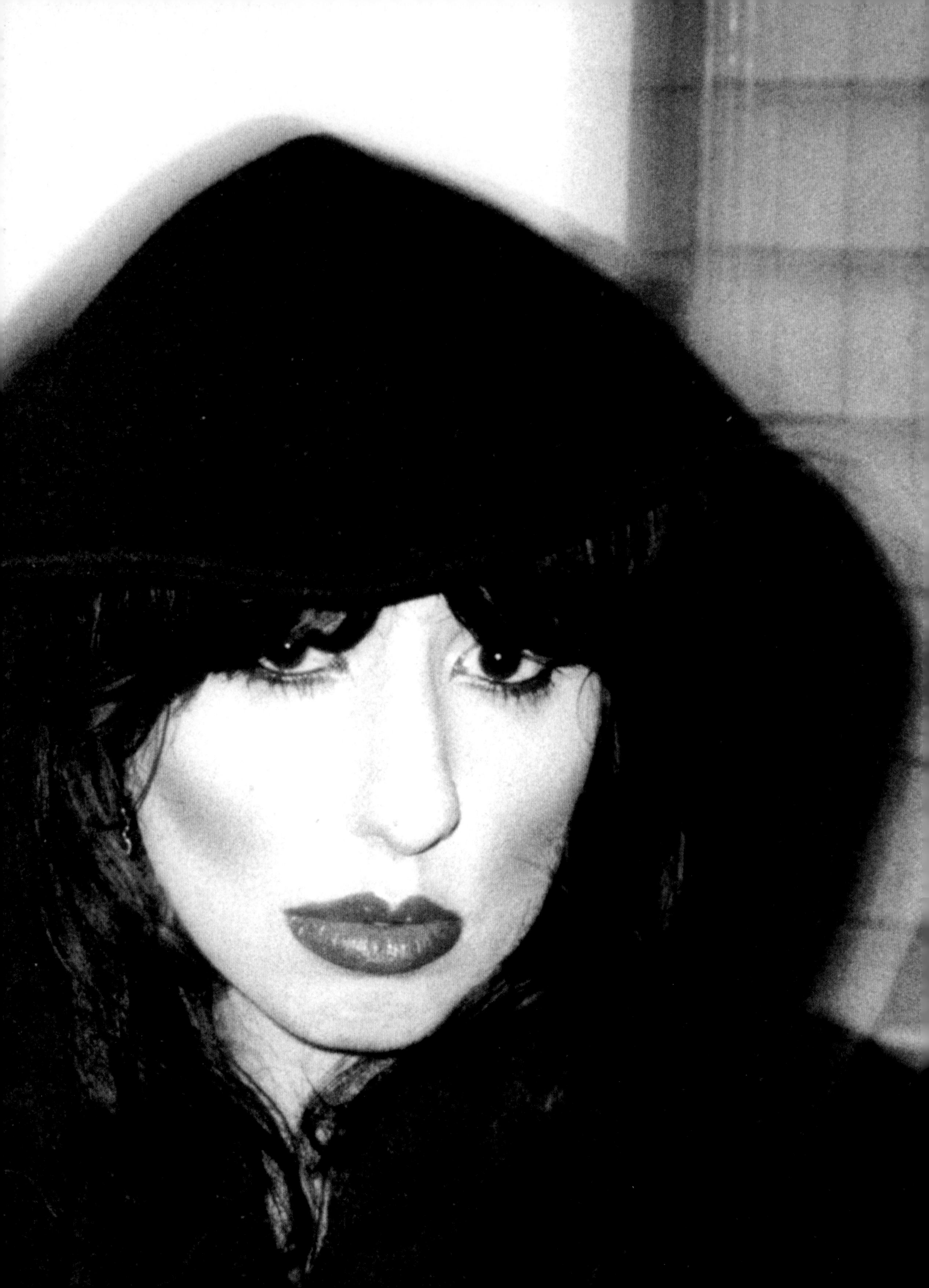

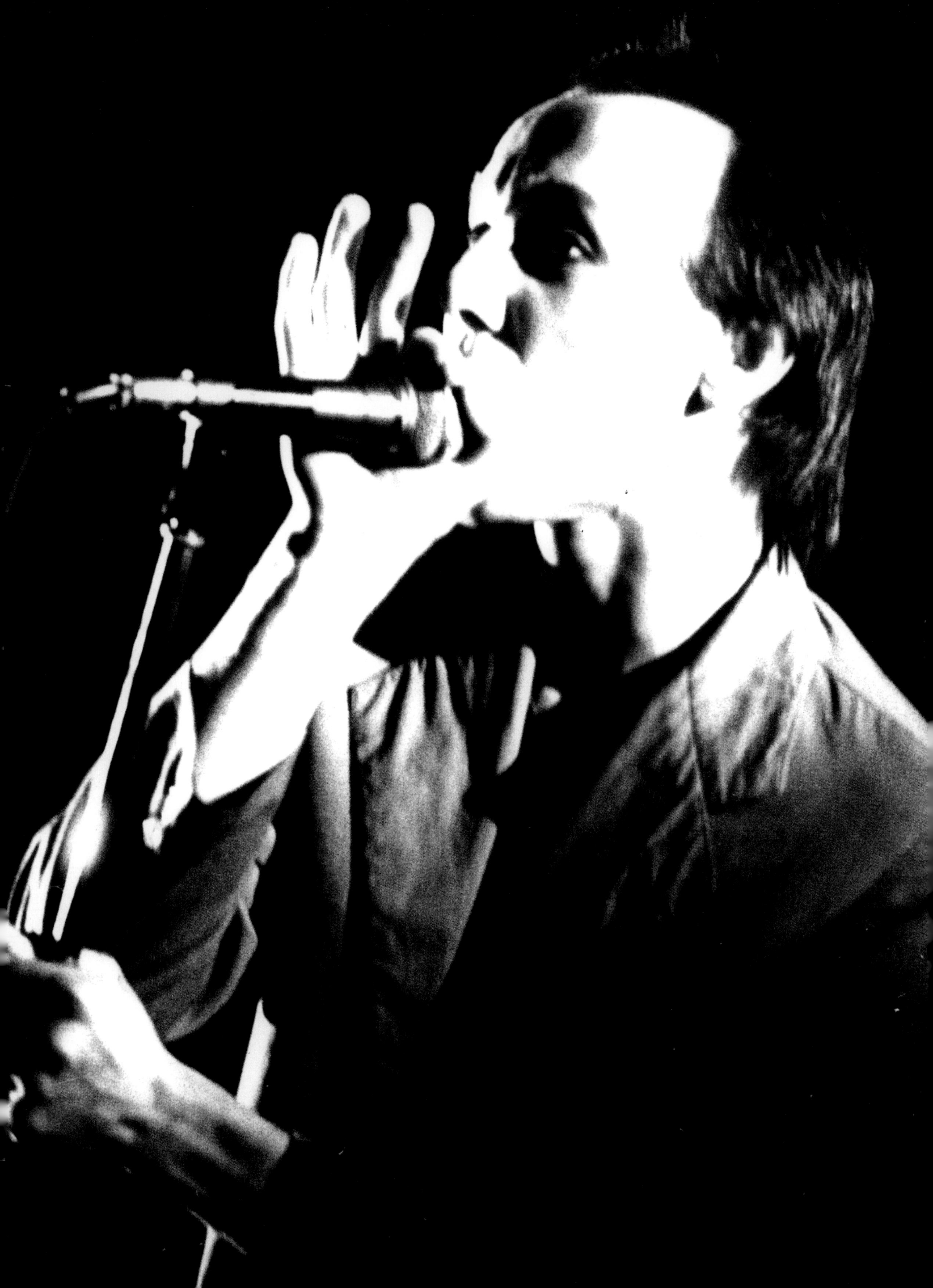

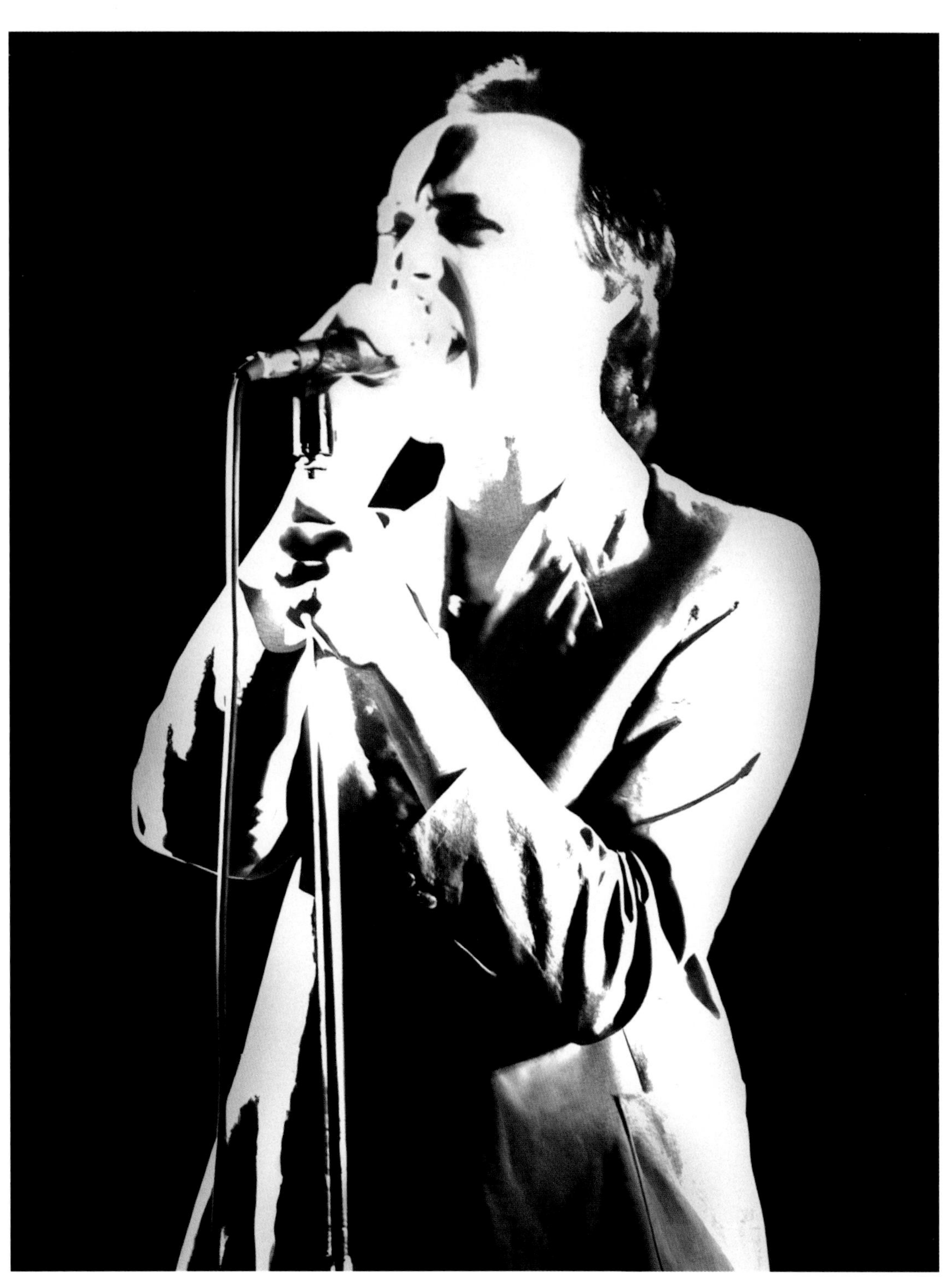

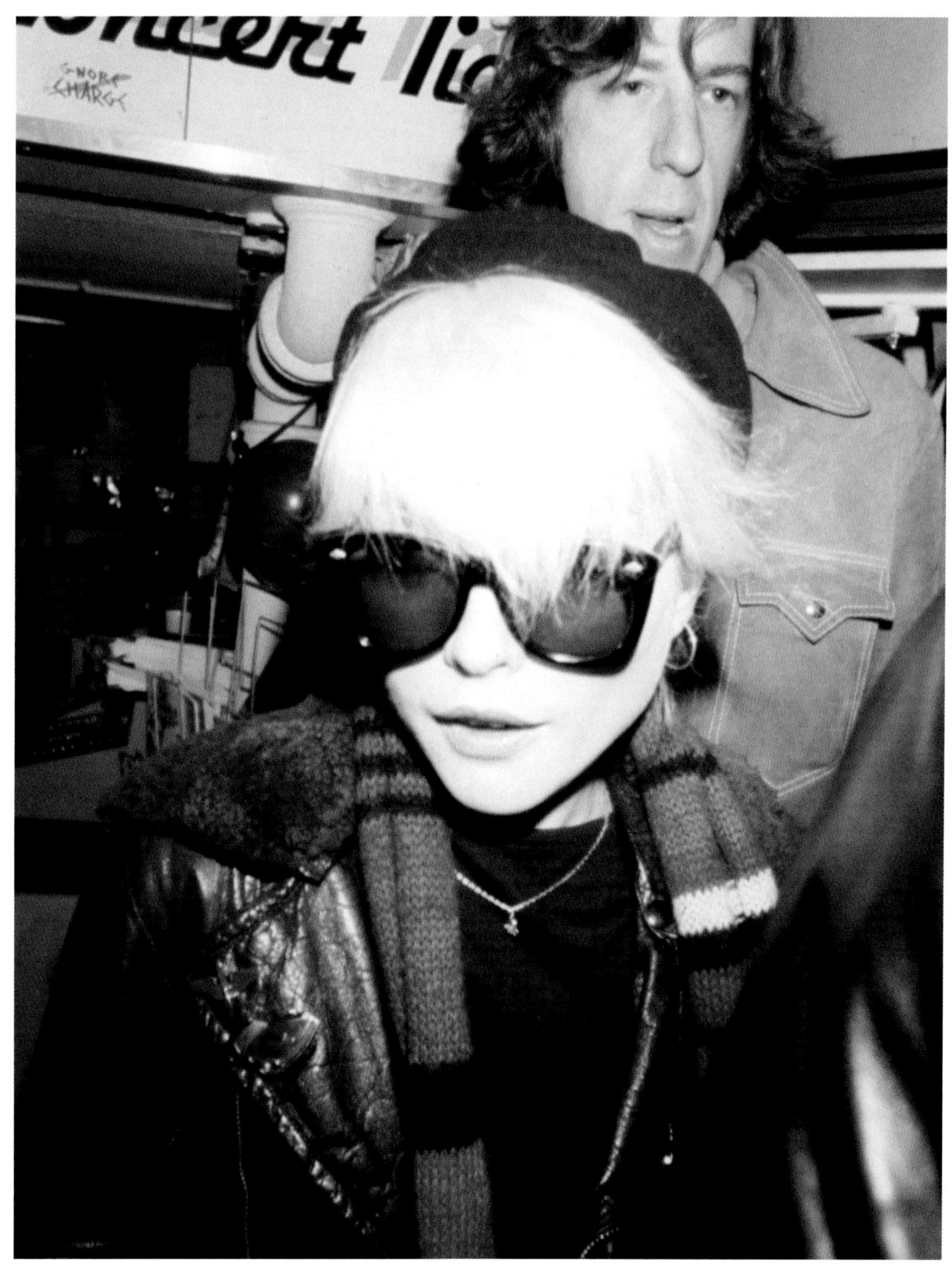

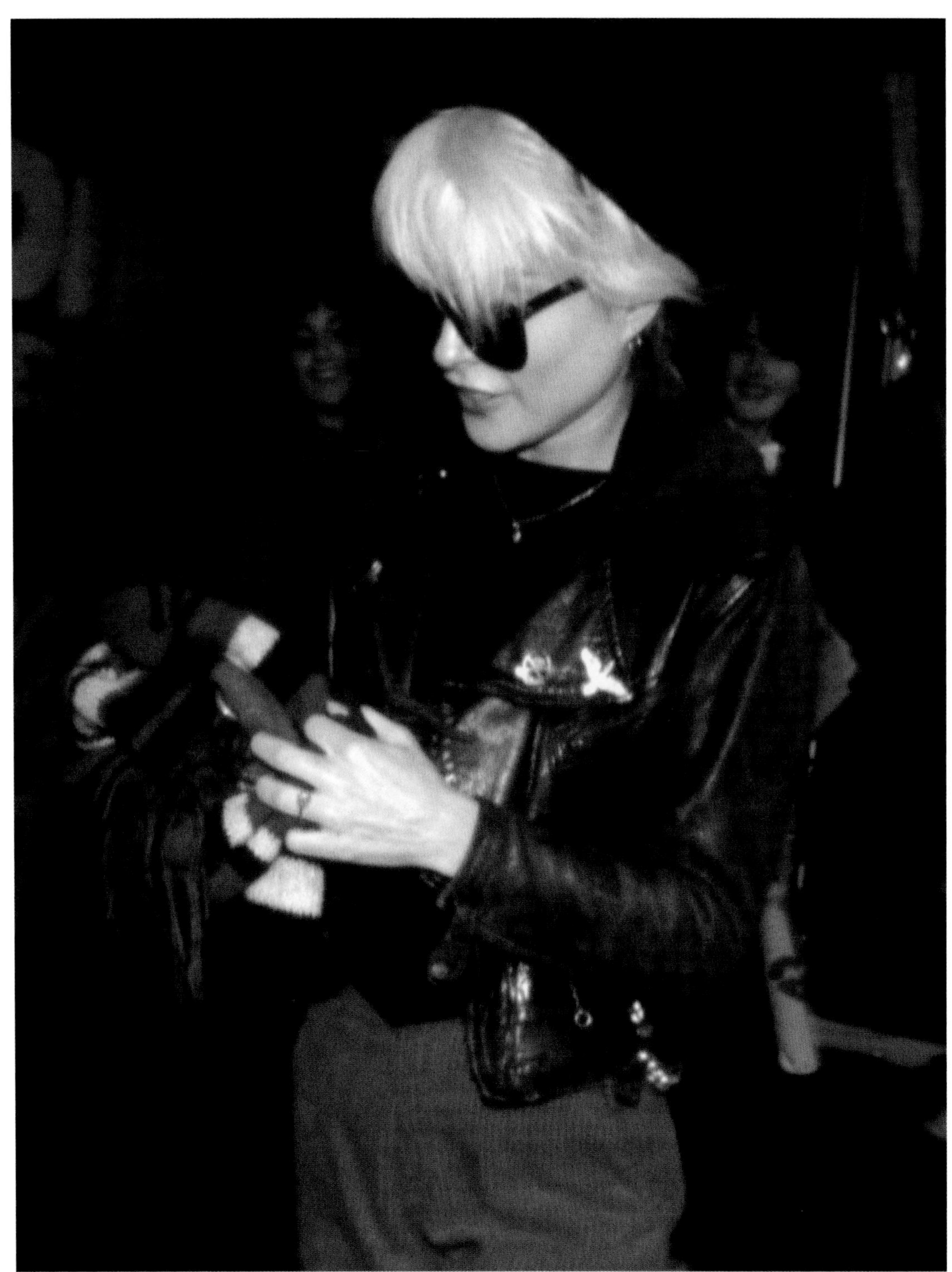

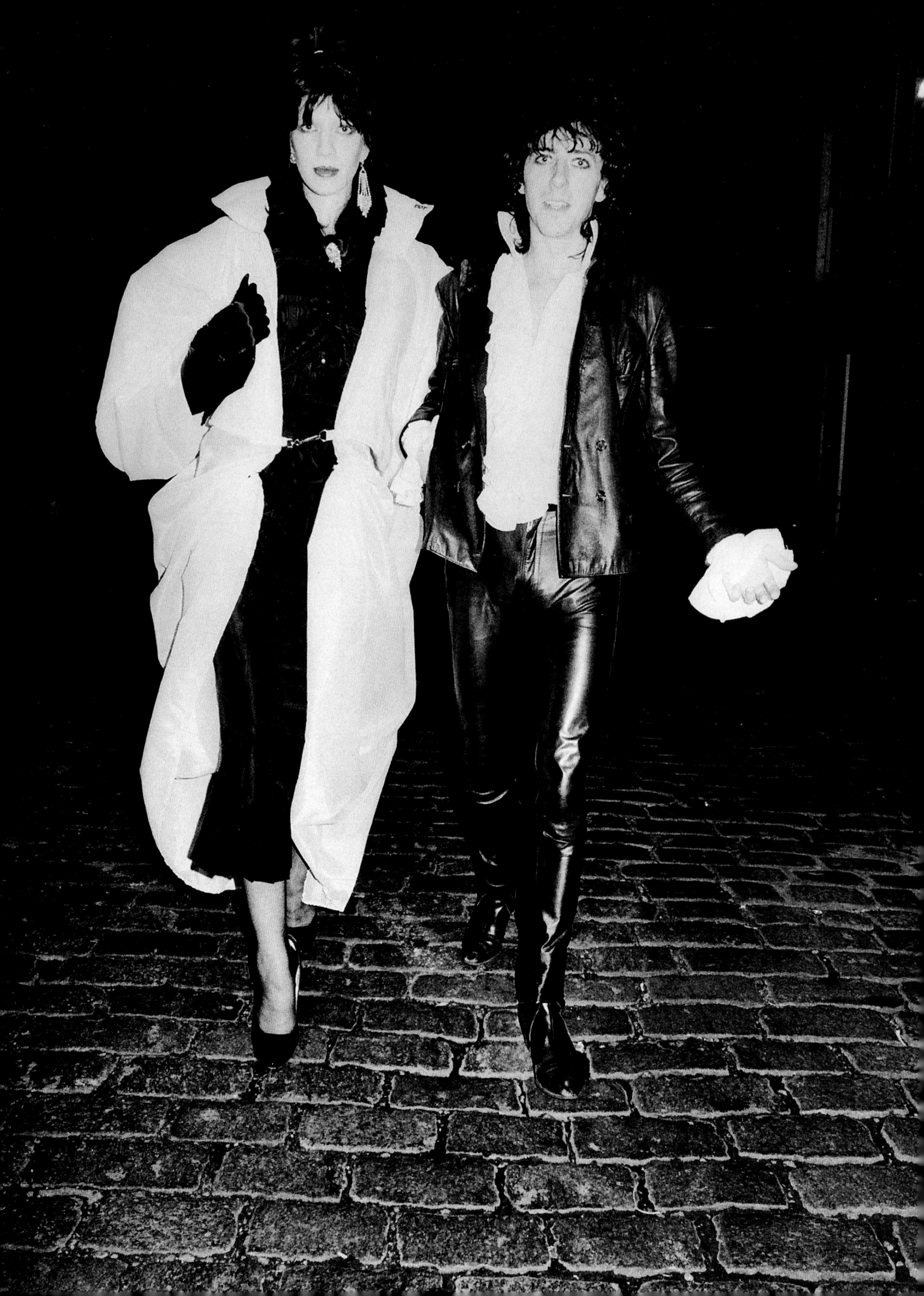

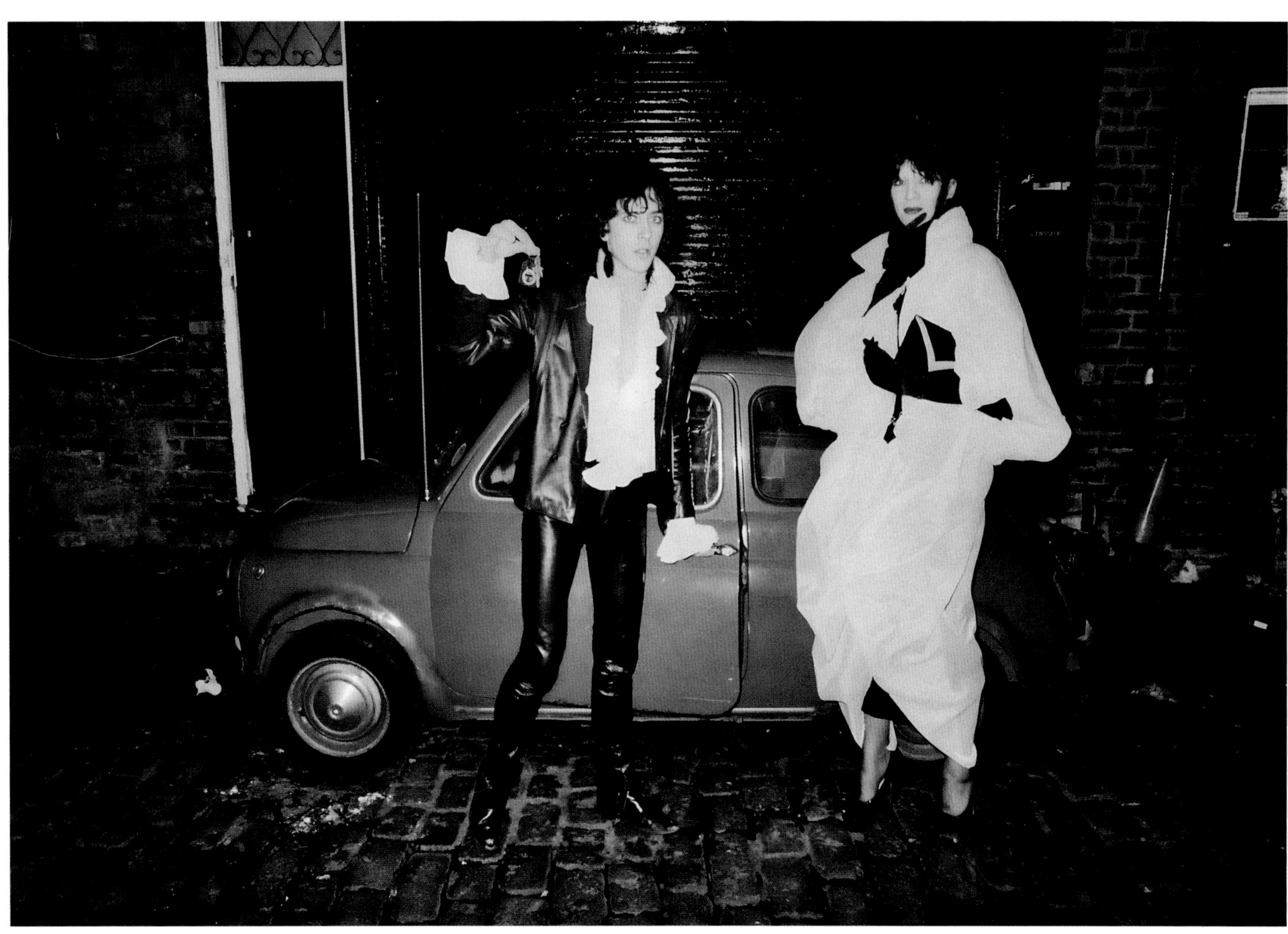

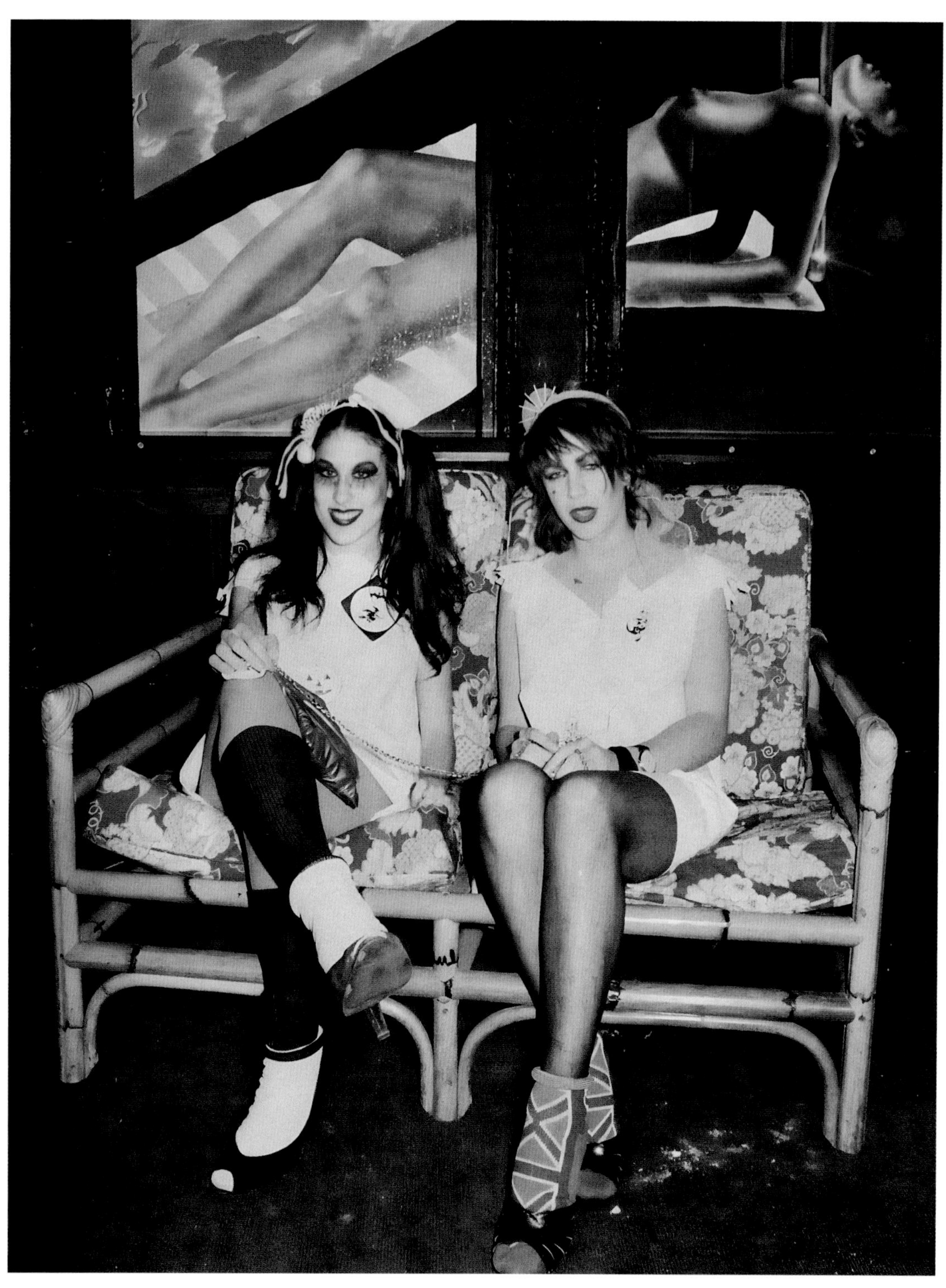

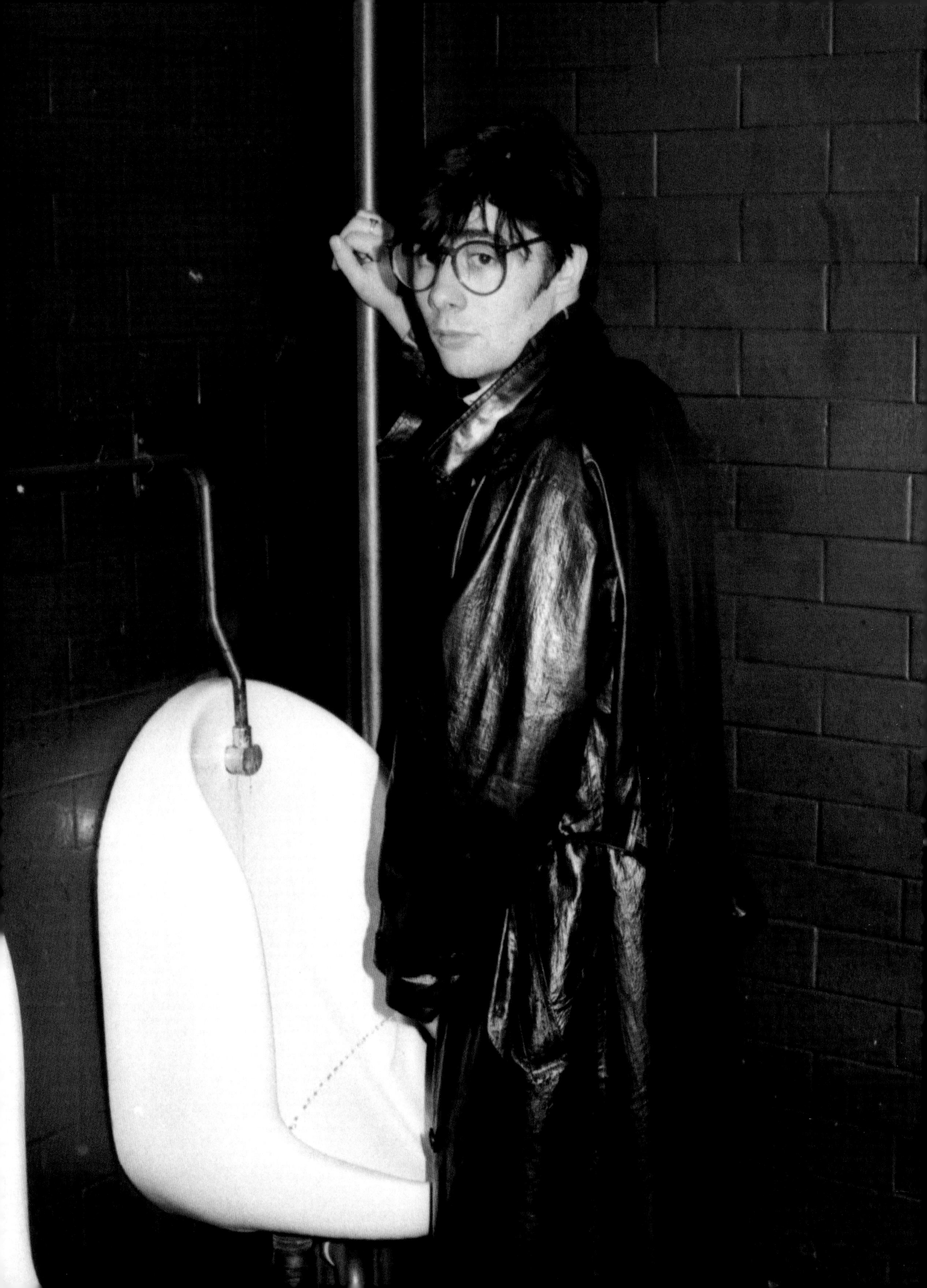

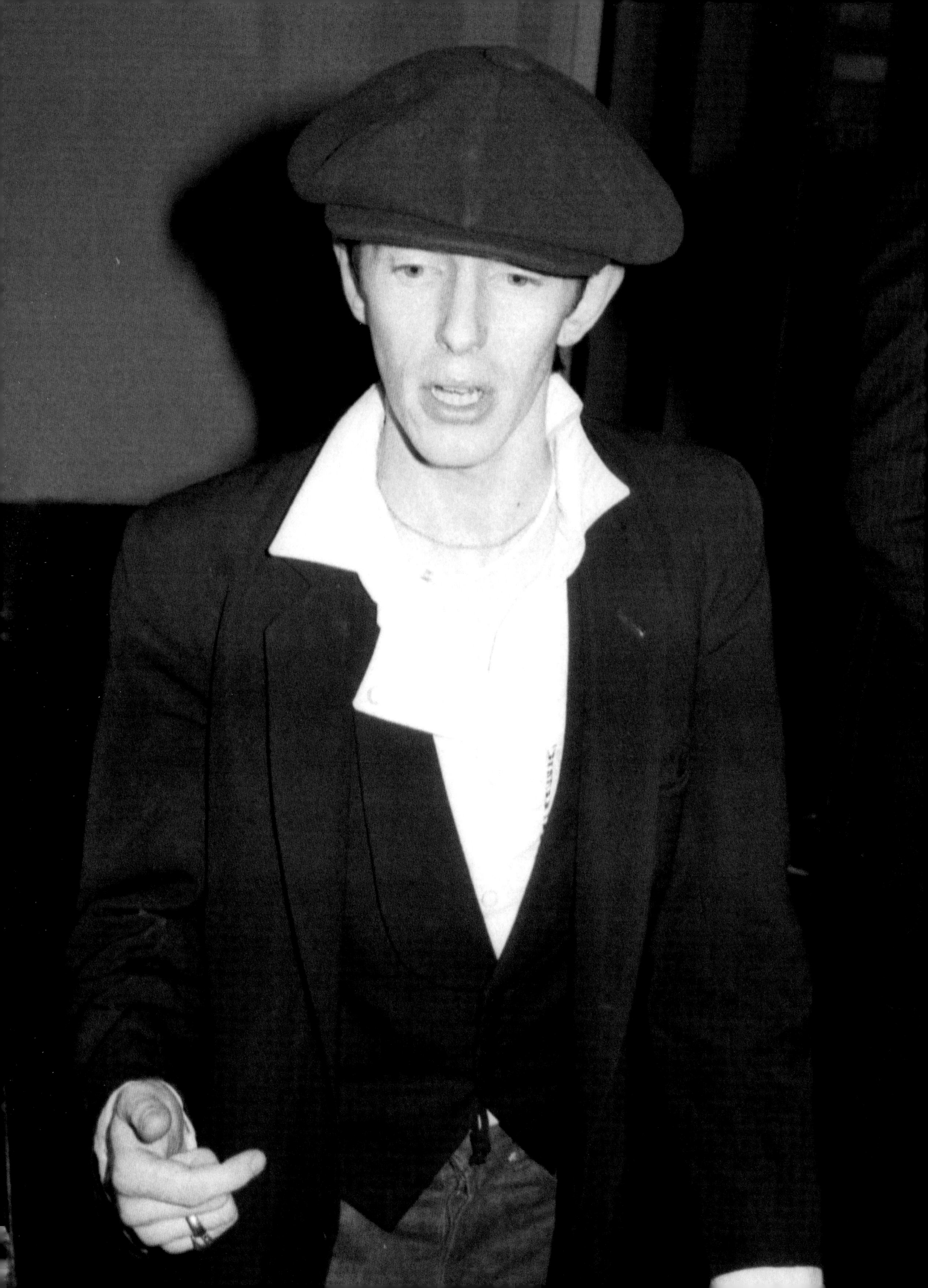

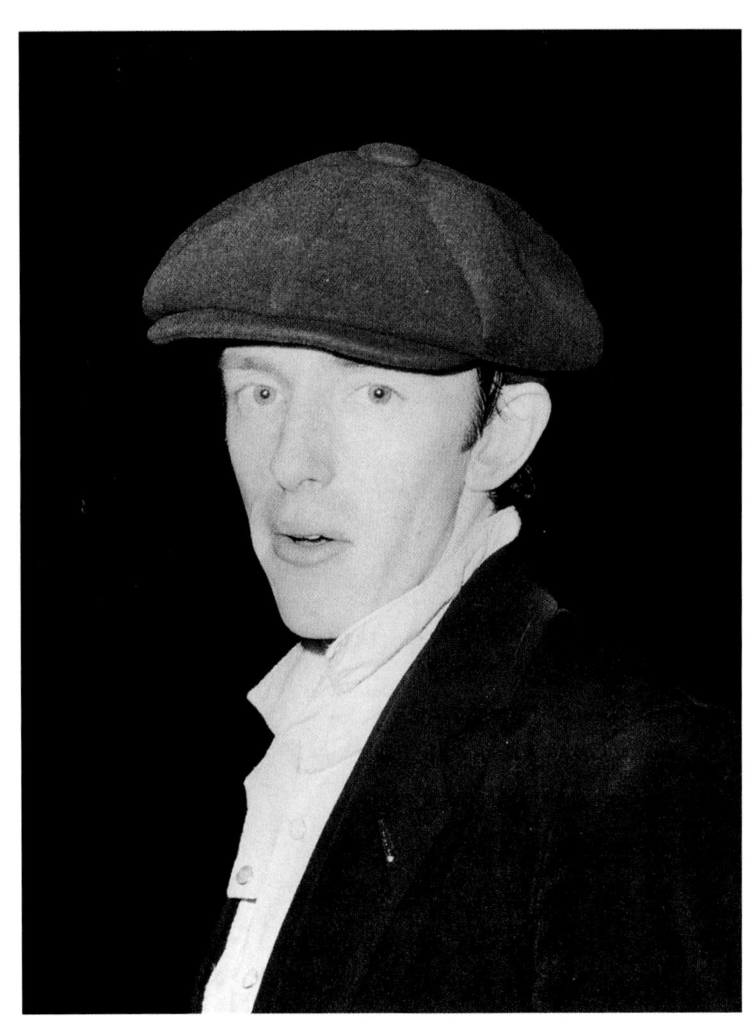

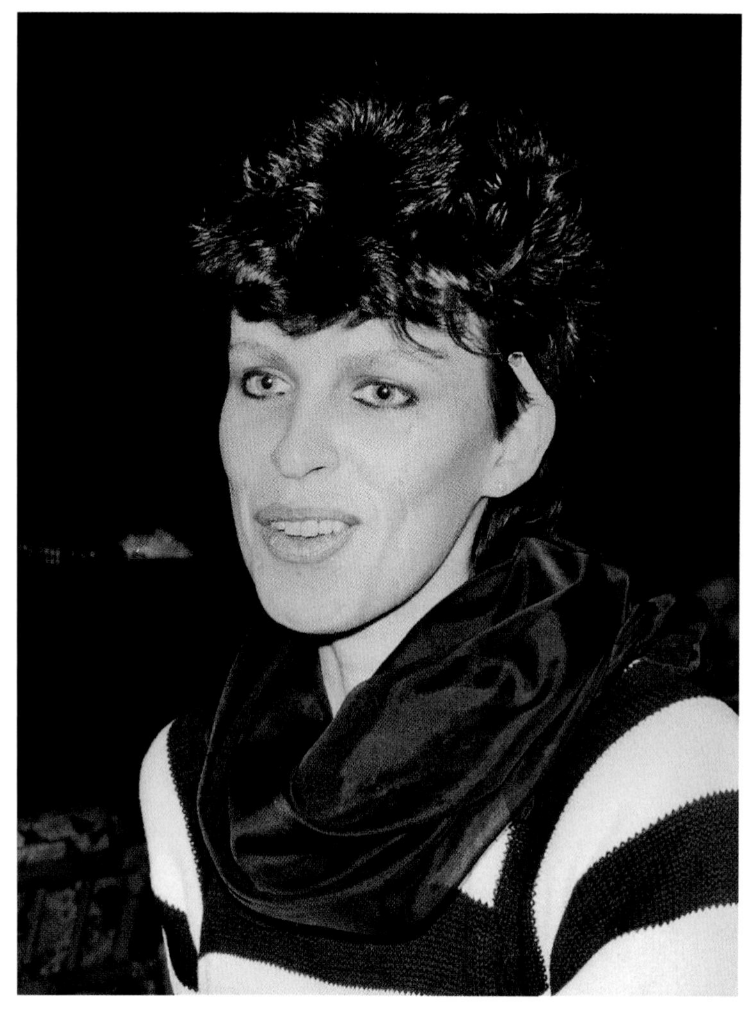

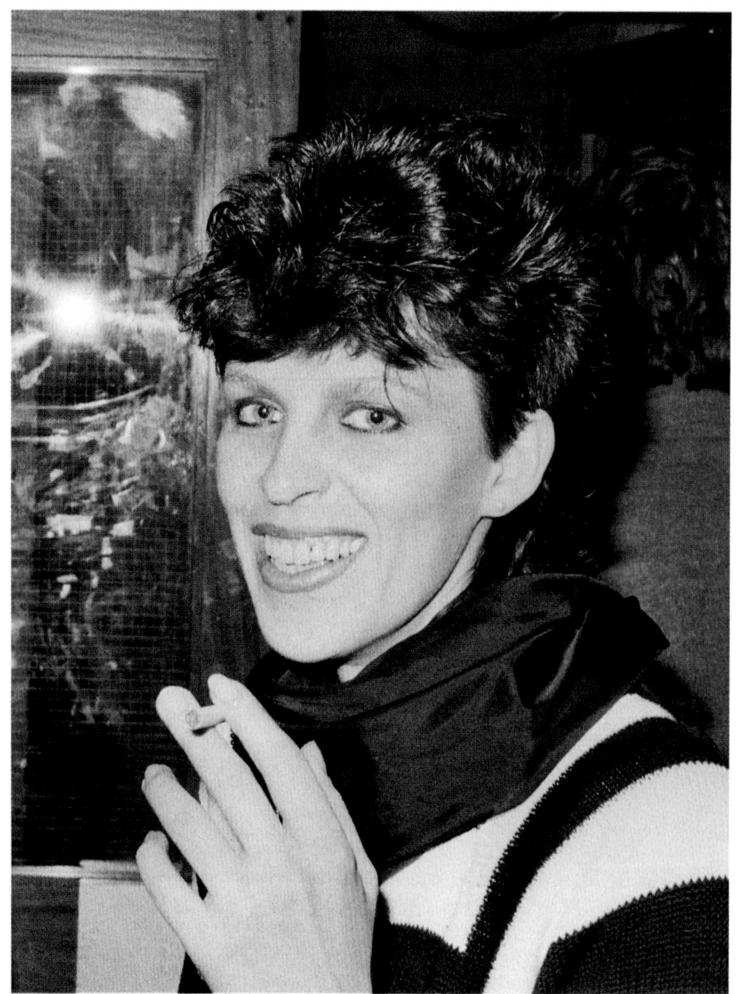

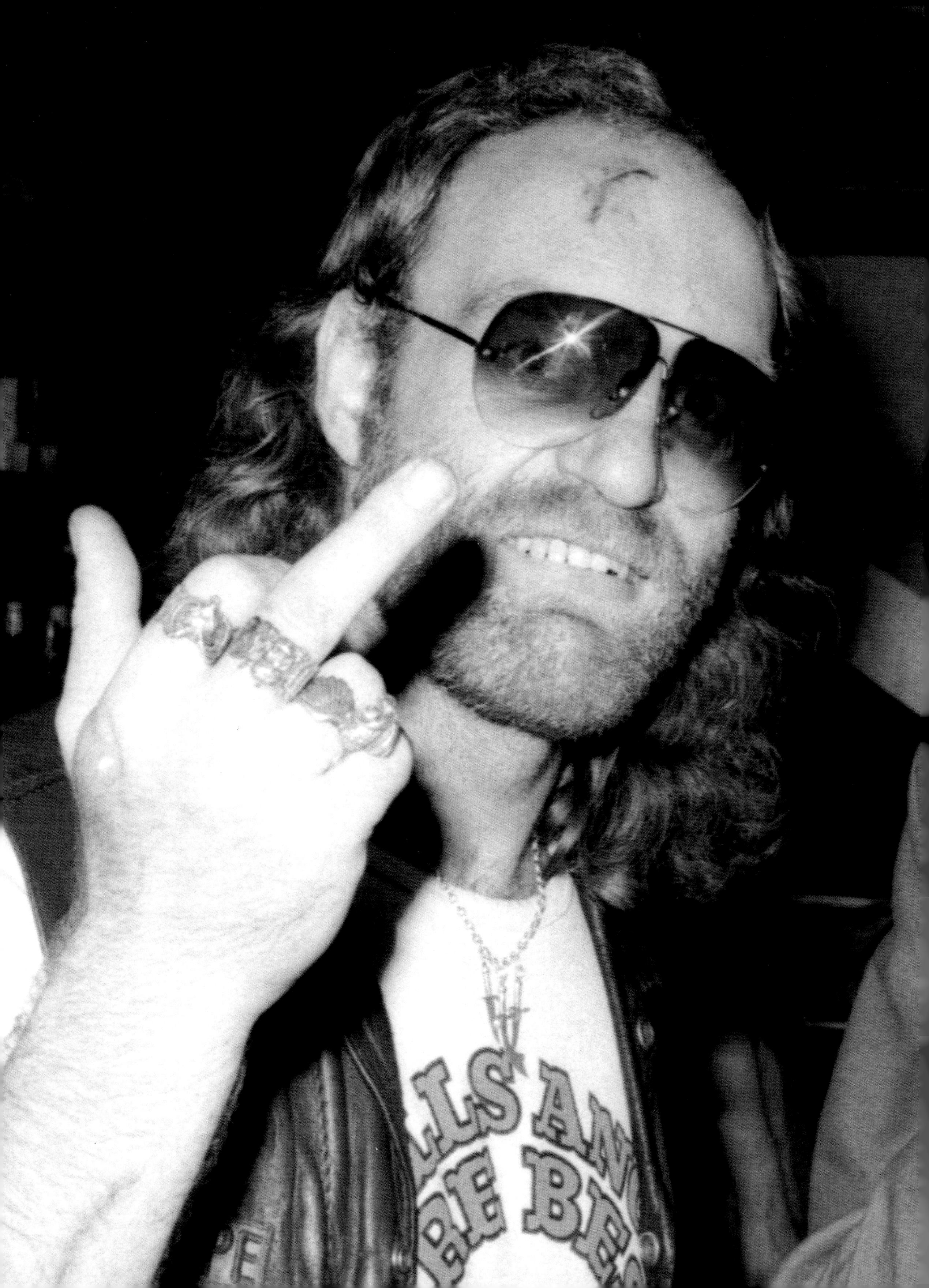
LS AN
E BIG
BE BR

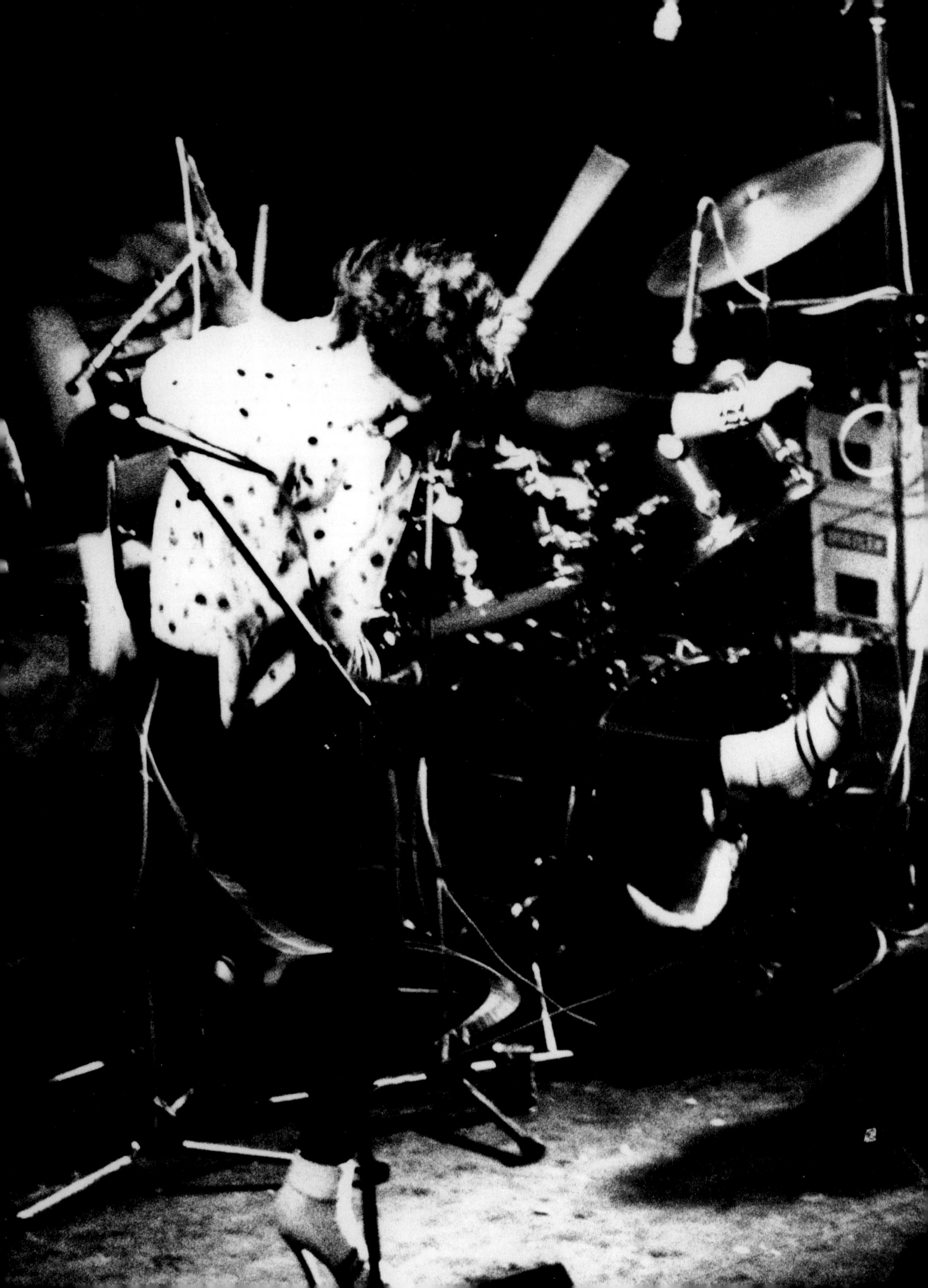

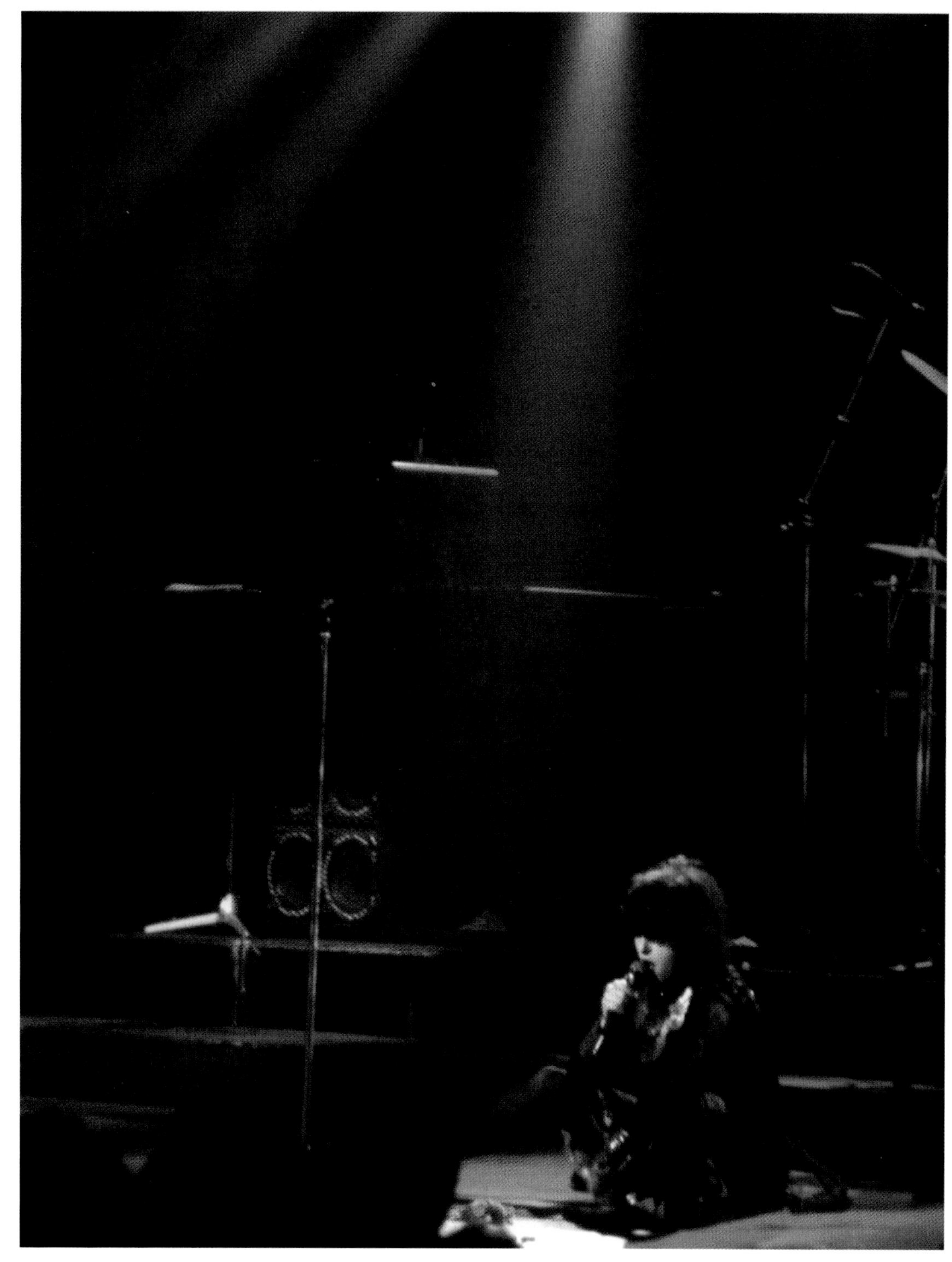

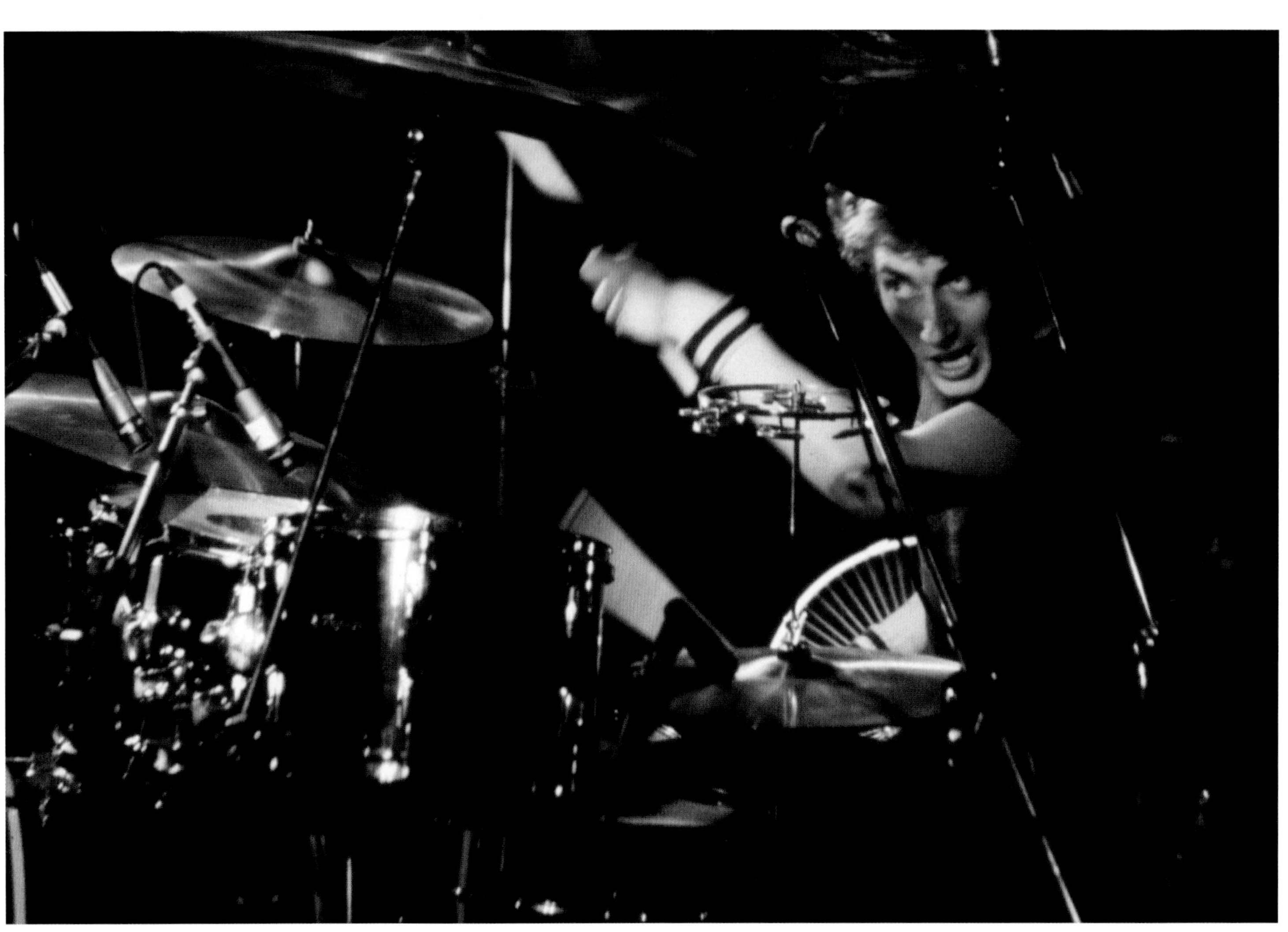

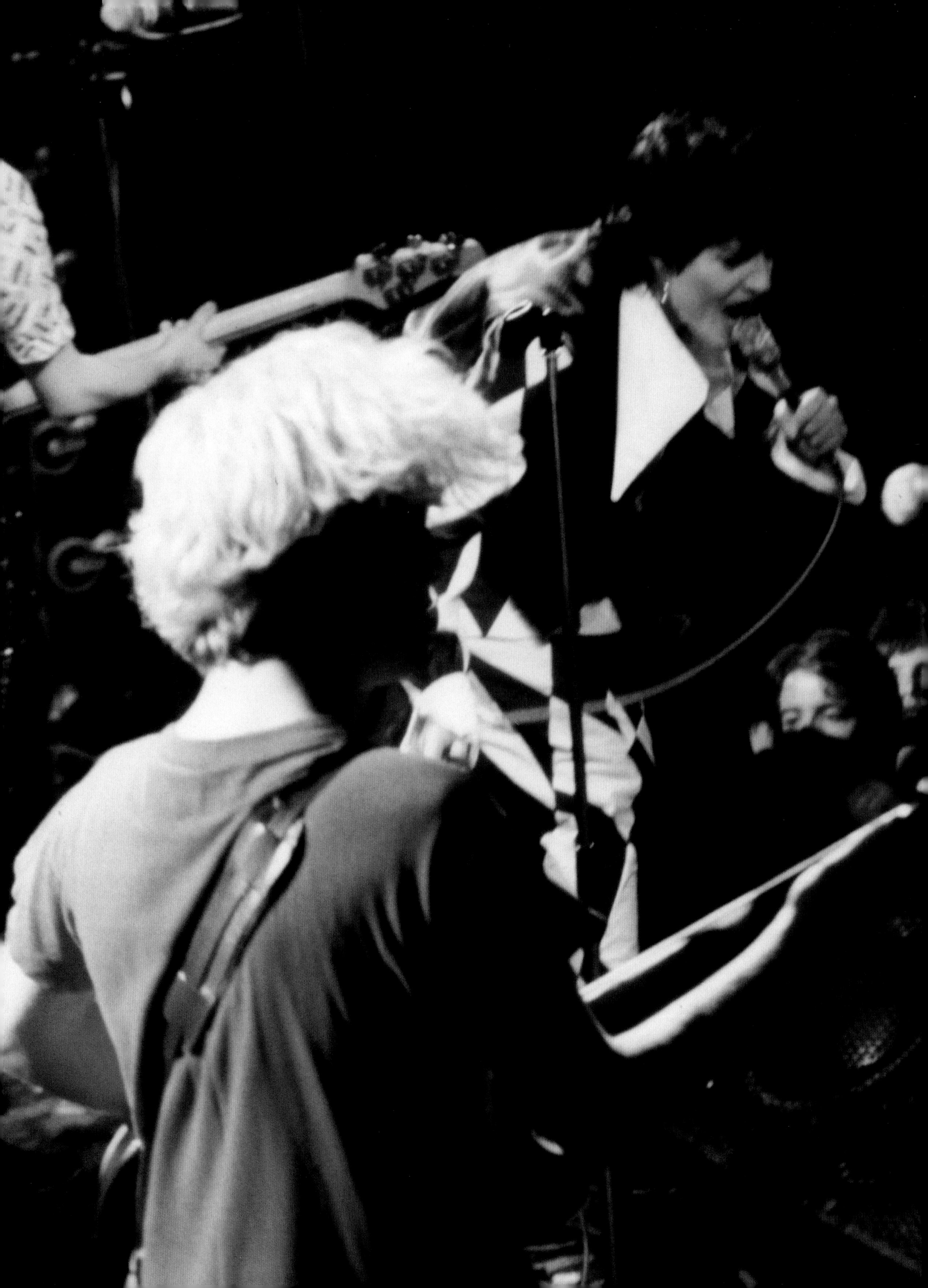

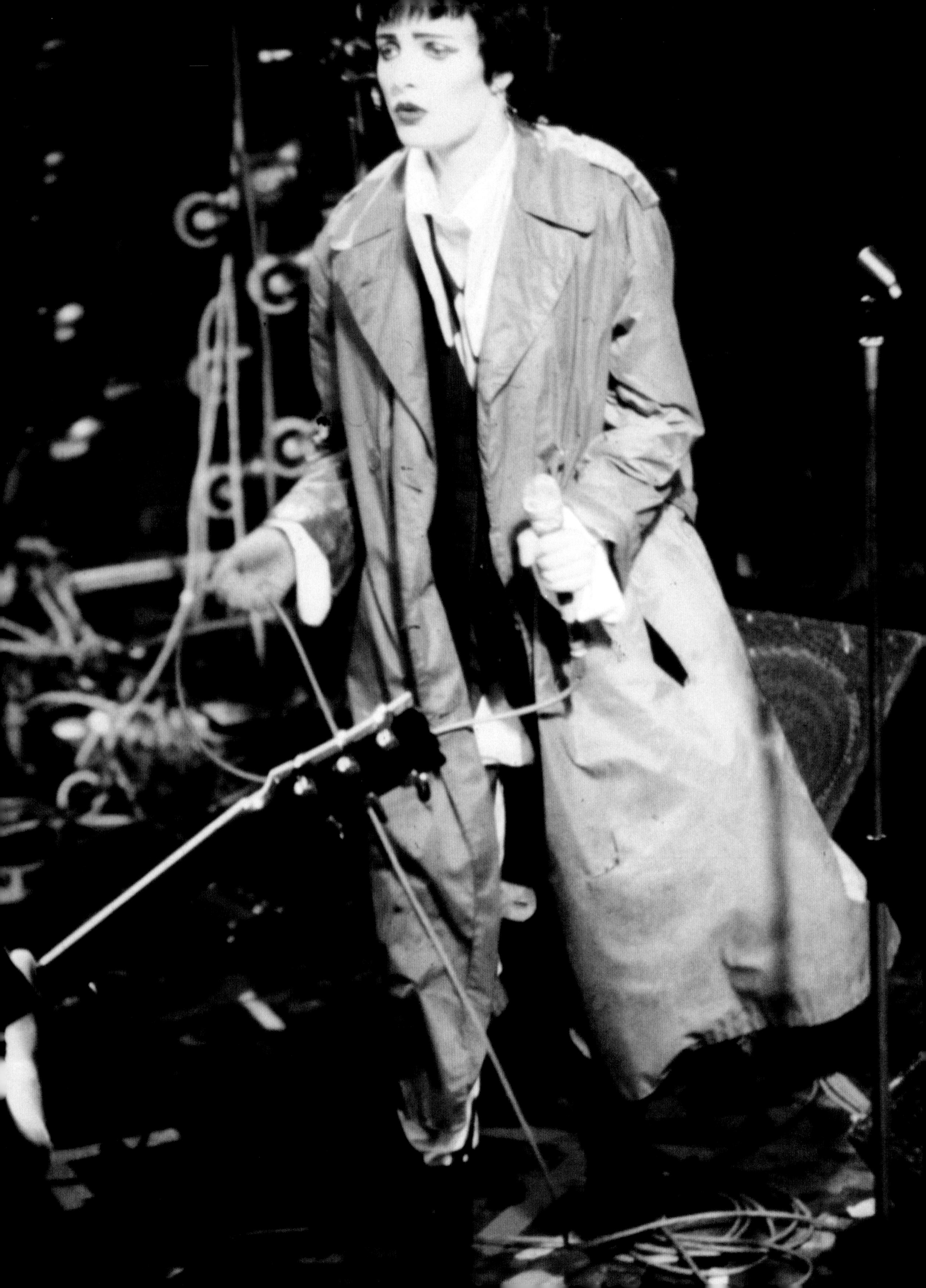

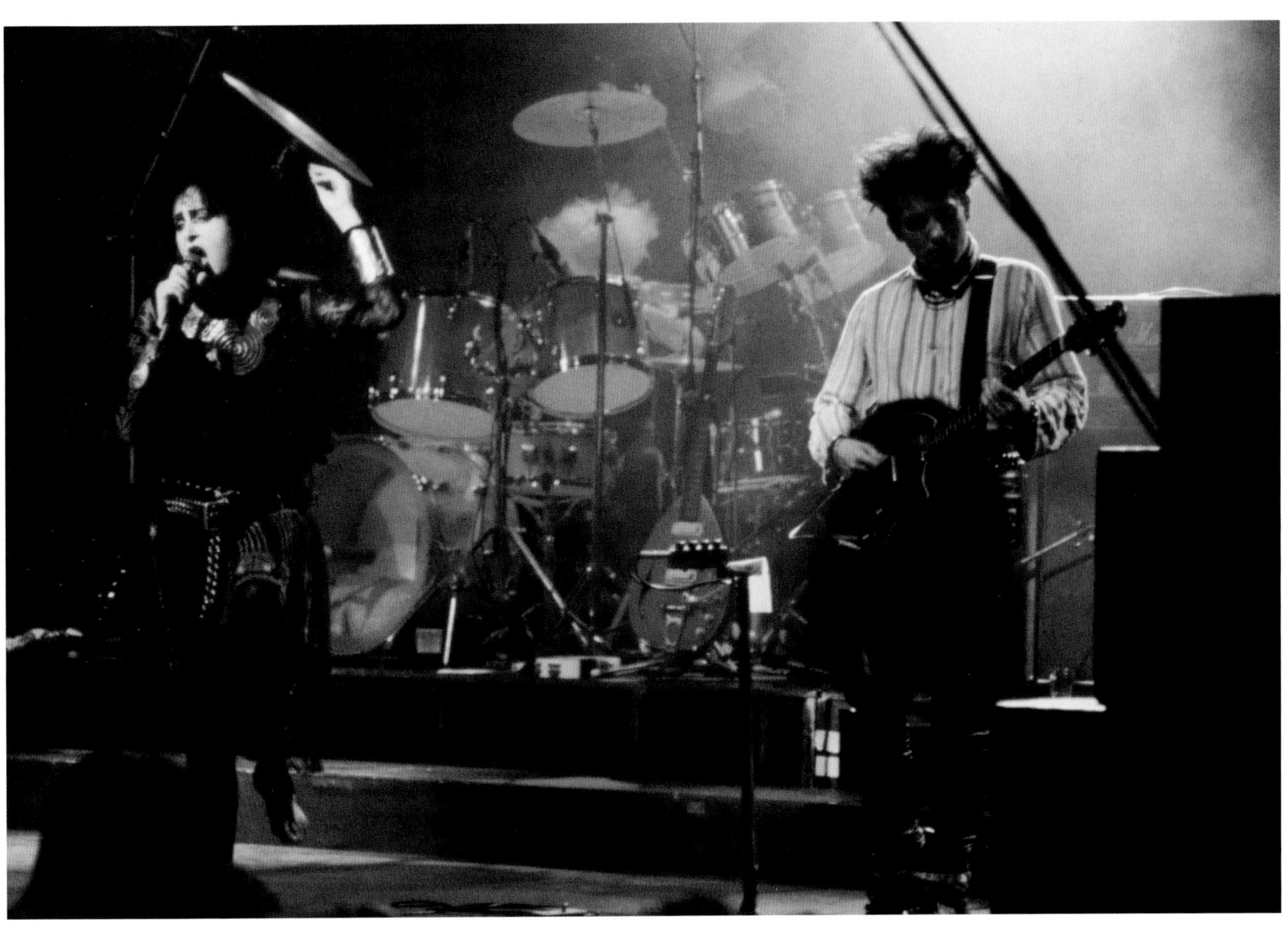

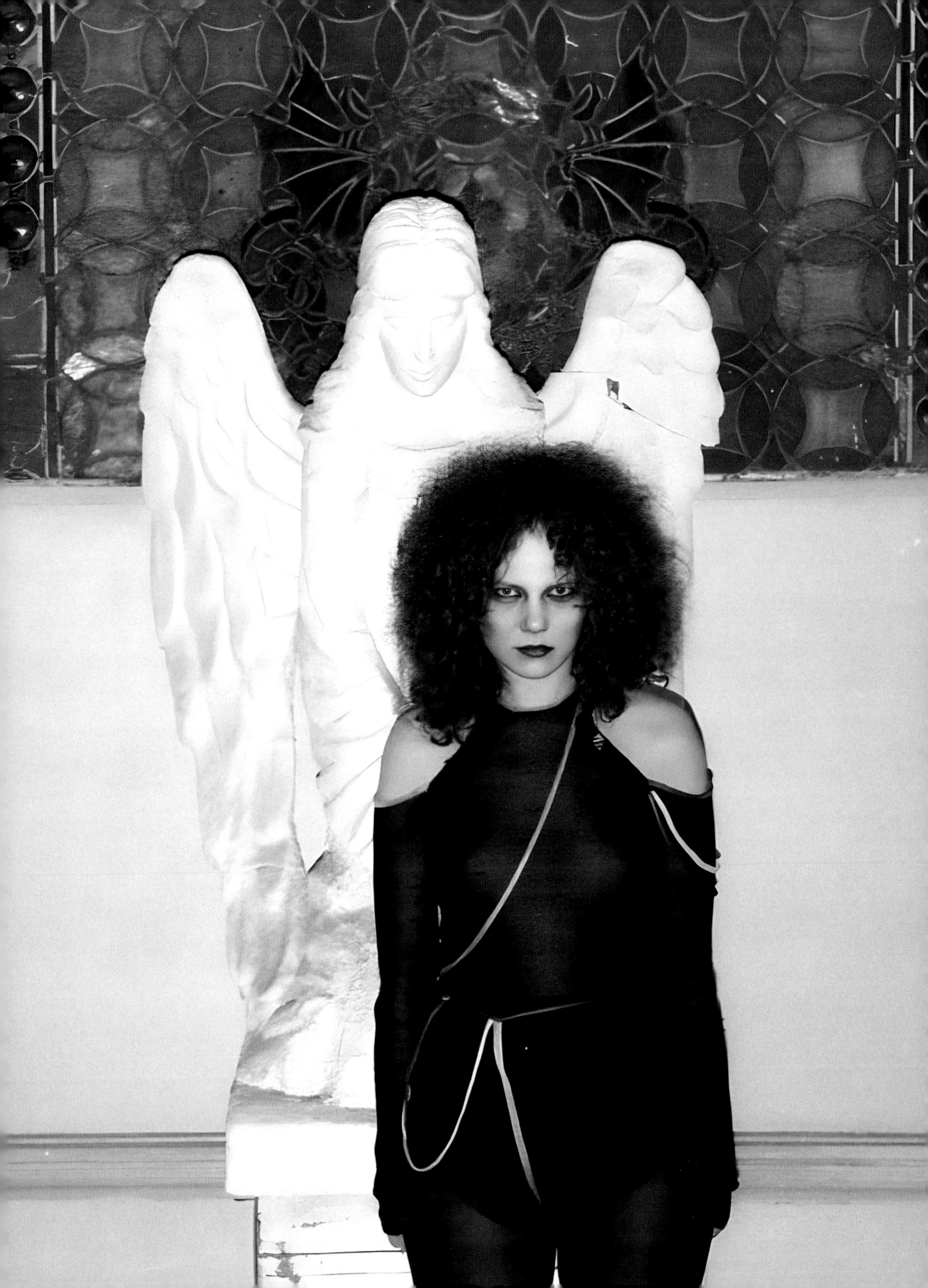

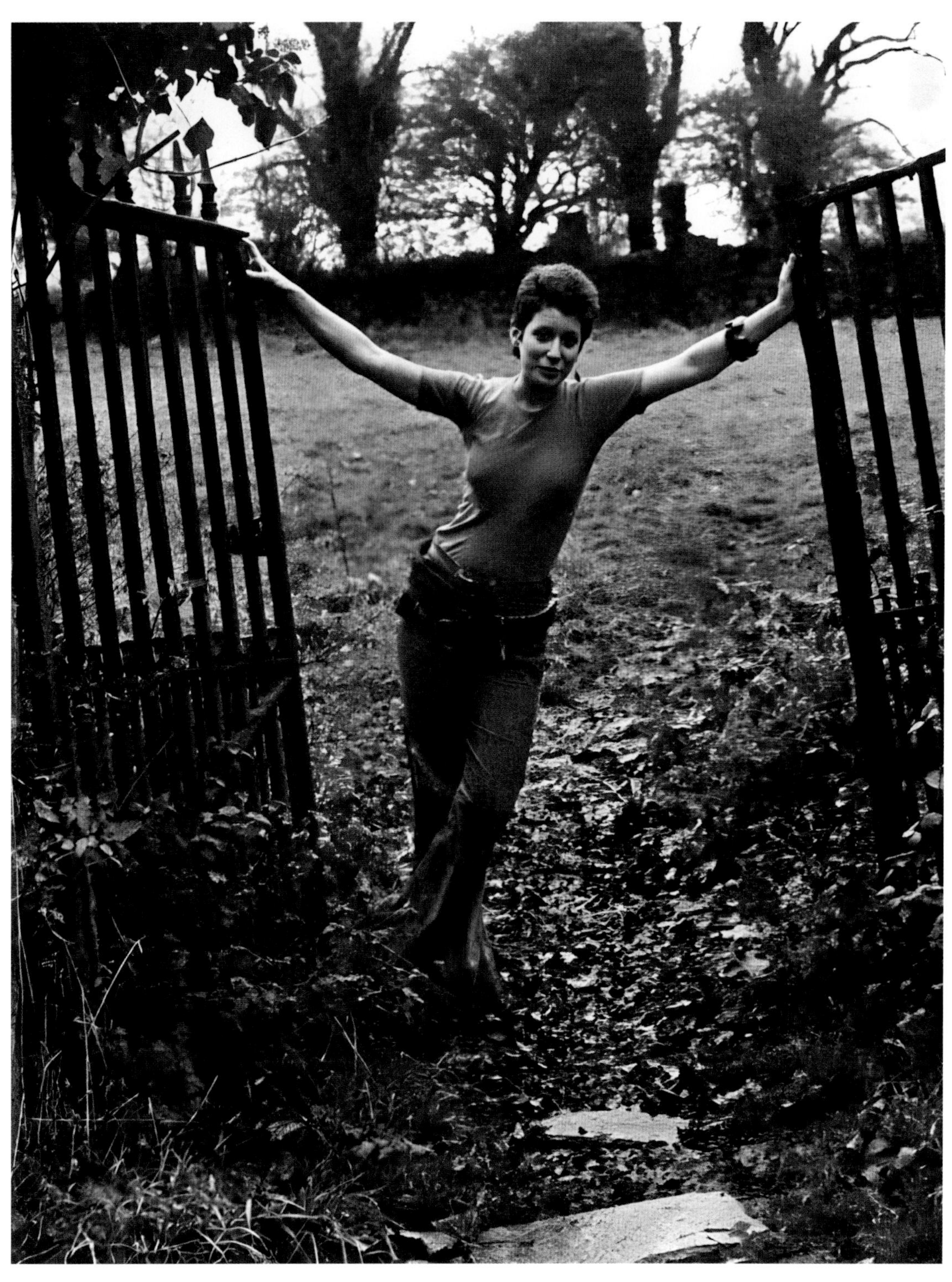

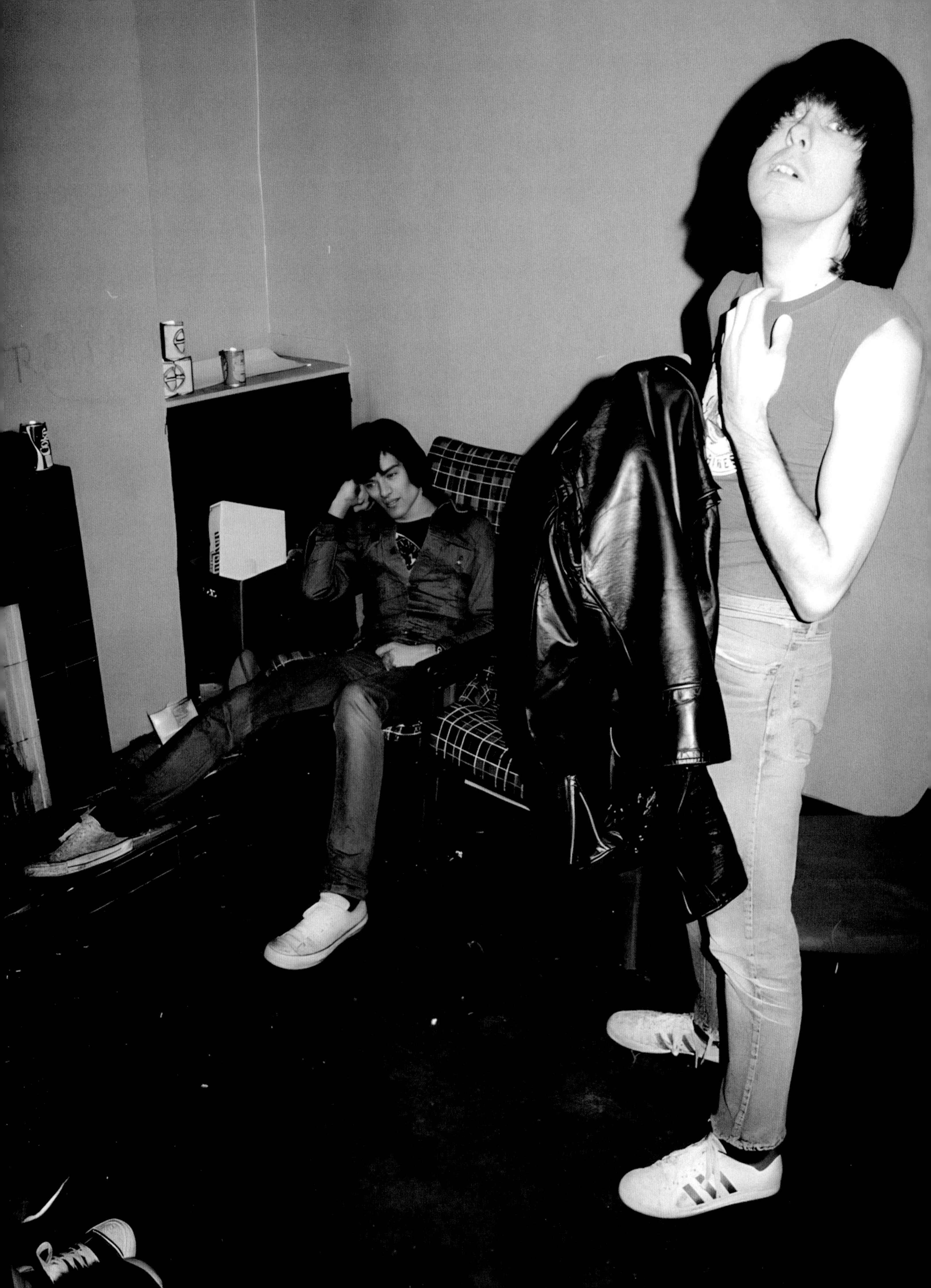

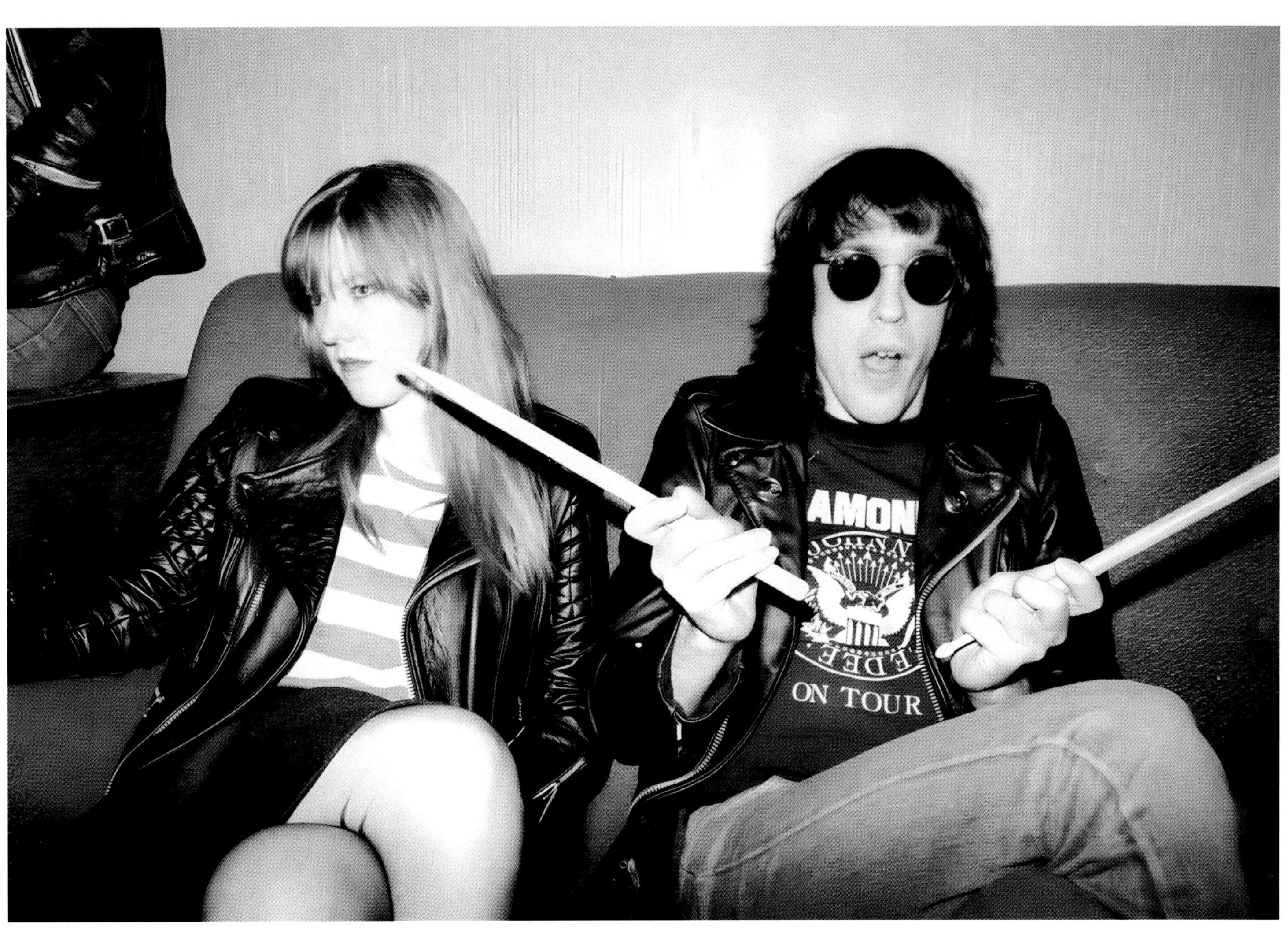

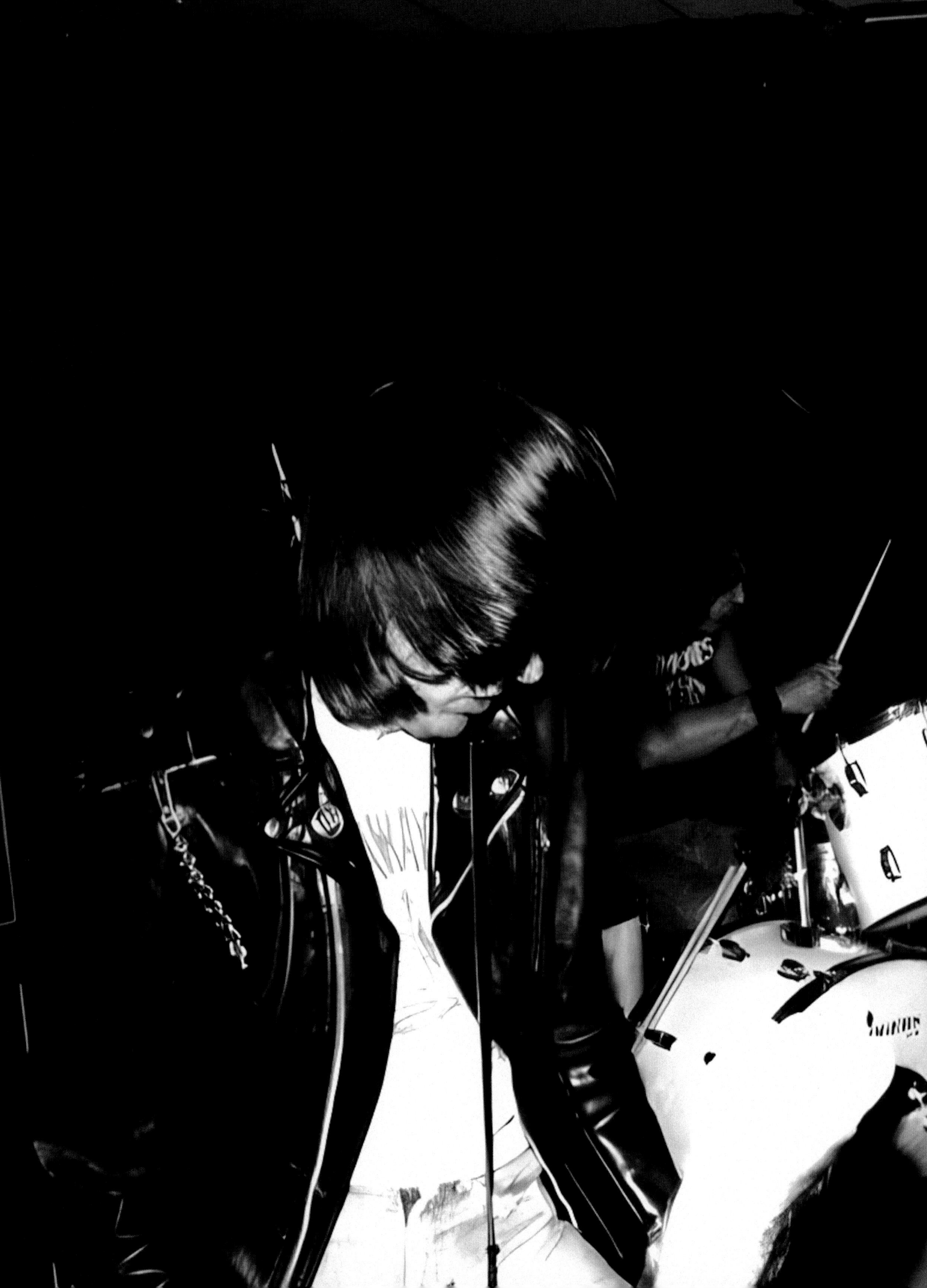

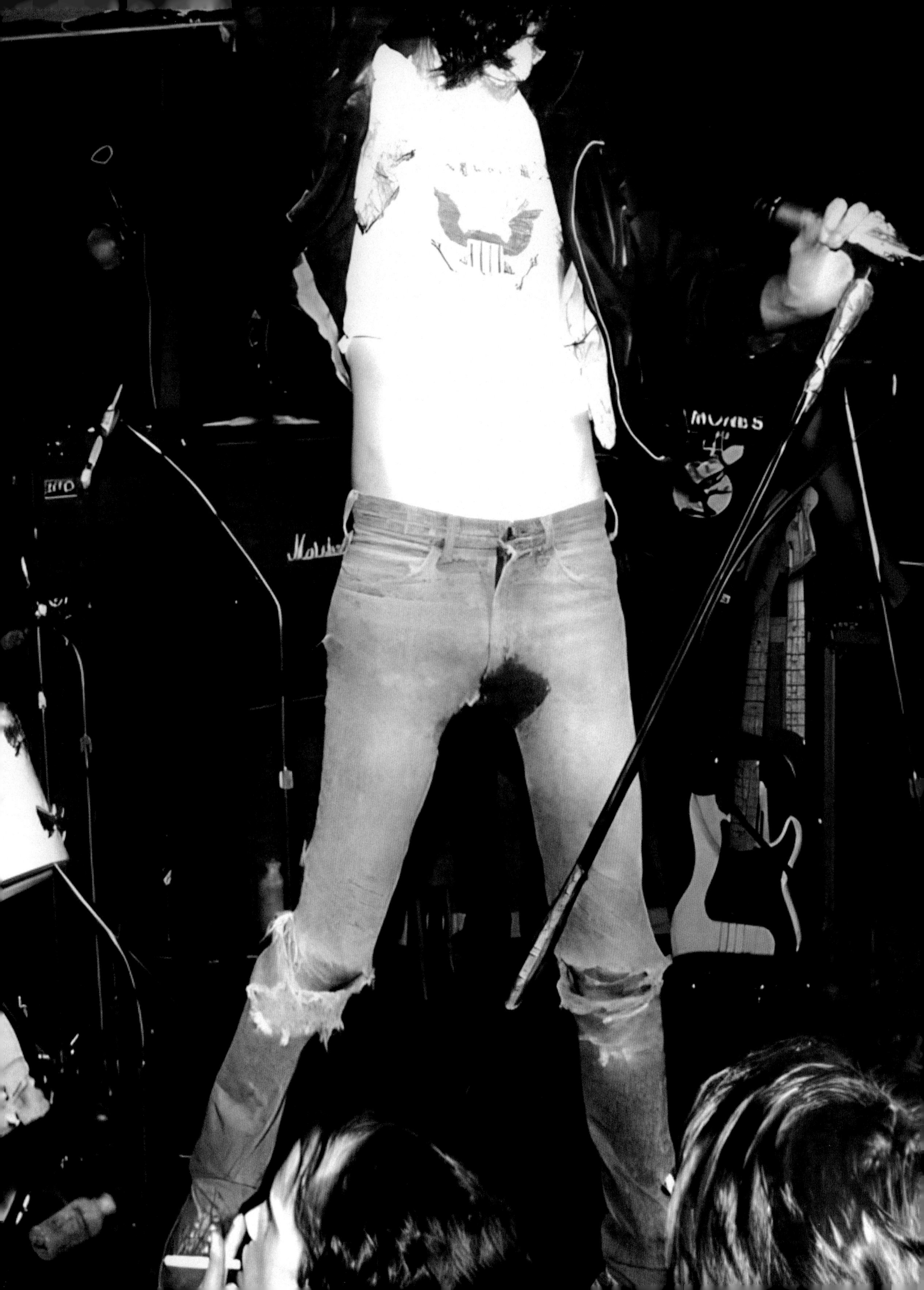

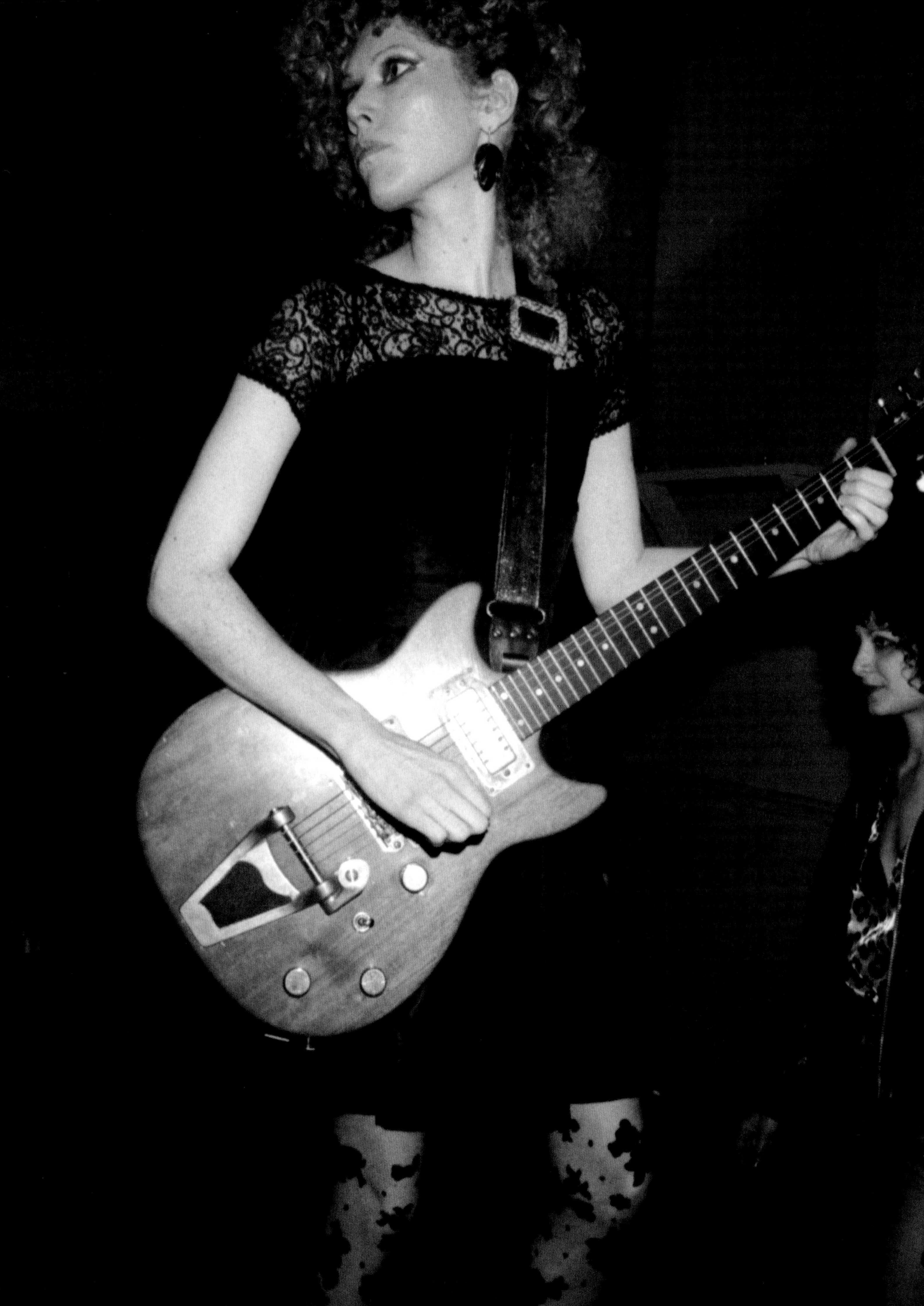

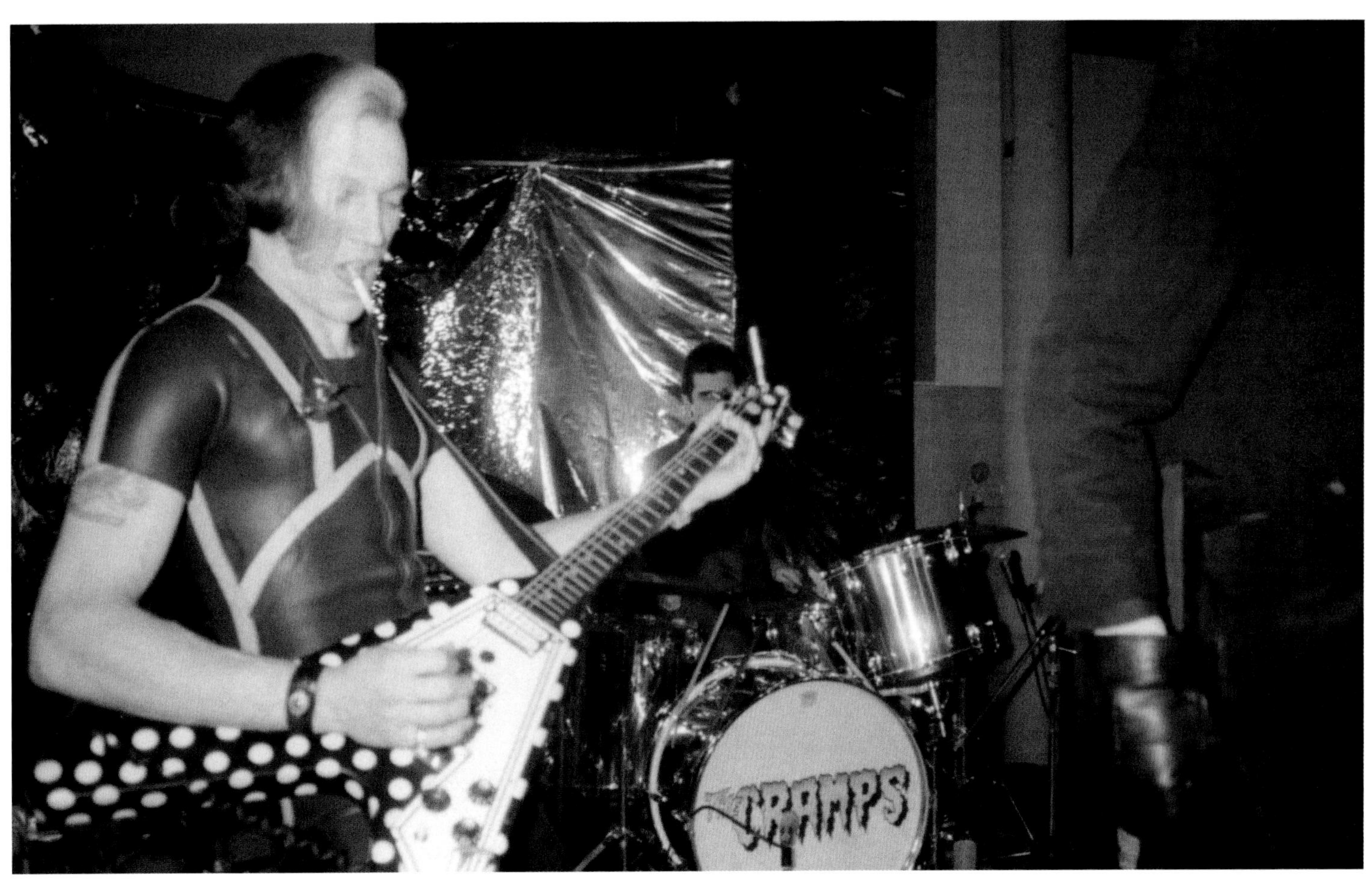
CRAMPS

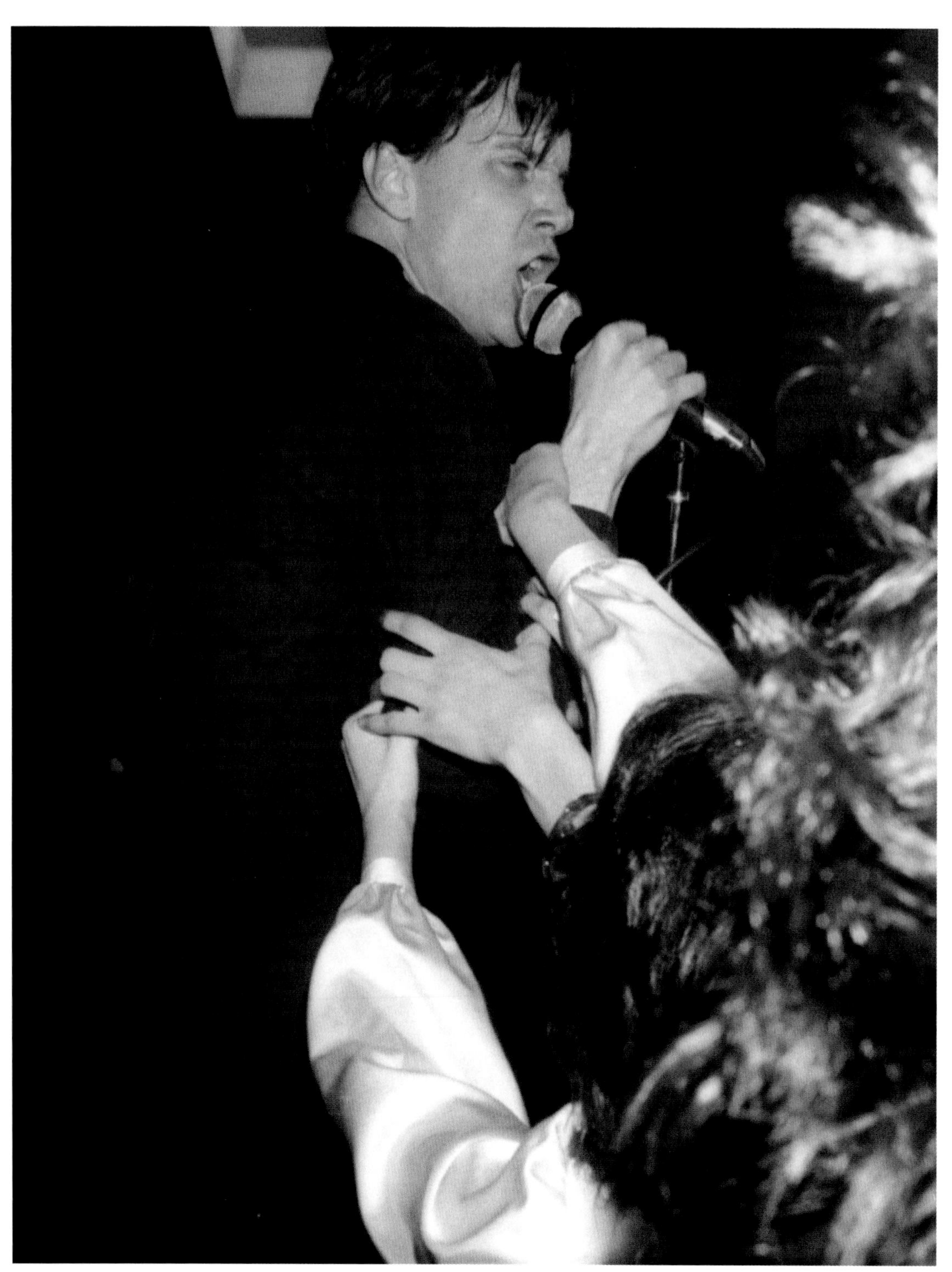

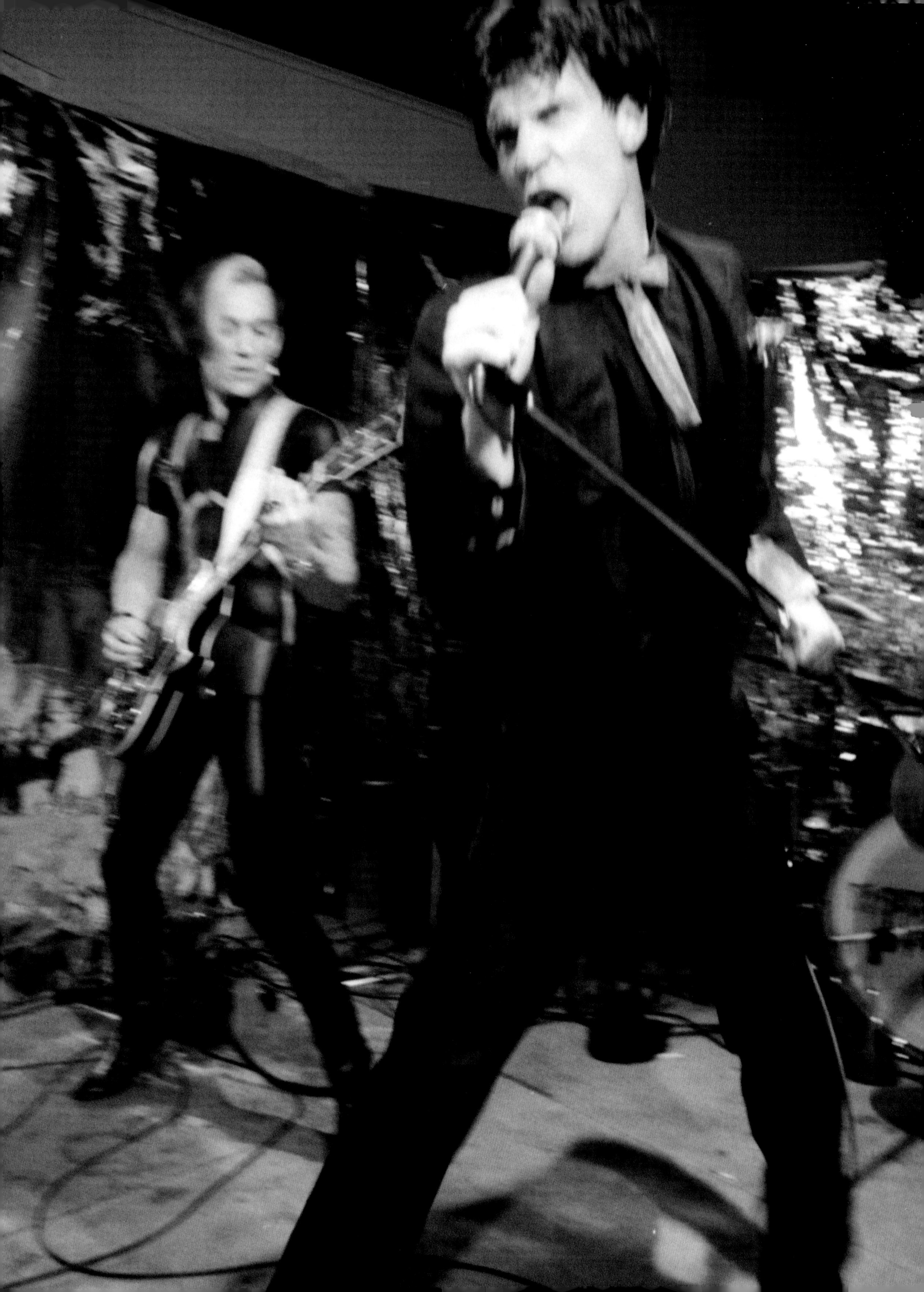

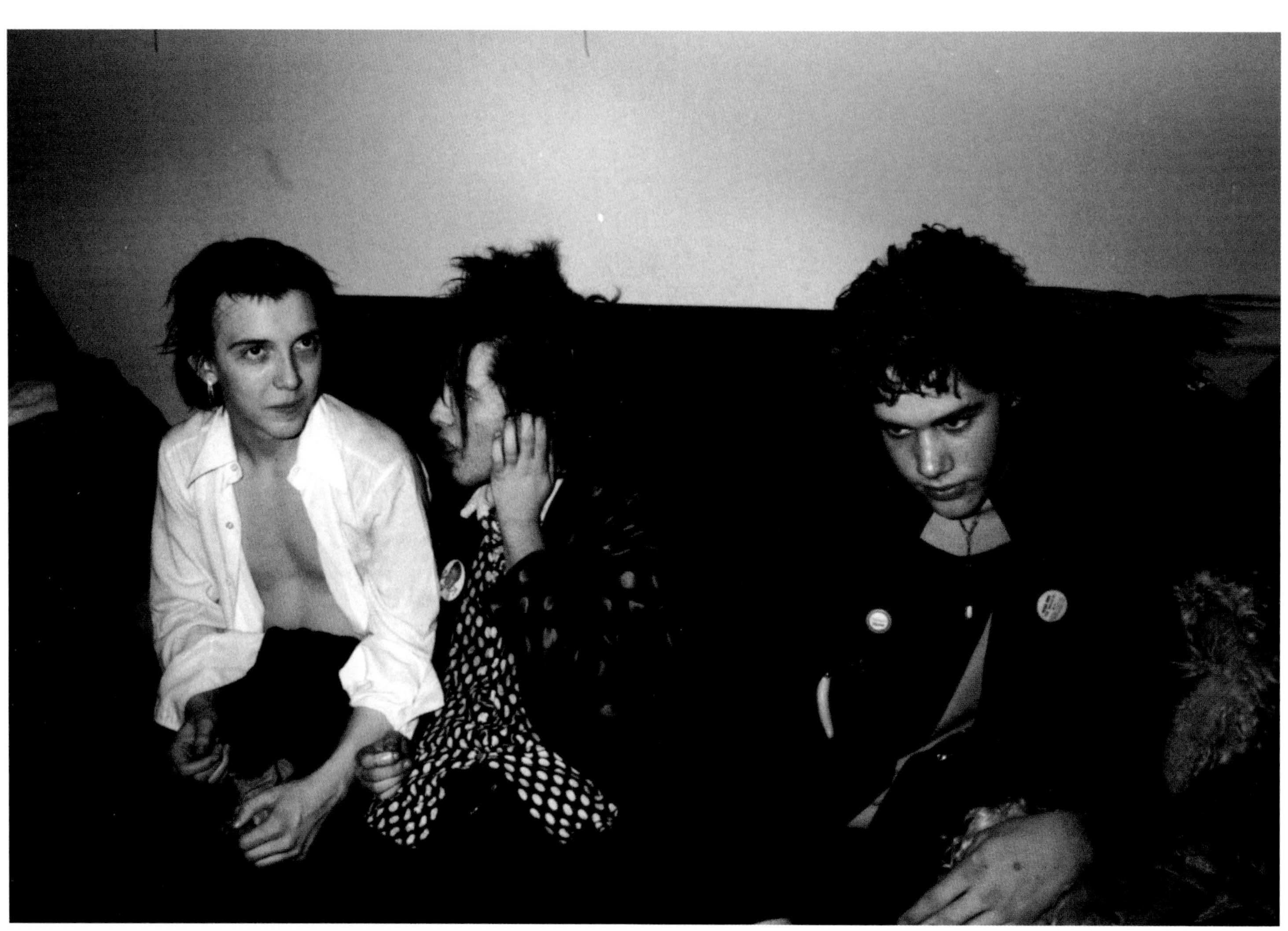

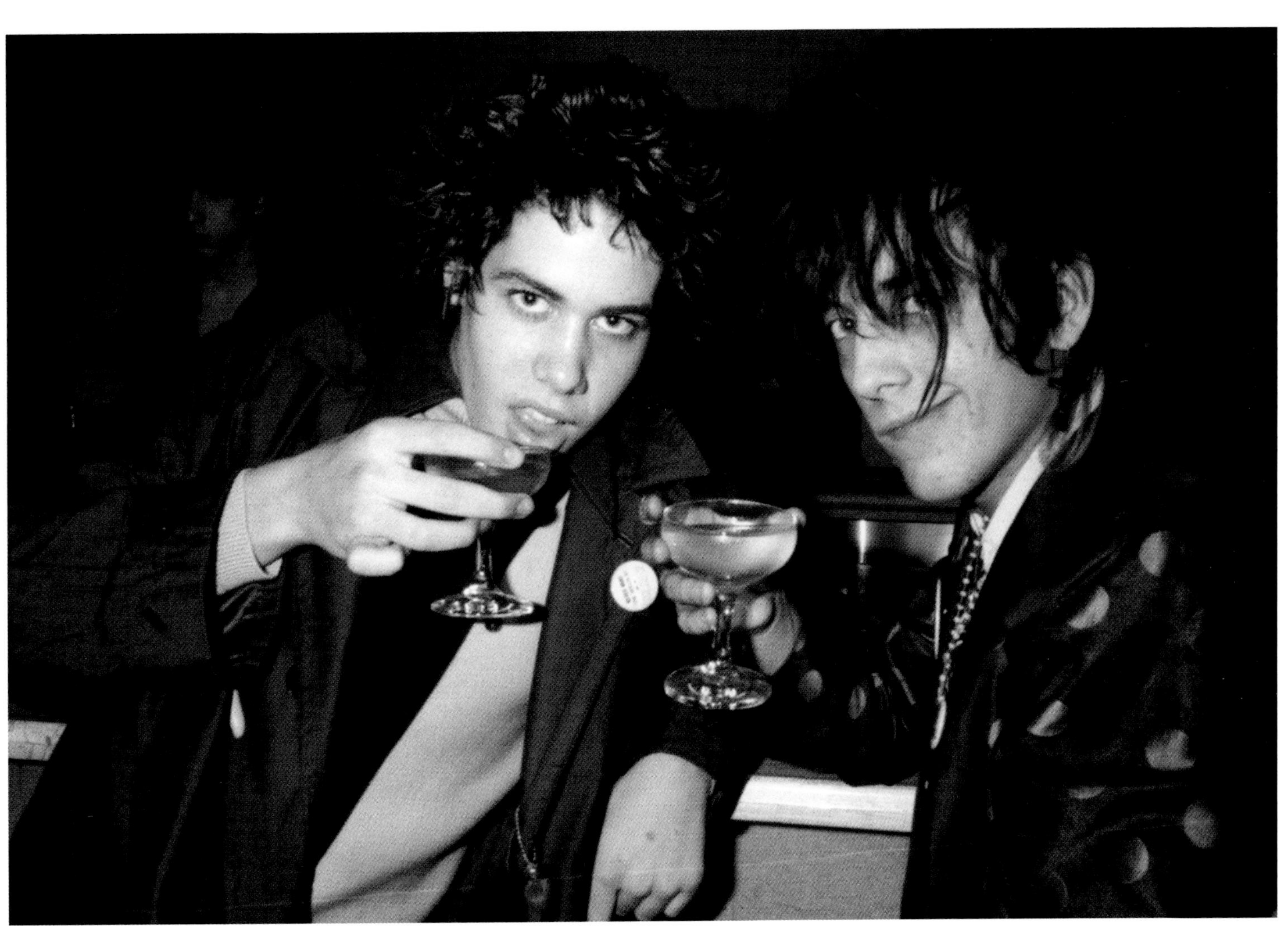

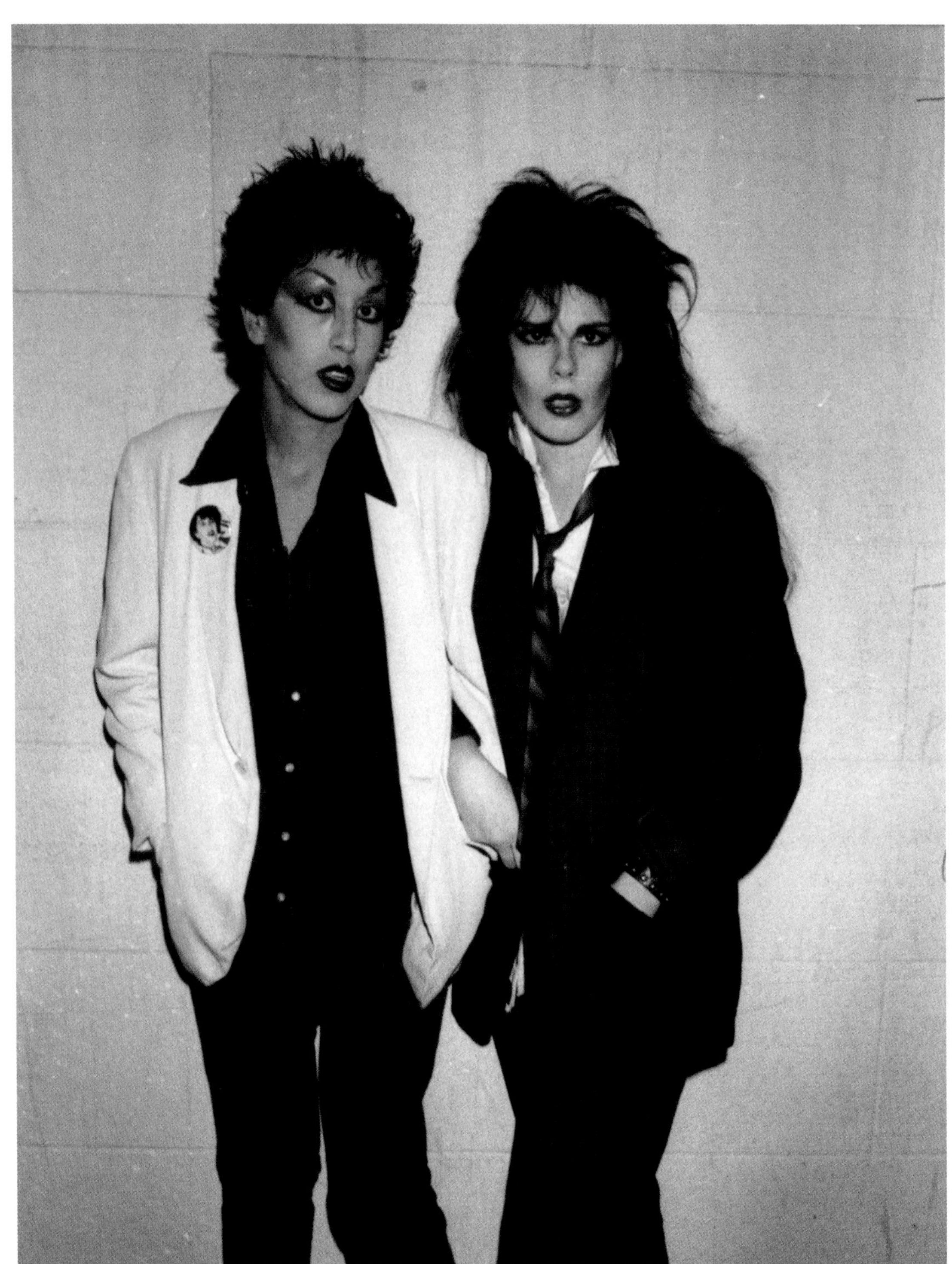

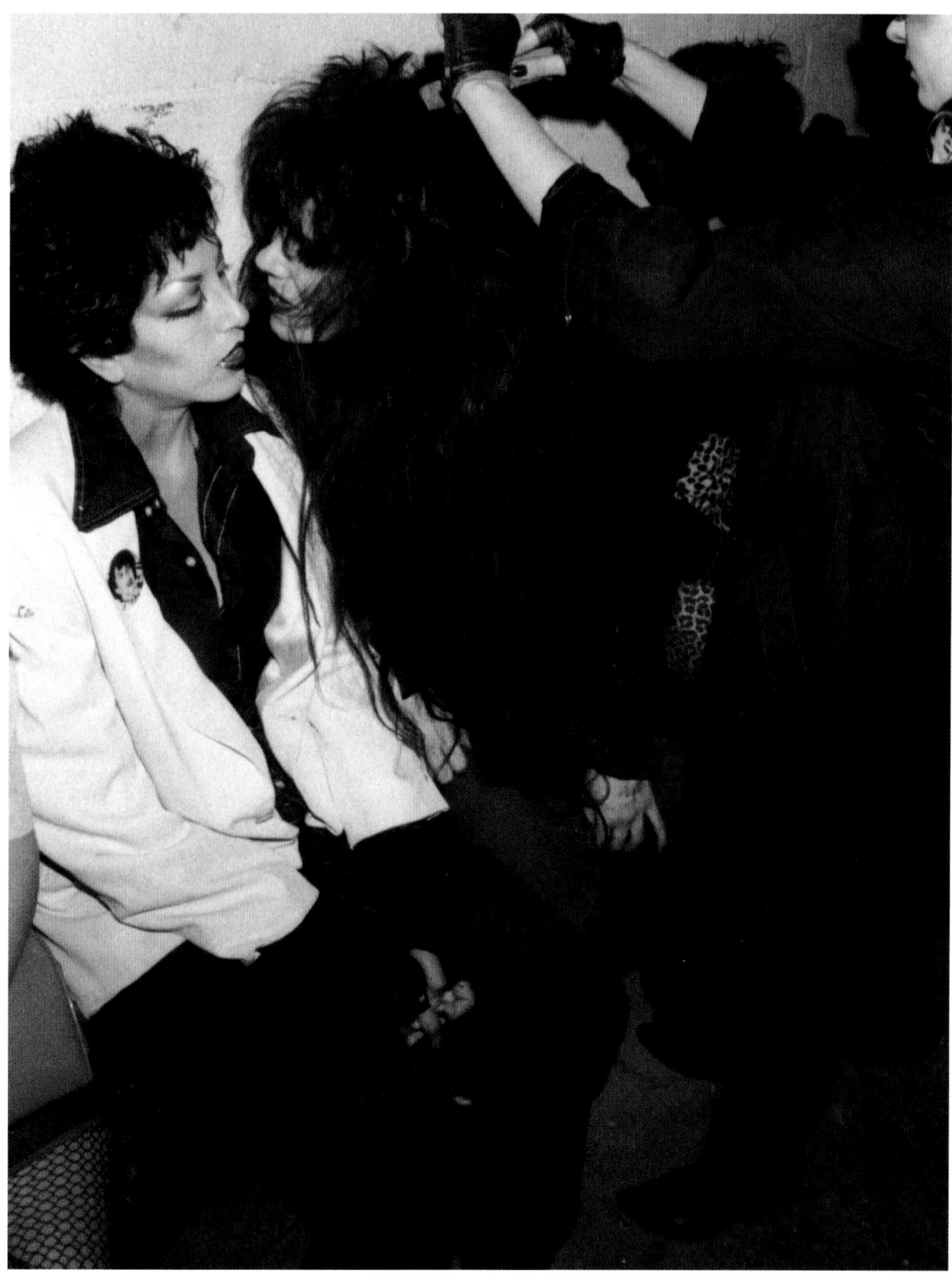

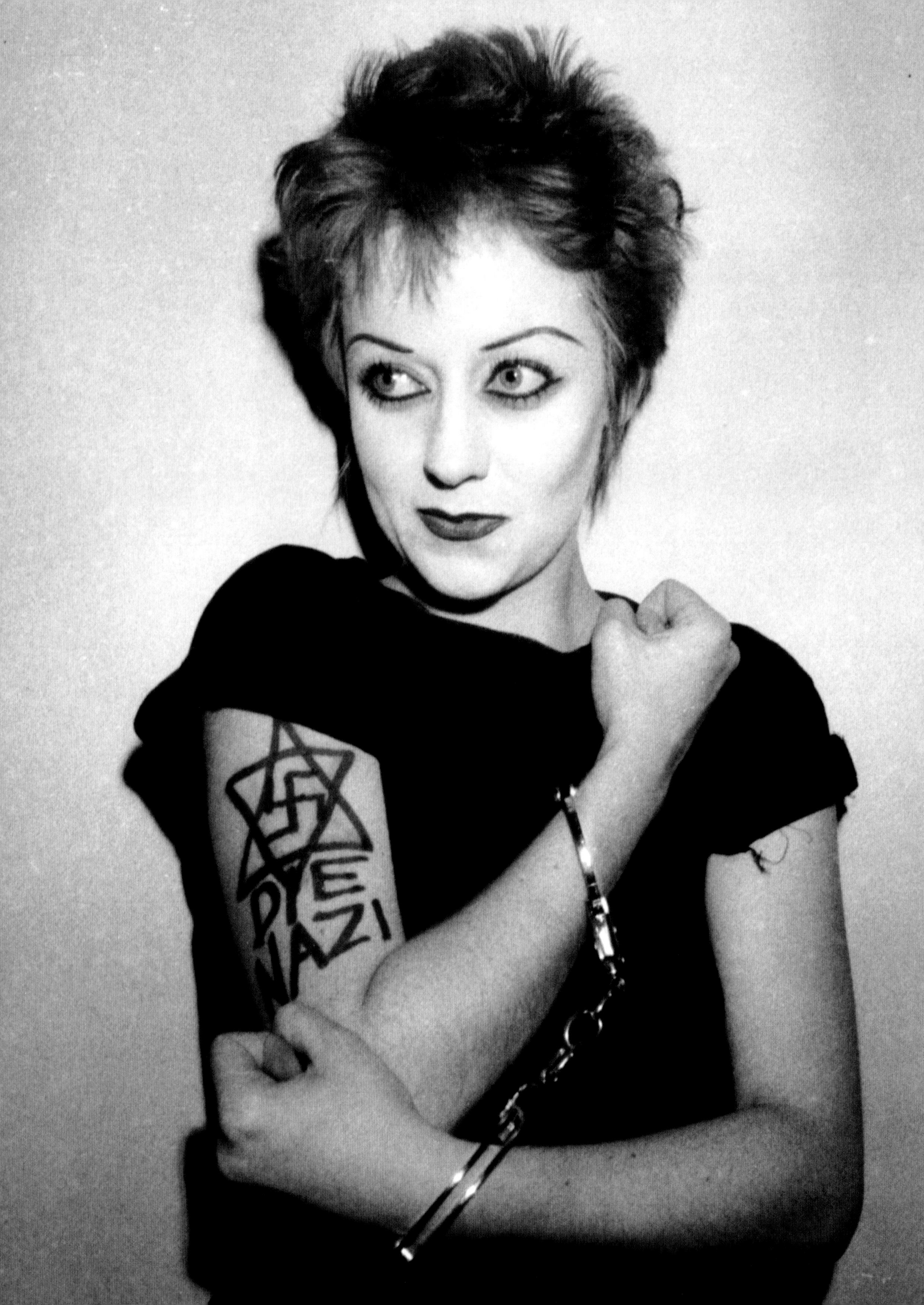
DYE
NAZI

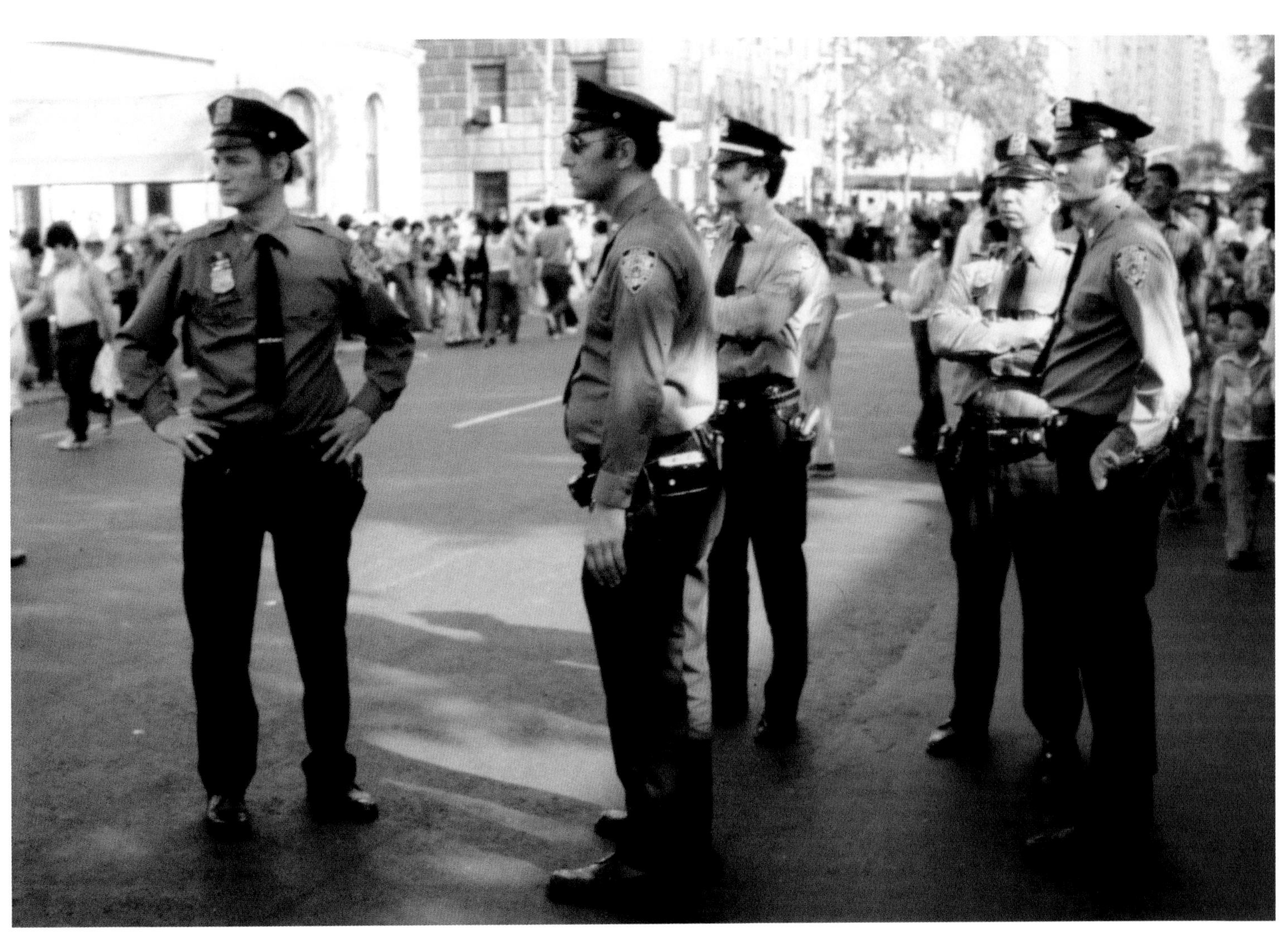

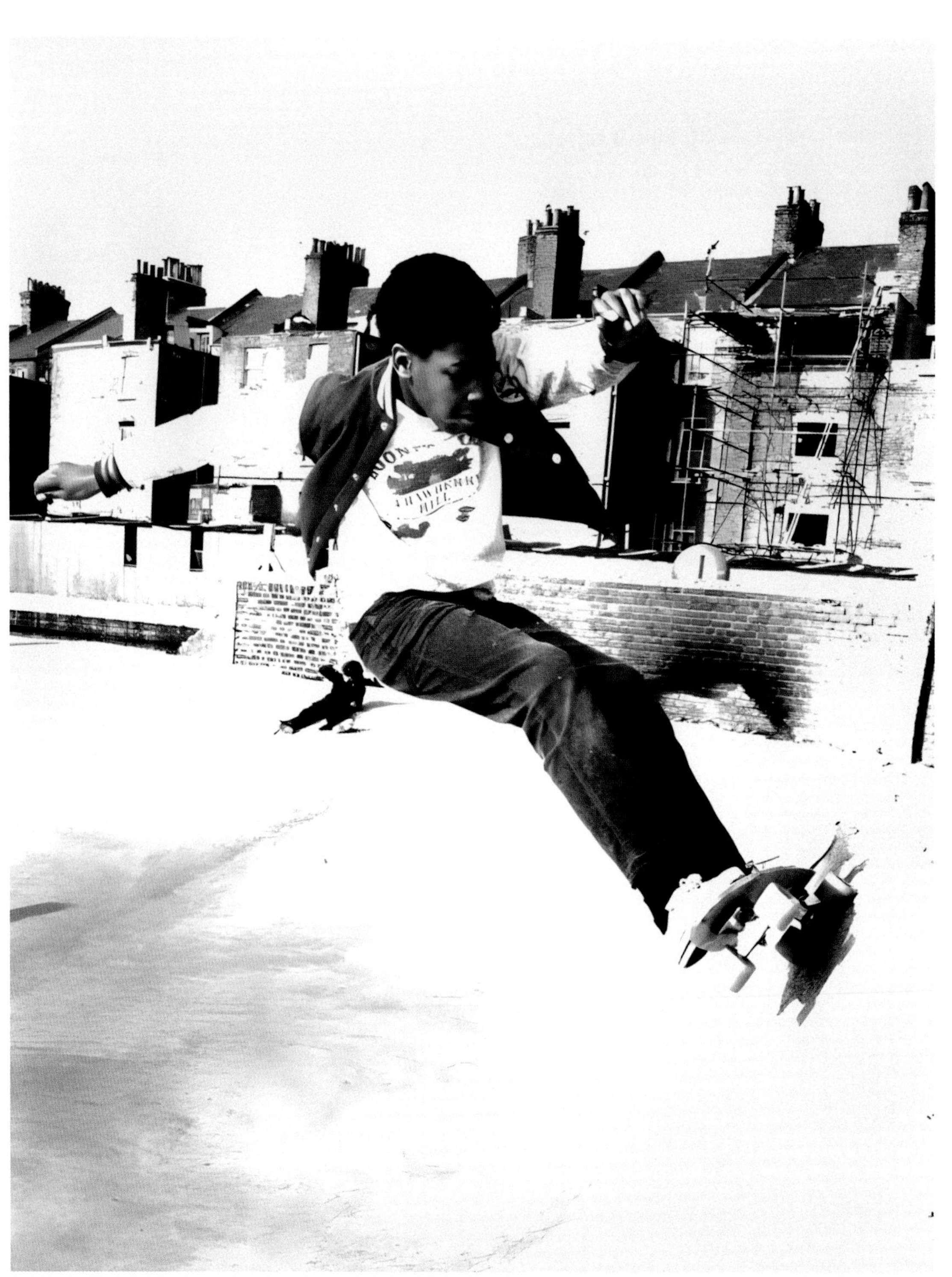

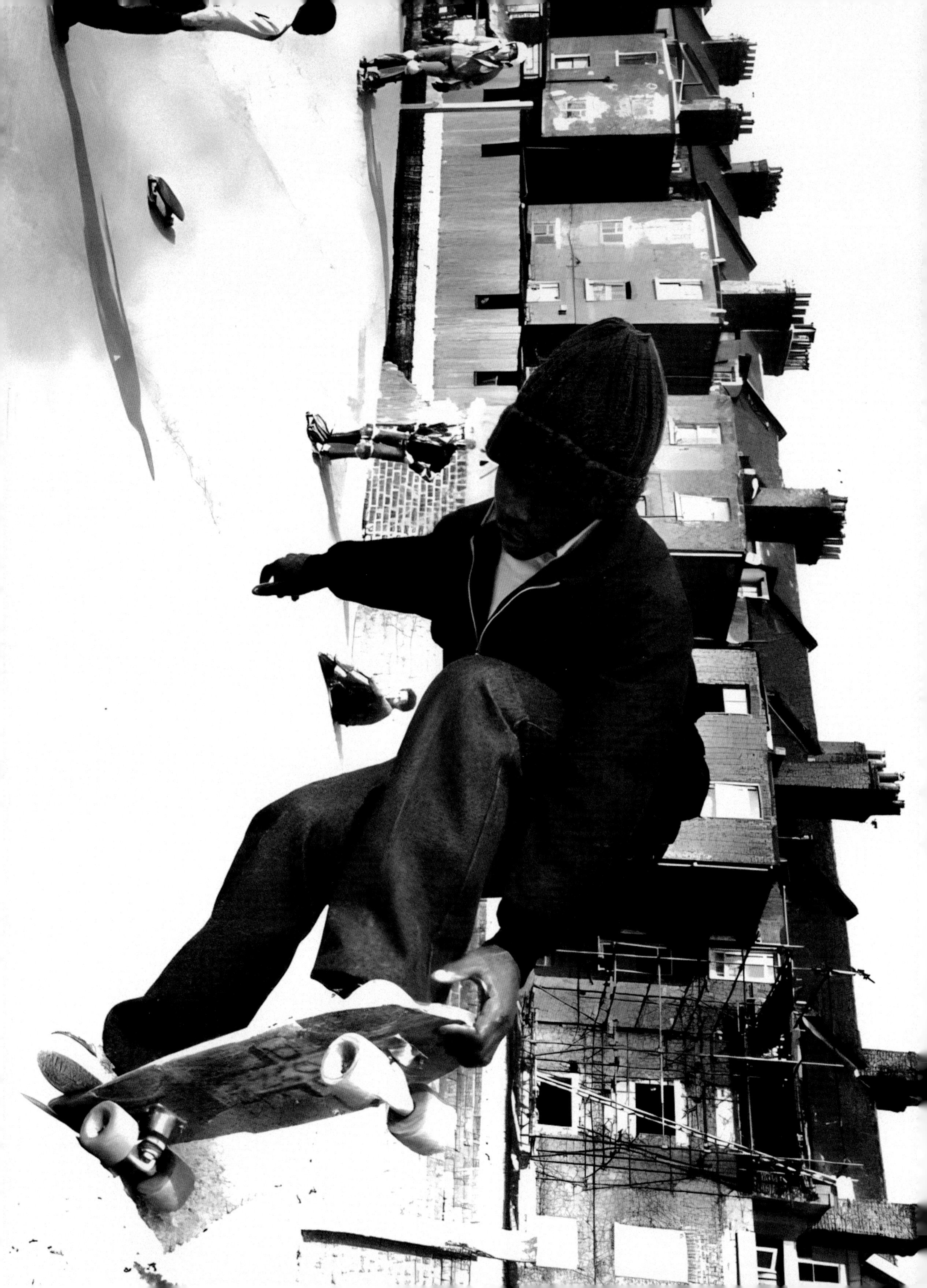

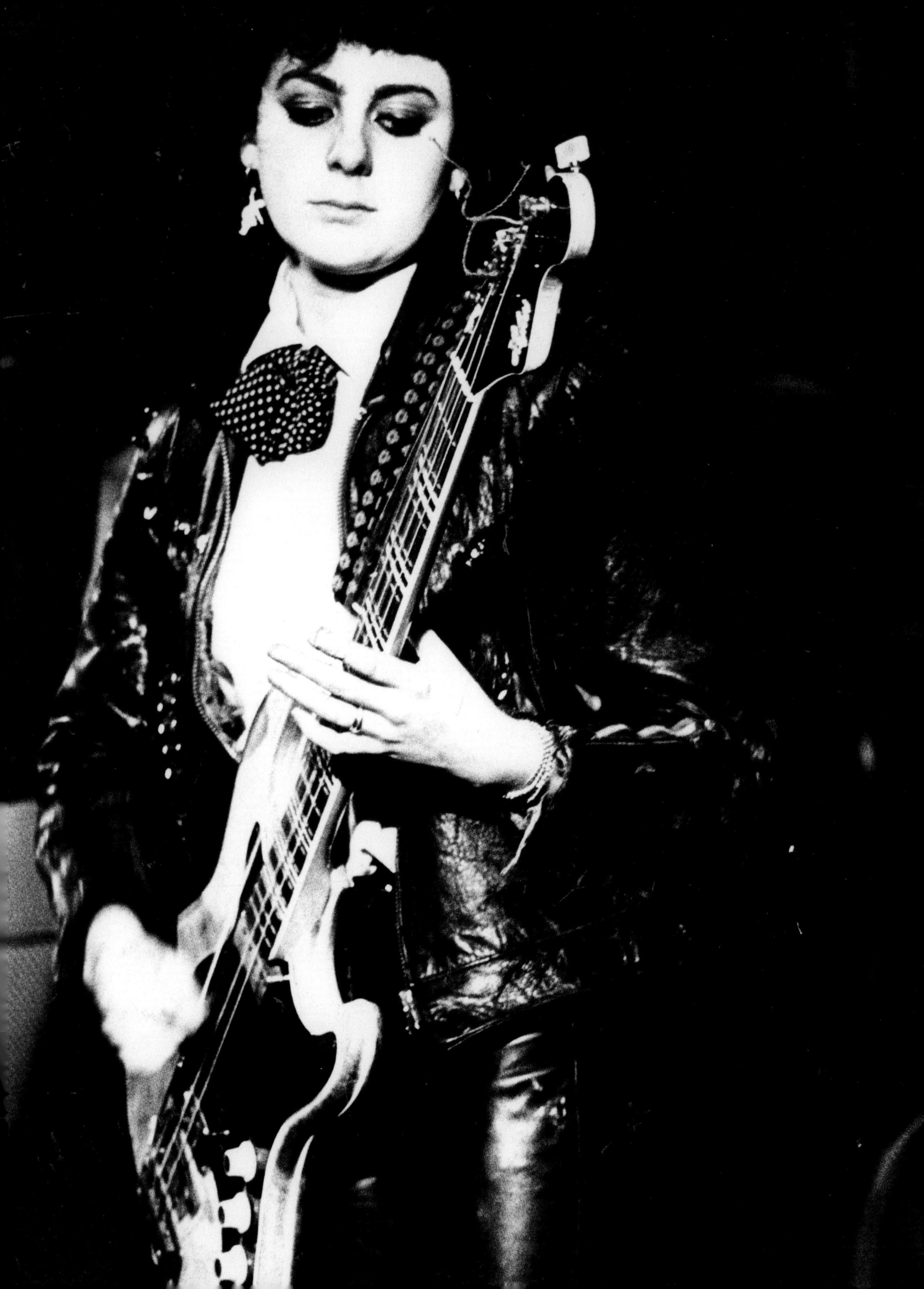

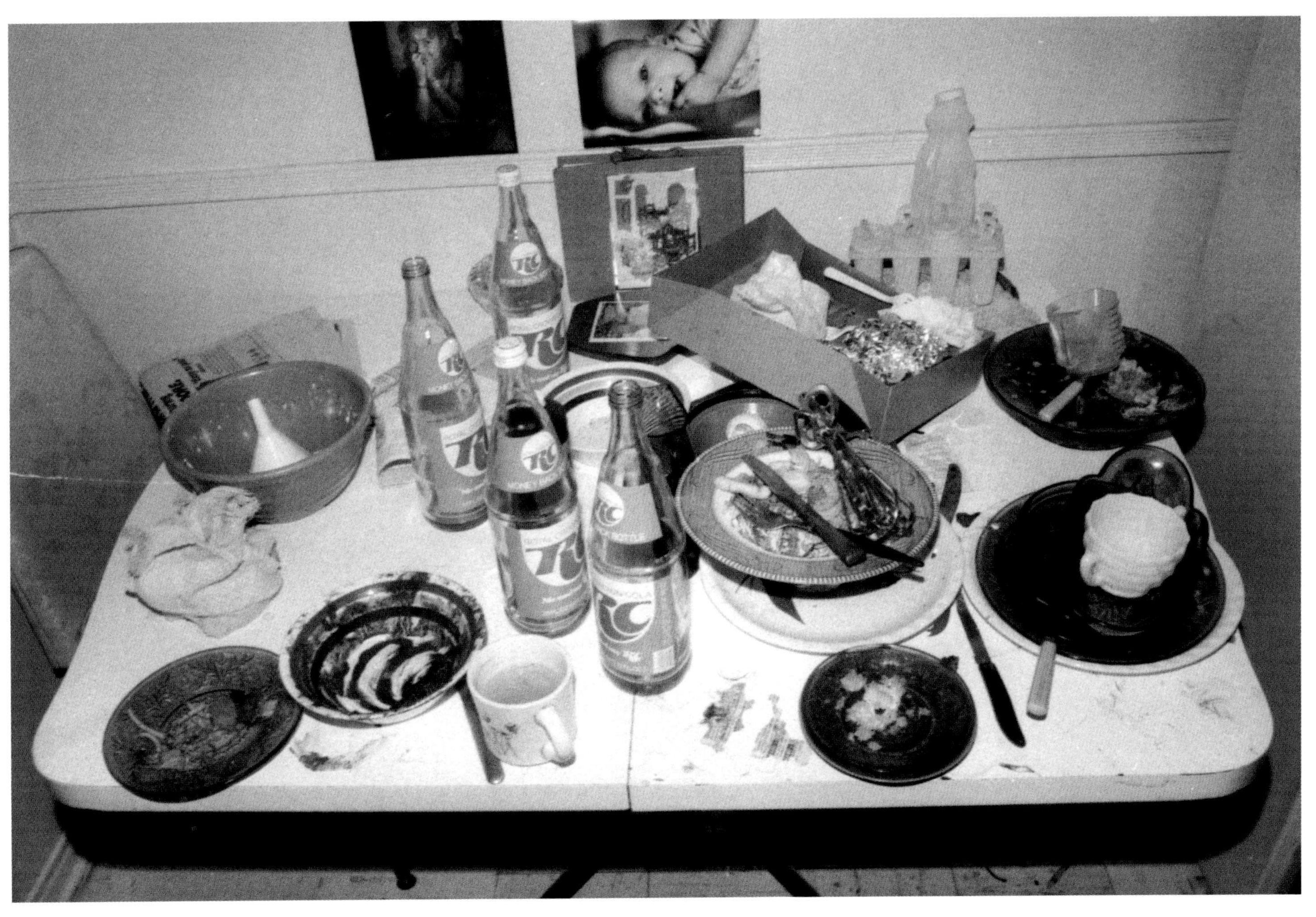

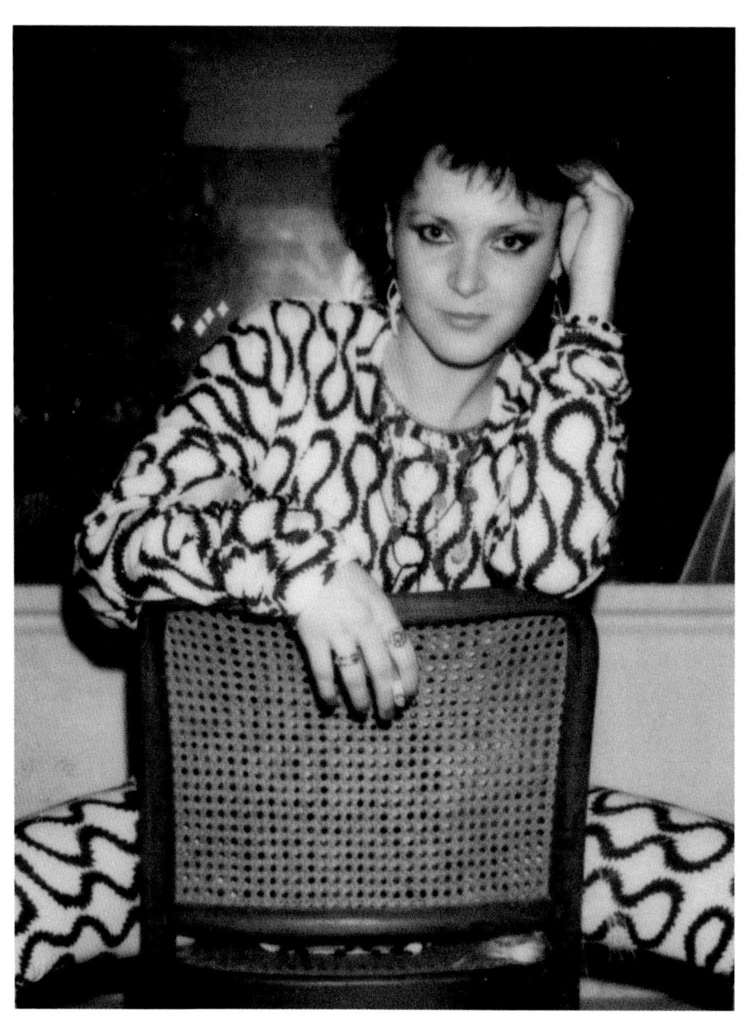

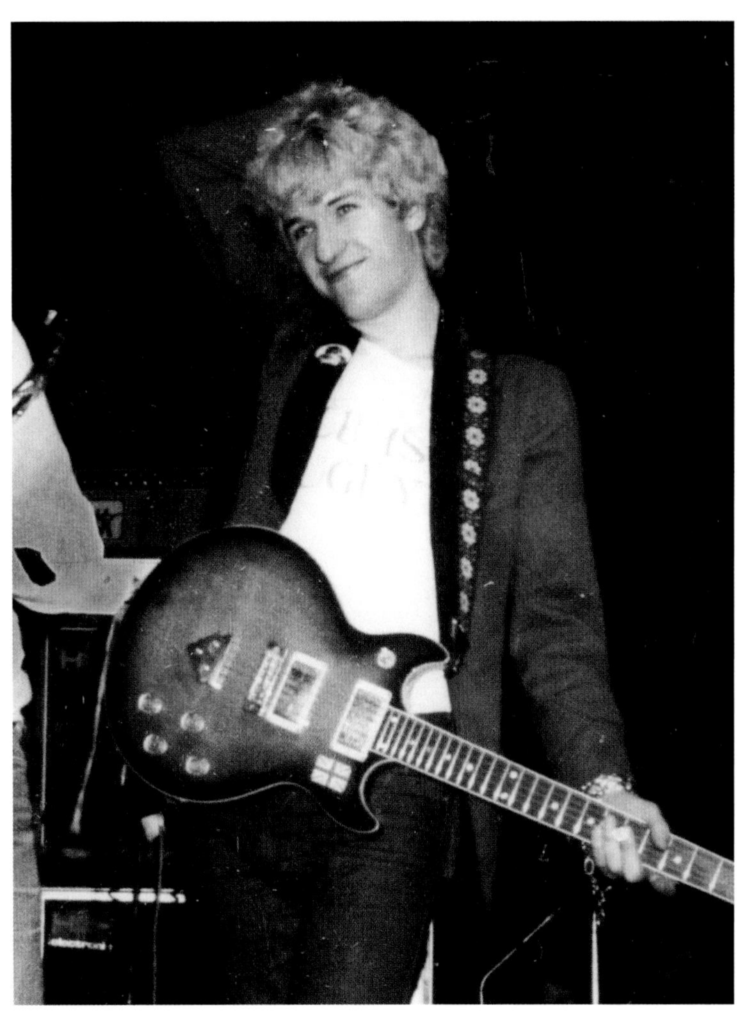

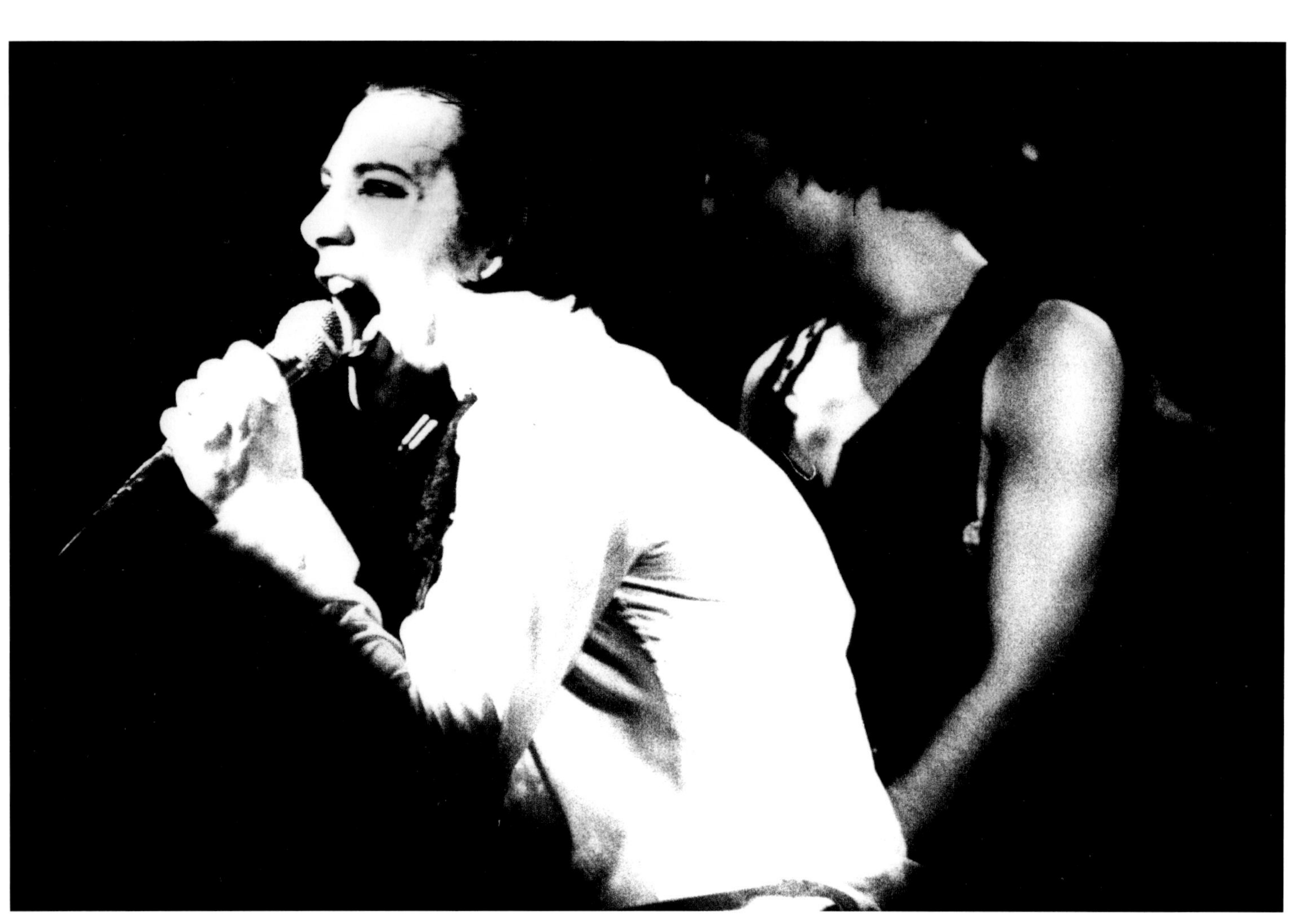

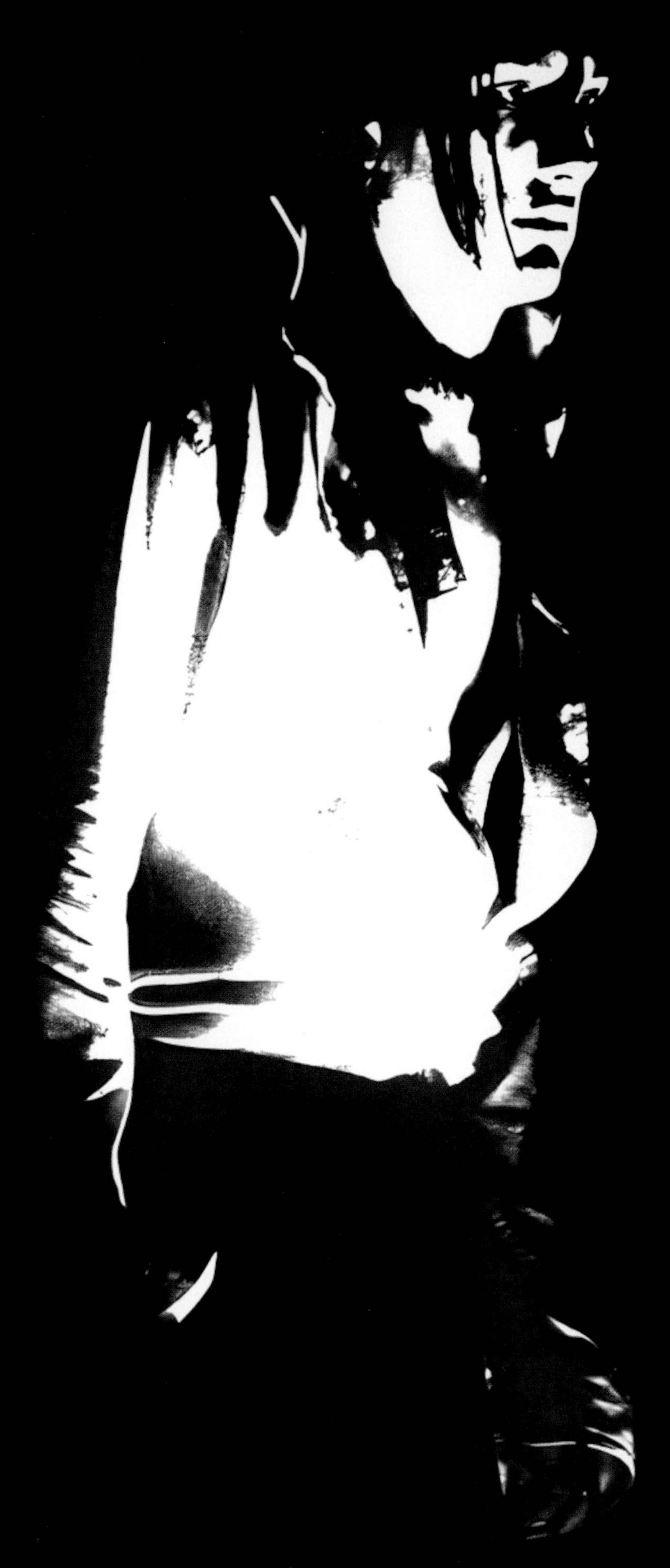

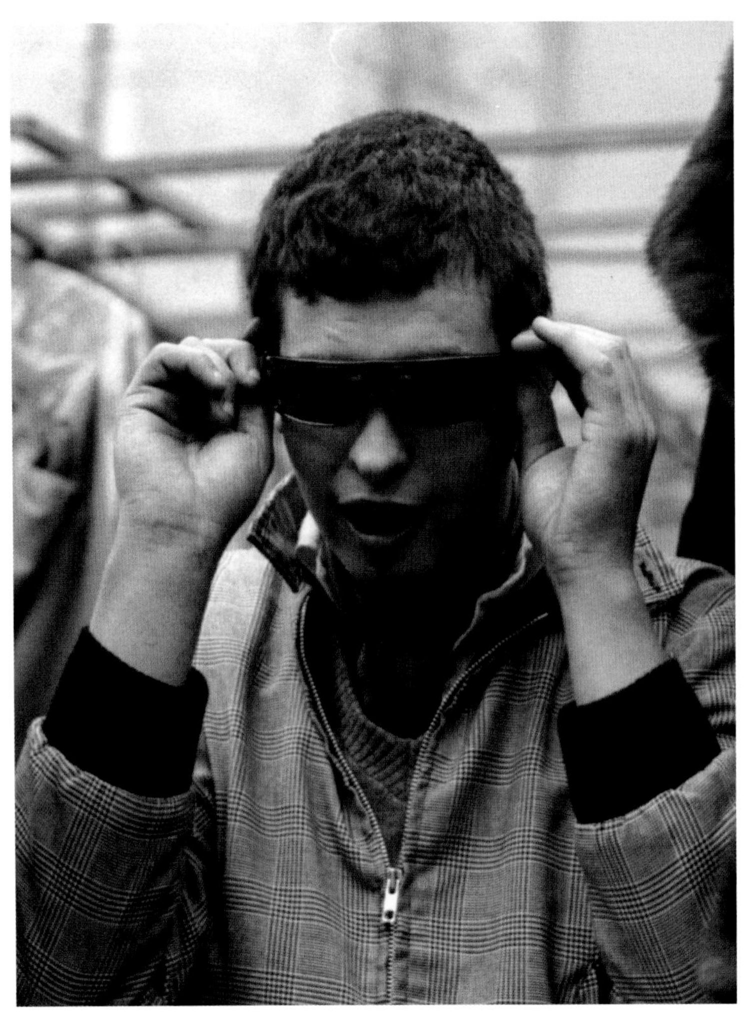

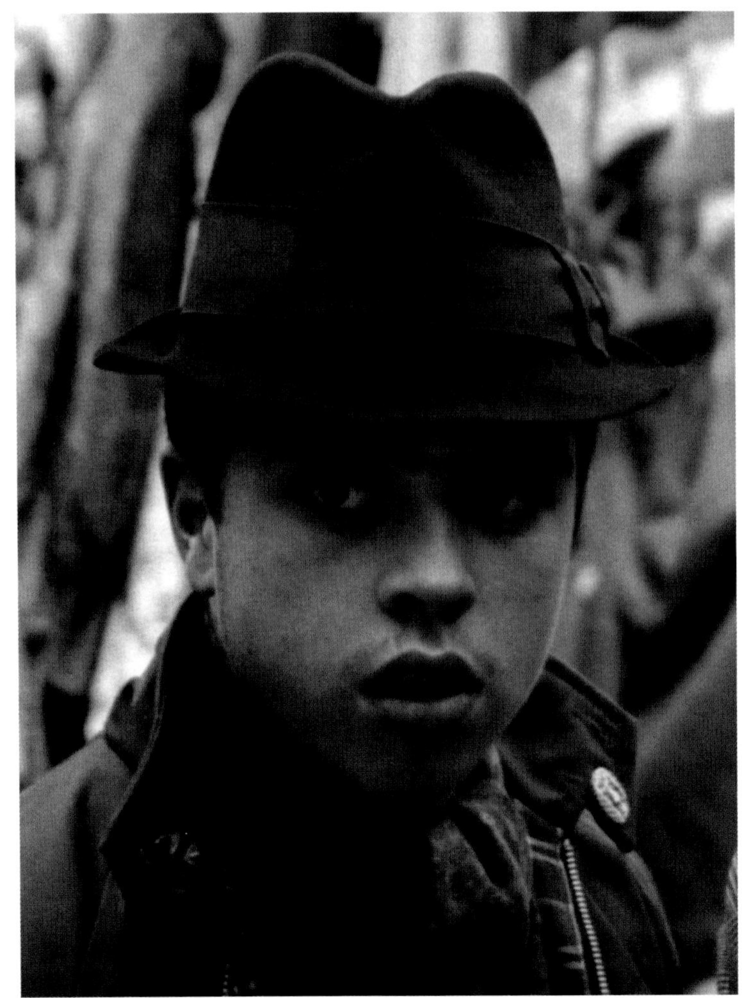

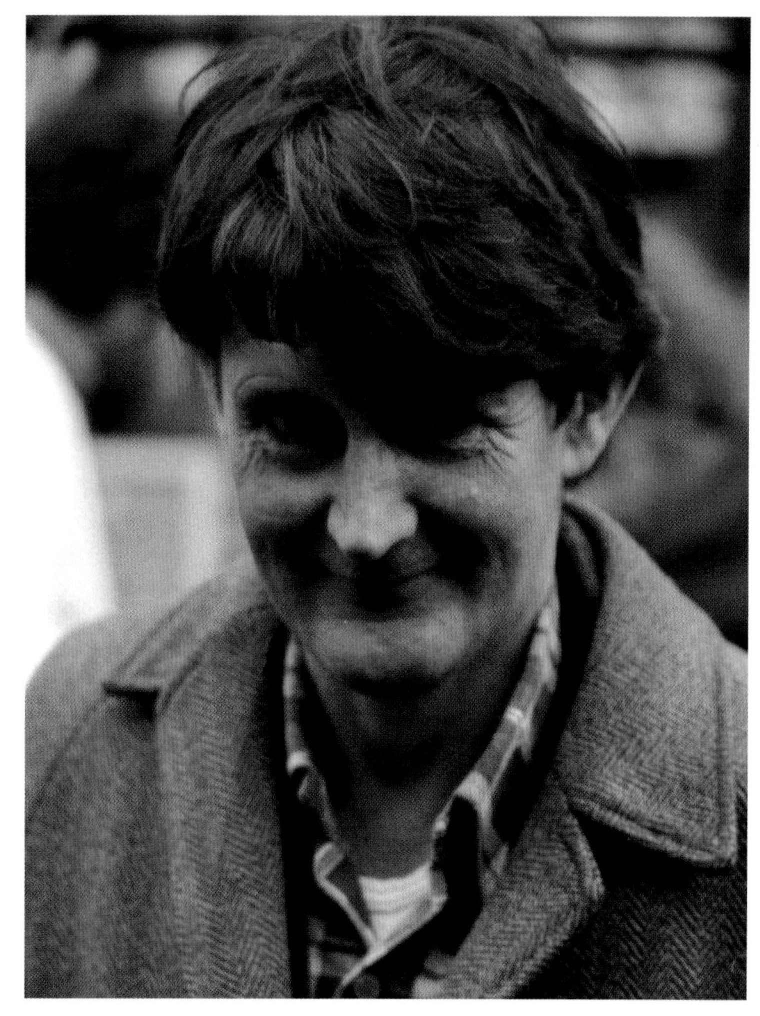

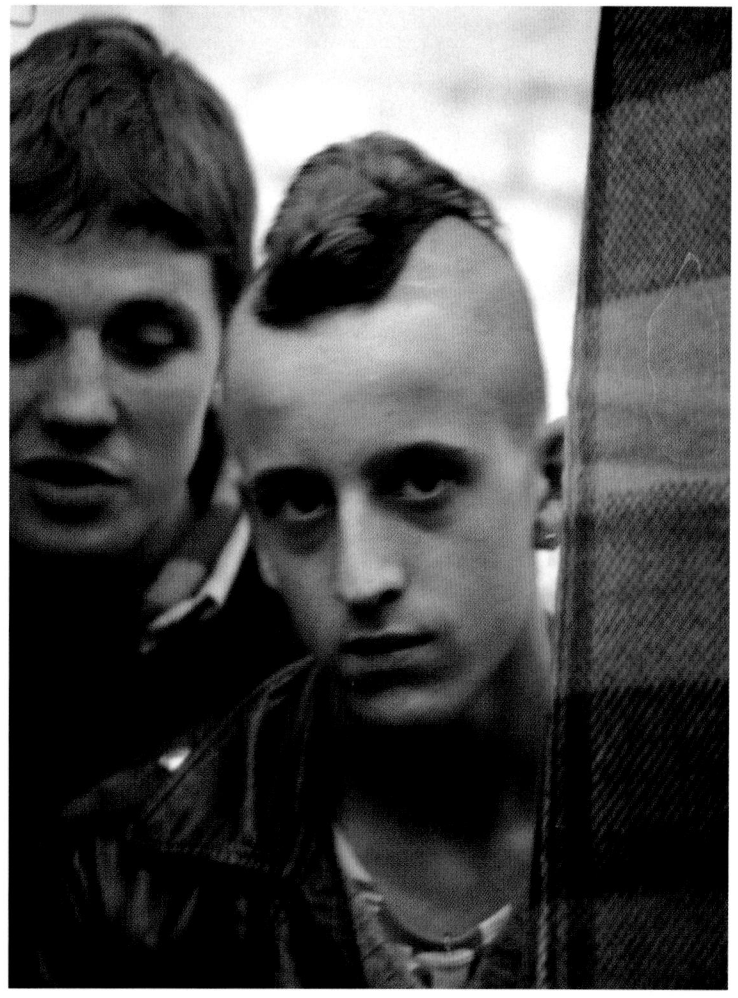

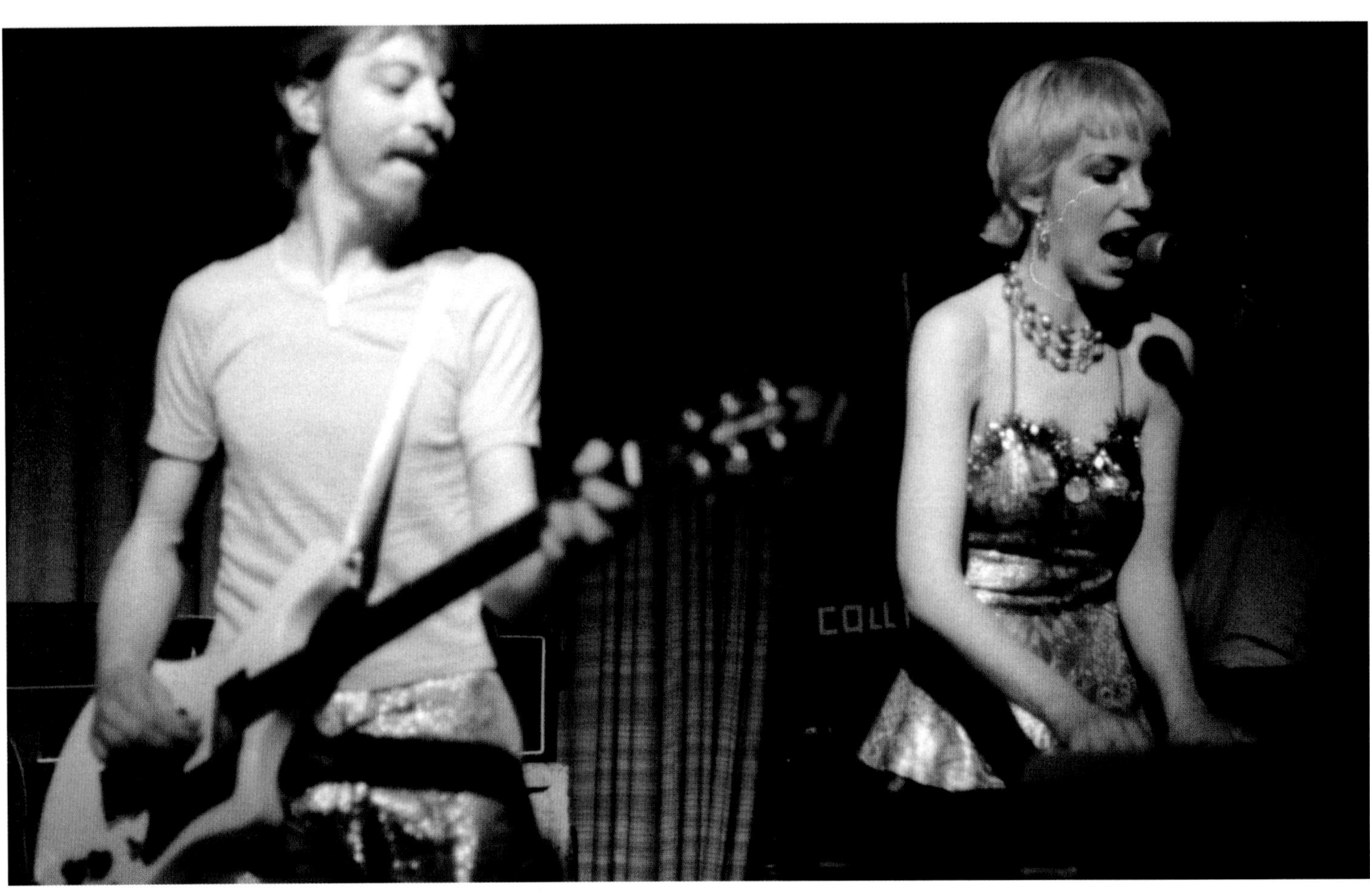

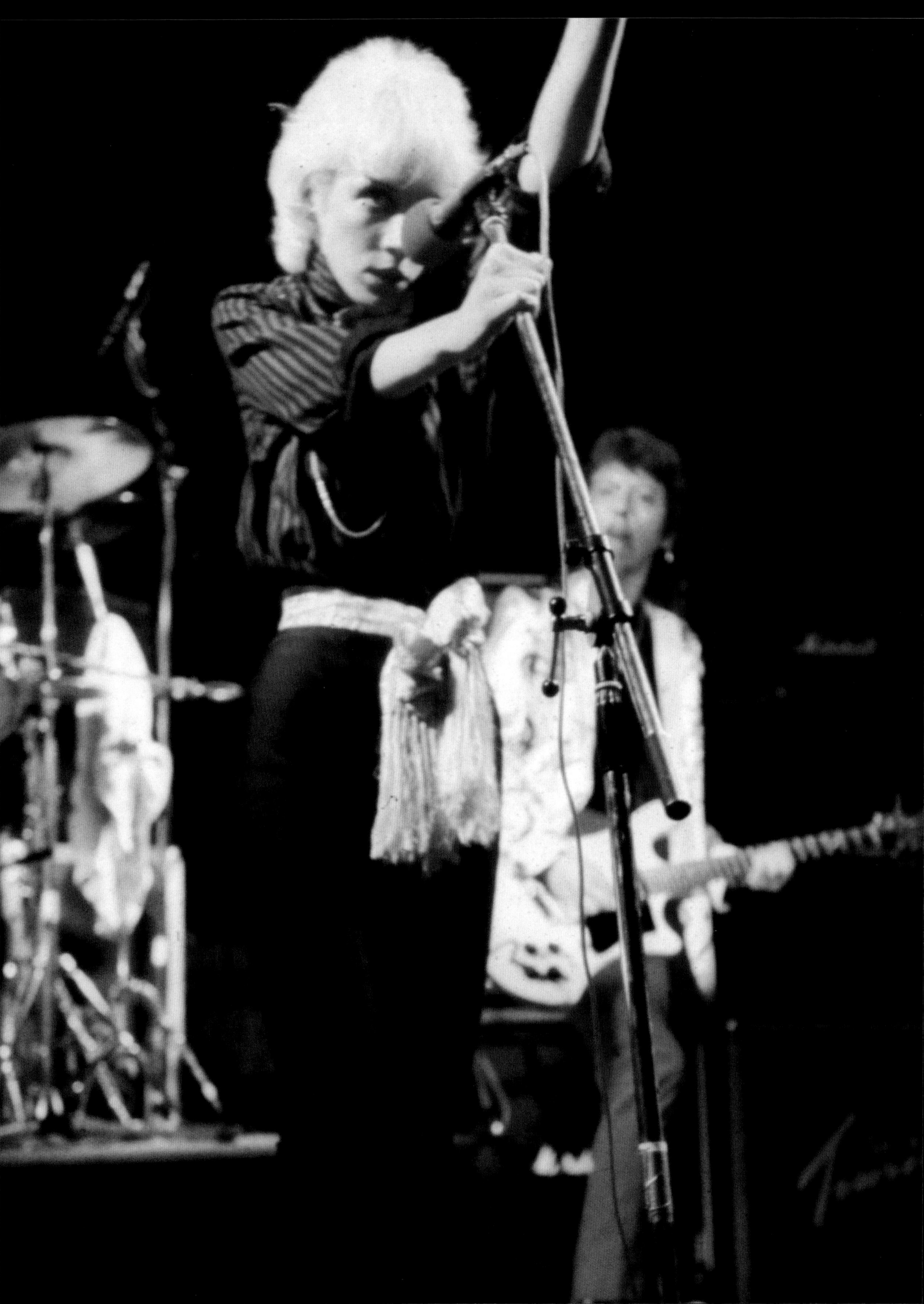

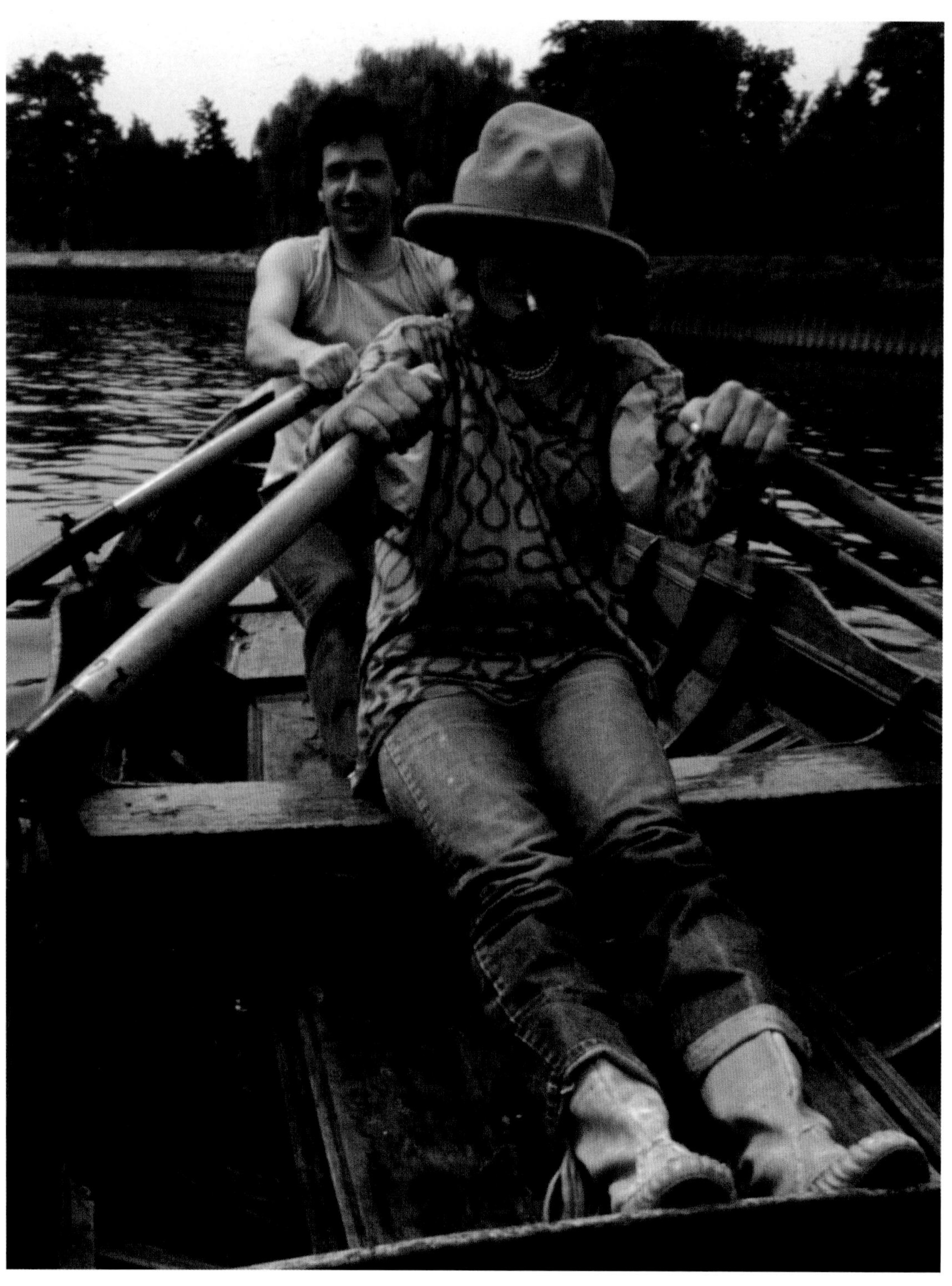

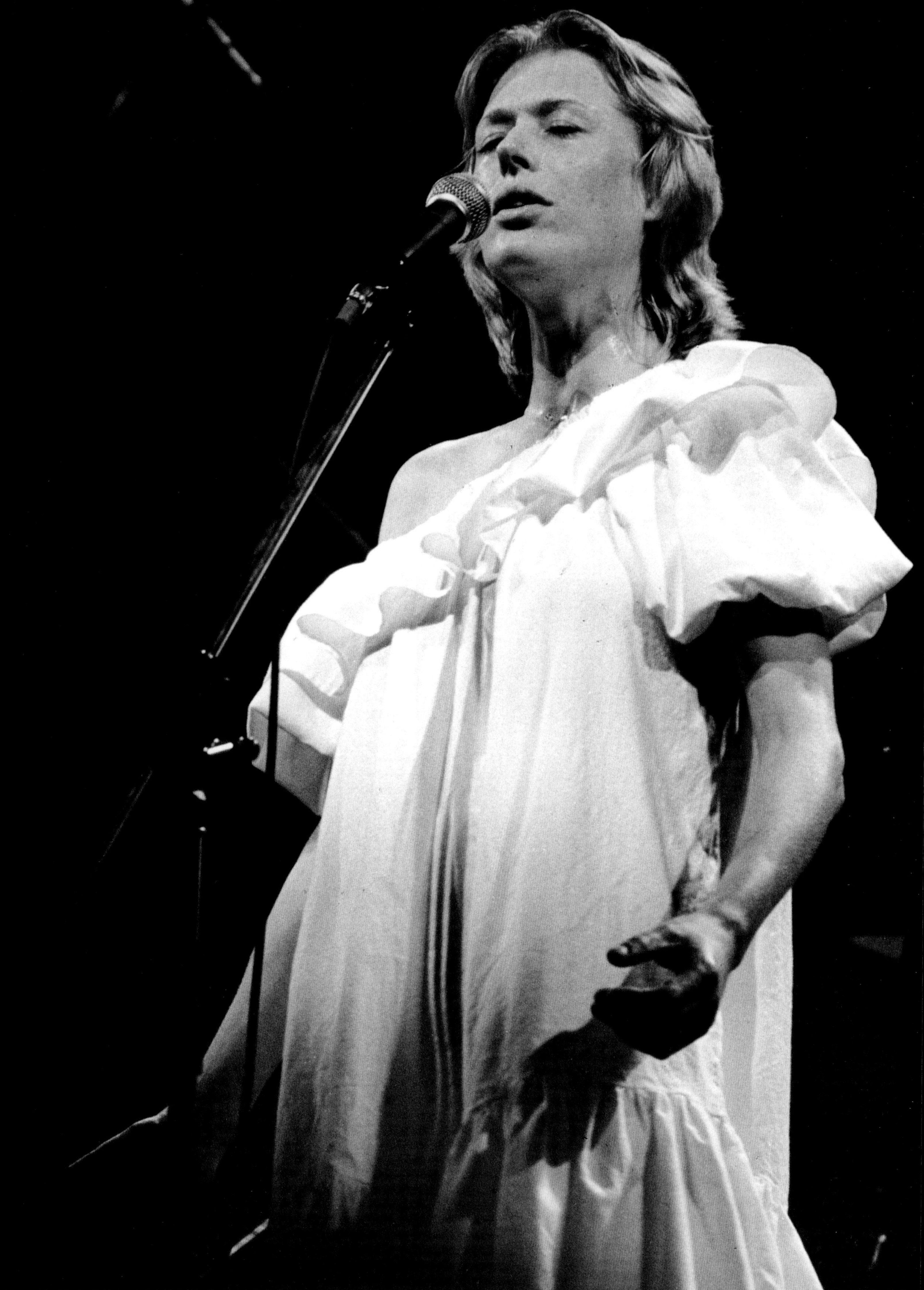

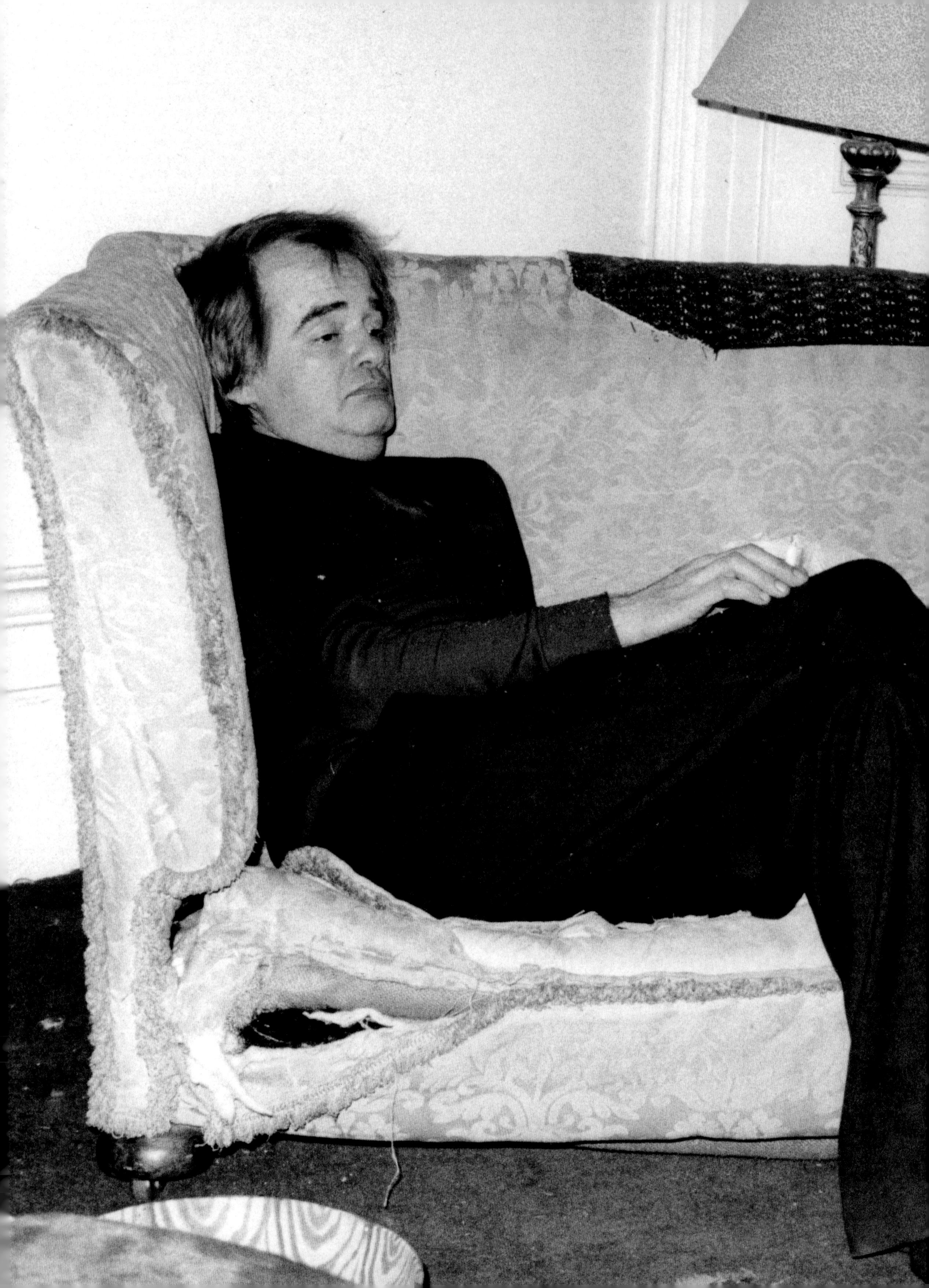

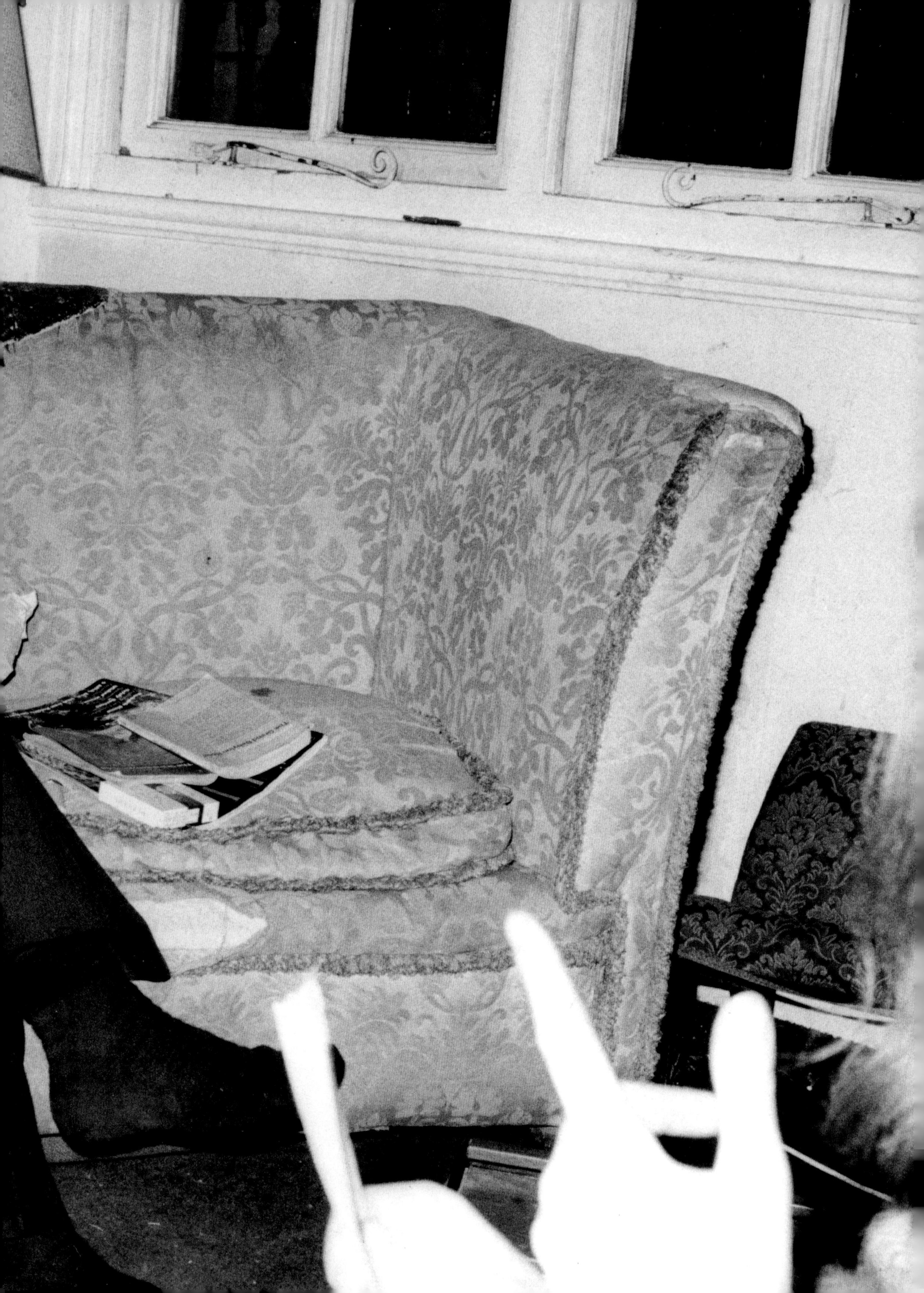

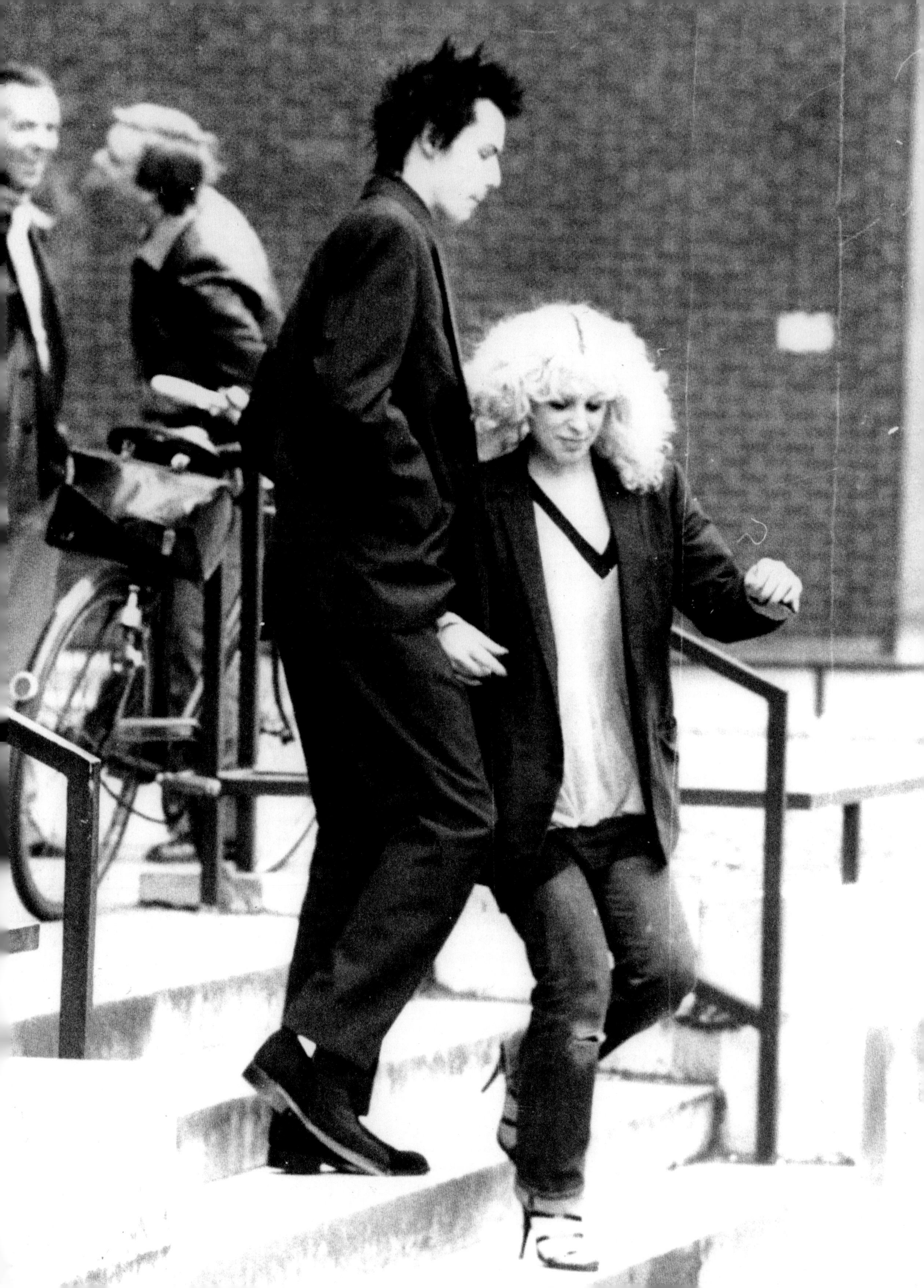

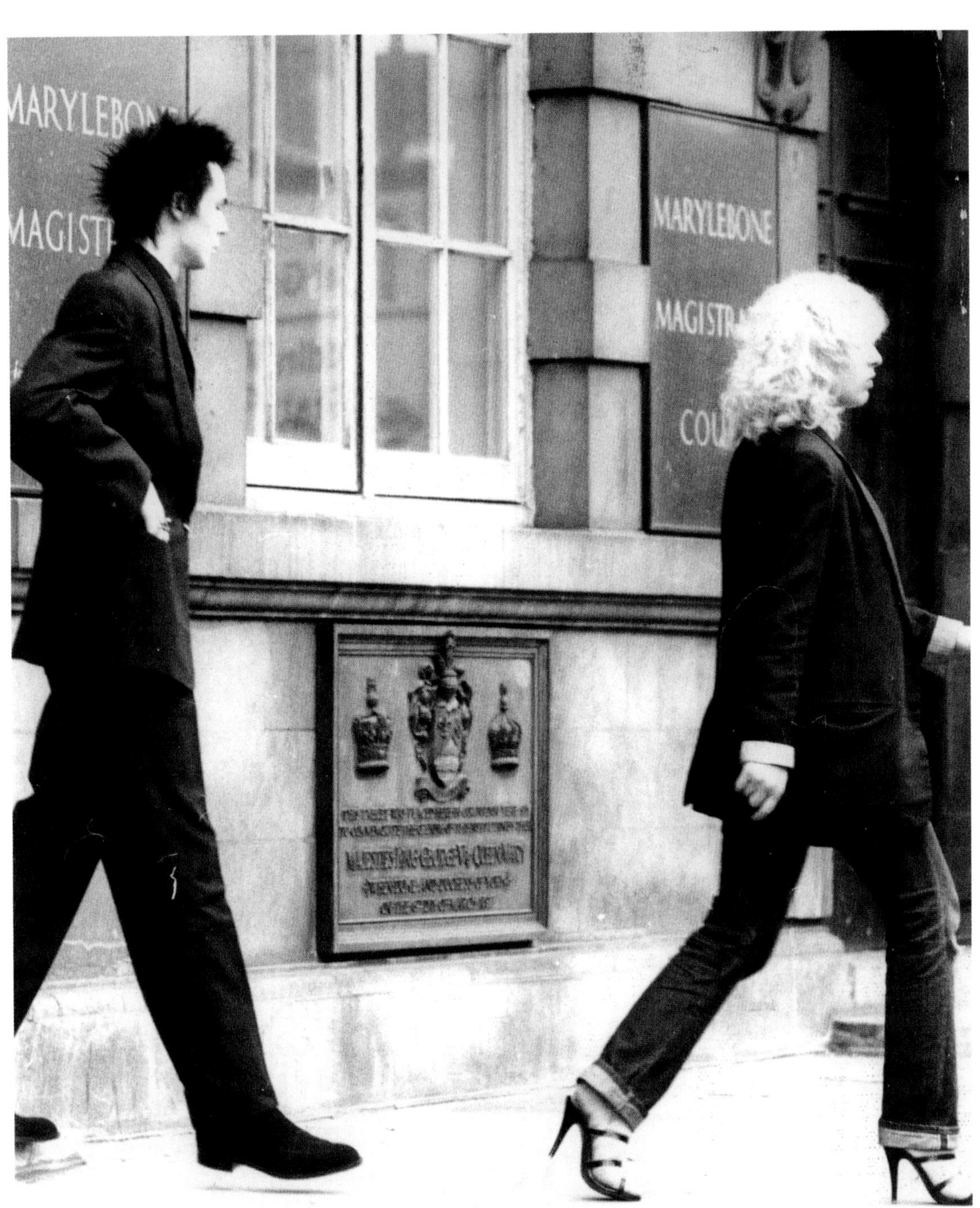

MARYLEBONE
MAGISTR
MARYLEBONE
MAGISTRA
COU

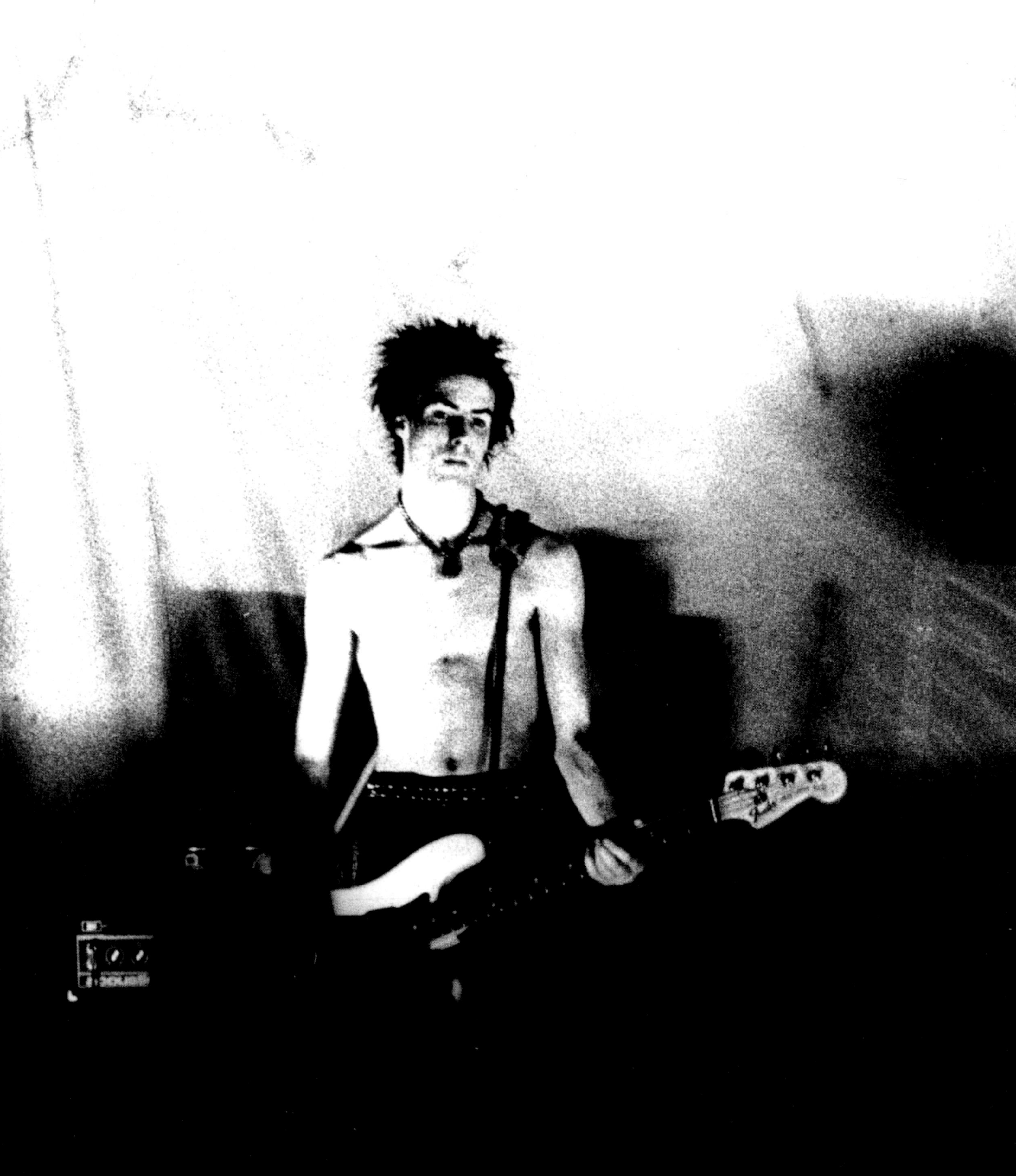

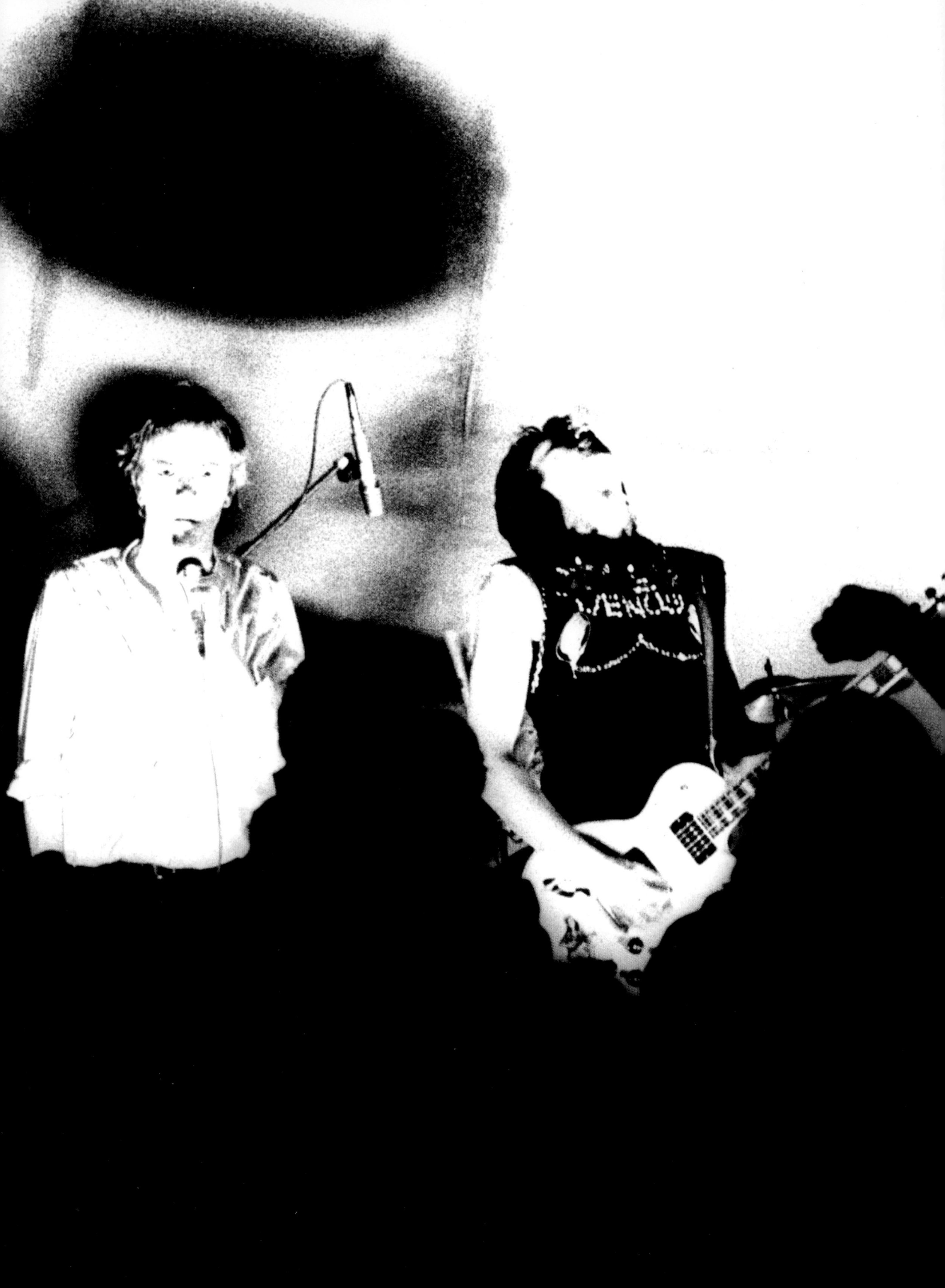

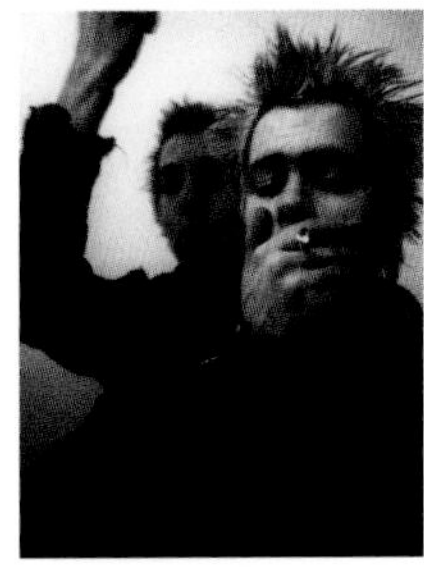

Danny & Nick,
London, 1976

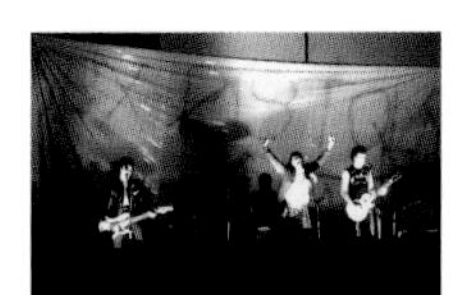

Sex Pistols, Brunel
University, London,
1977

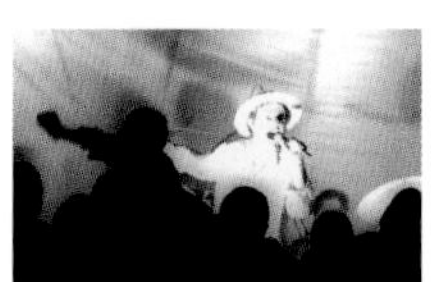

Sex Pistols, Brunel
University, London,
1977

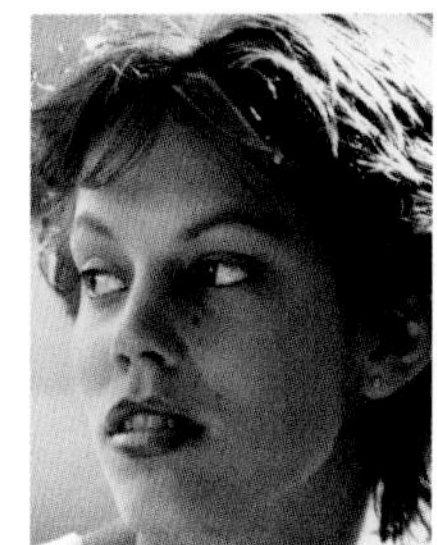

Liz, London, 1977

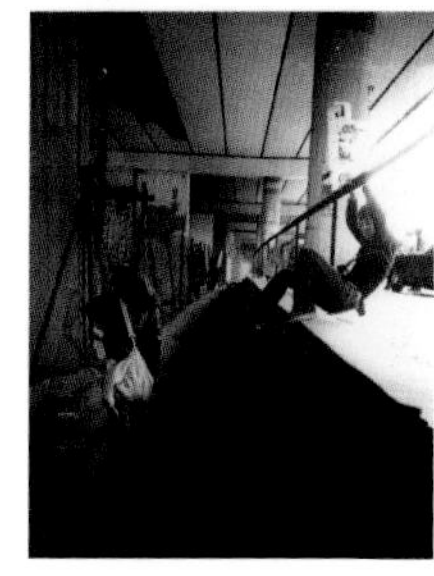

Liz & Toby, London,
1976

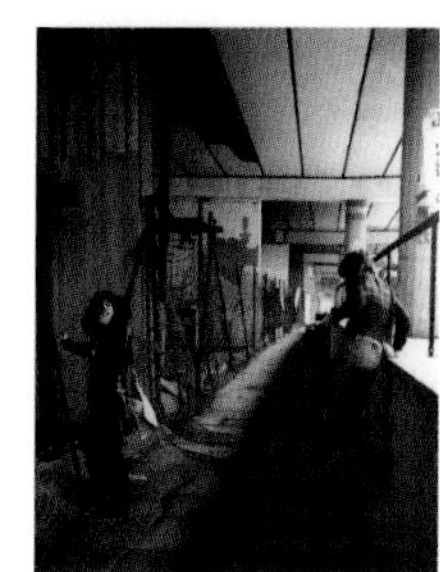

Liz & Toby, London,
1976

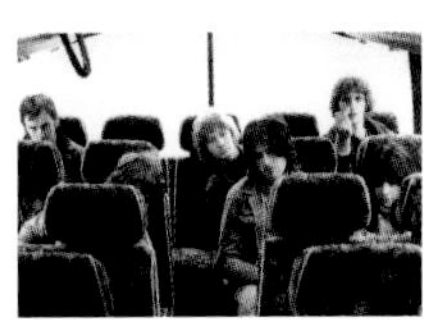

Split Rivet & Janice,
UK, 1976

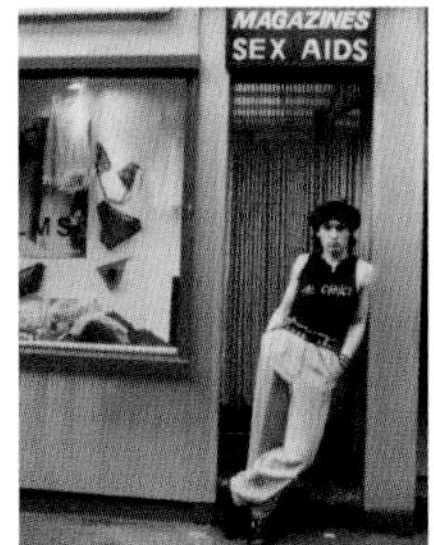

Steve Dior, London,
1981

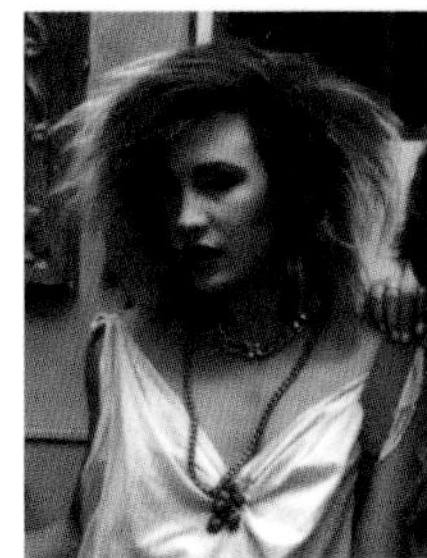

Marilyn, London,
1980

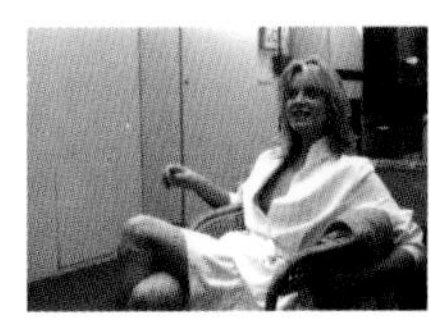

London, 1980

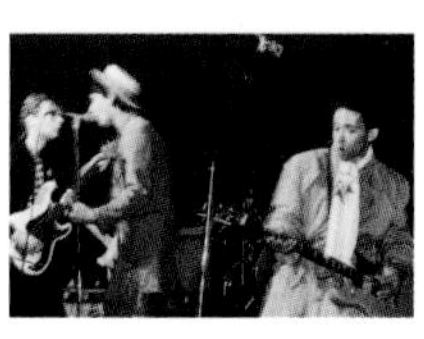

Glen Matlock &
London Cowboys,
London, 1981

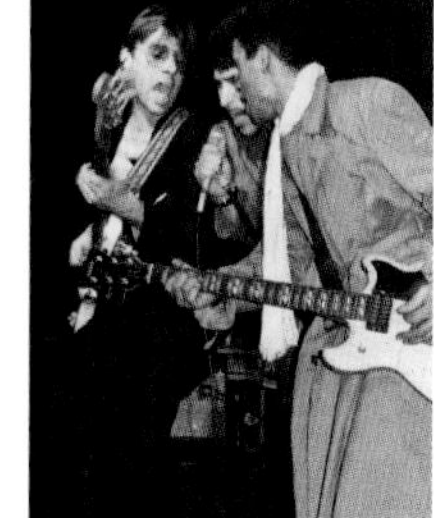

Glen Matlock &
London Cowboys,
London, 1981

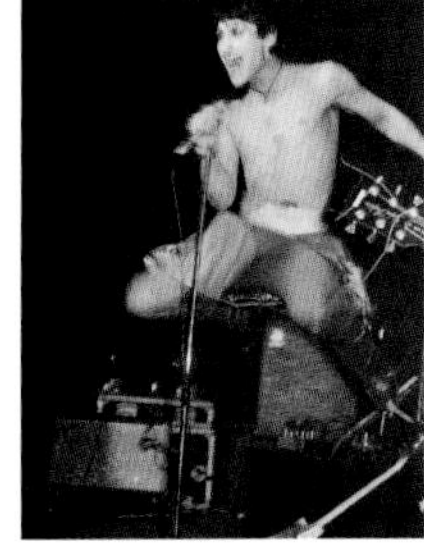

Steve Dior: London
Cowboys, London,
1981

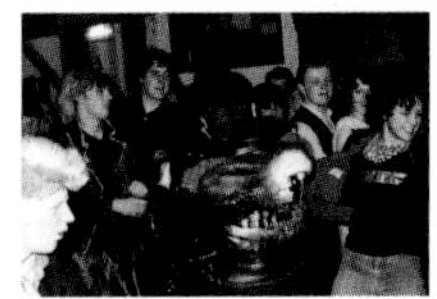

London, 1978

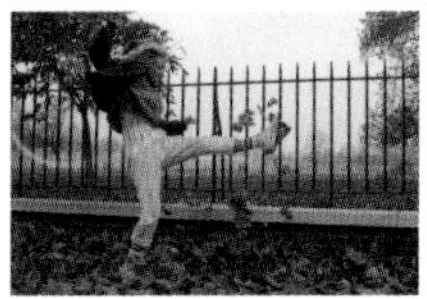

Marilyn, London,
1982

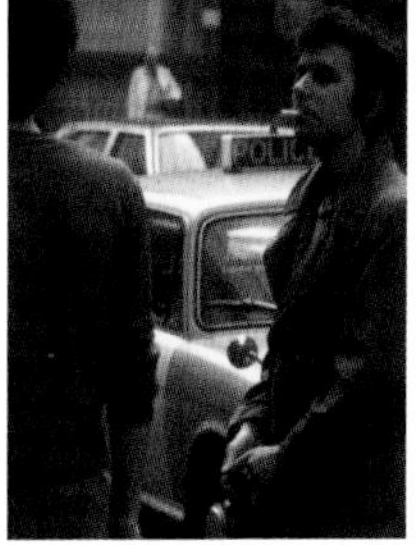

Jerry Nolan,
London, 1981

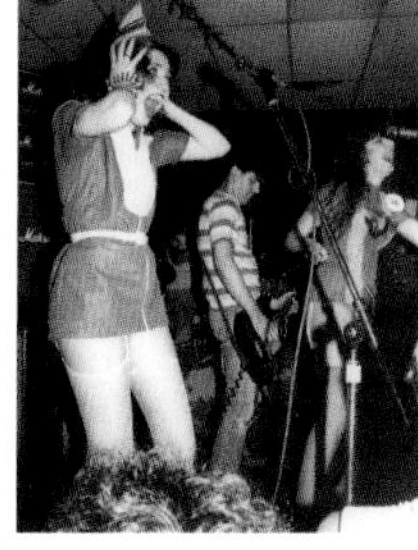

Sic F*cks,
New York, 1979

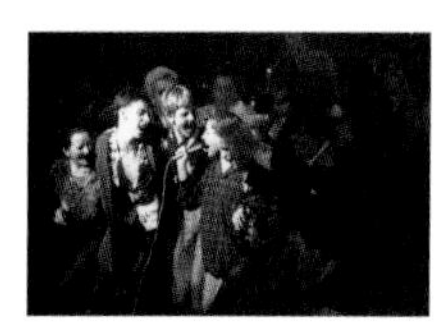

X-Ray Spex,
The Roundhouse,
London, 1978

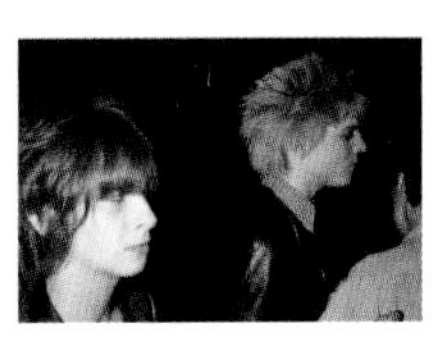

New York, 1979

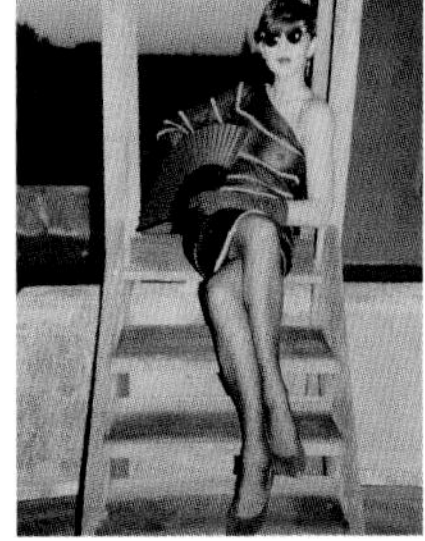

Celia, London, 1981

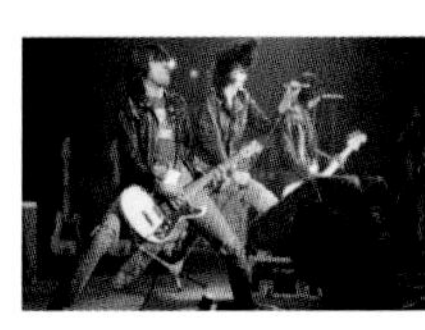

Ramones,
The Rainbow,
London, 1977

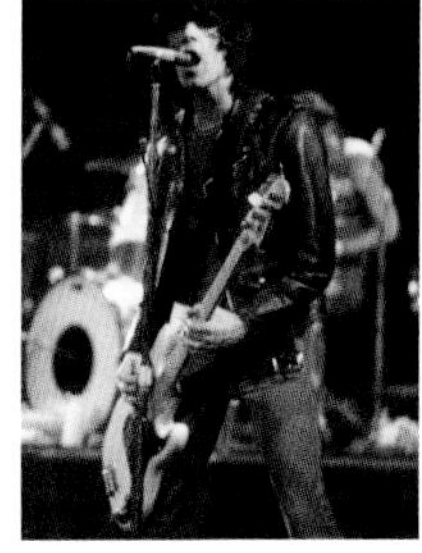

Ramones,
The Rainbow,
London, 1977

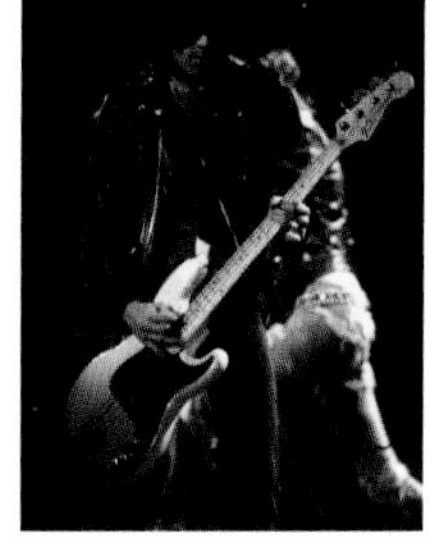

Ramones,
The Rainbow,
London, 1977

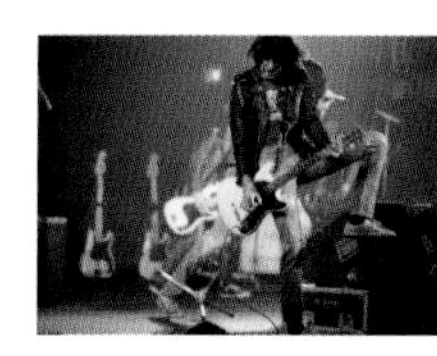

Ramones,
The Rainbow,
London, 1977

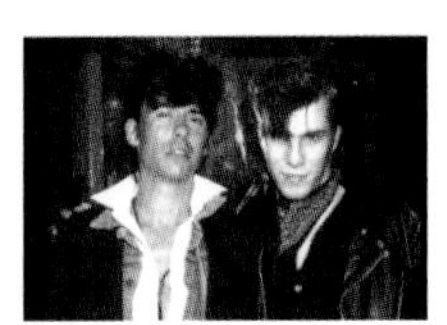

Pete Farndon &
Slim Jim Phantom,
London, 1980

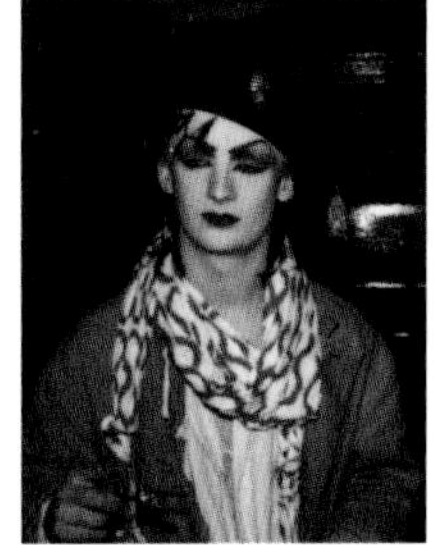

Boy George, London,
1980

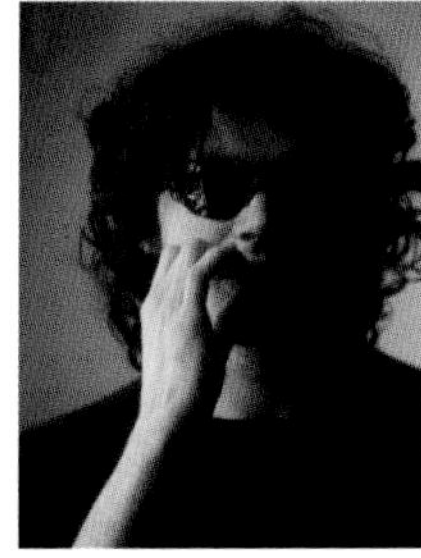

Allan, London, 1976

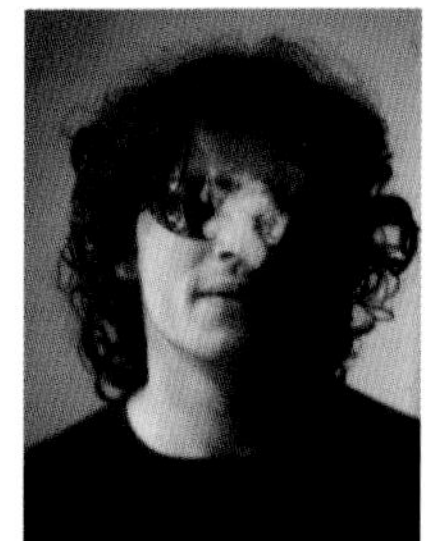

Allan, London, 1976

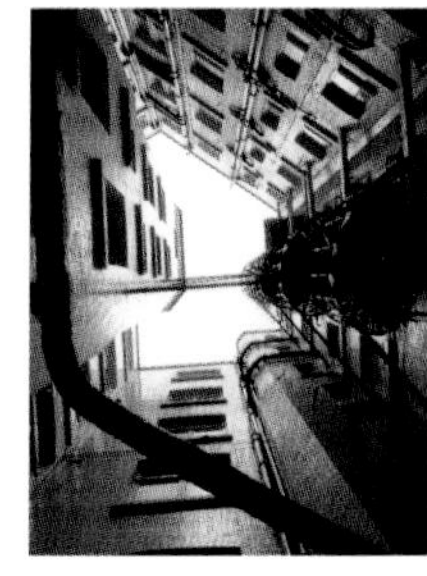

Neville Court,
London, 1976

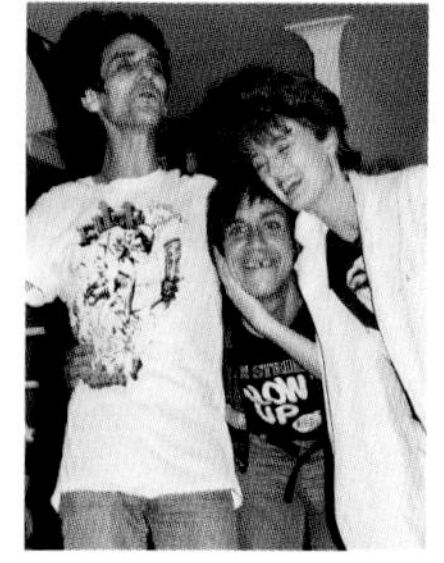

Iggy Pop & friends,
London, 1980

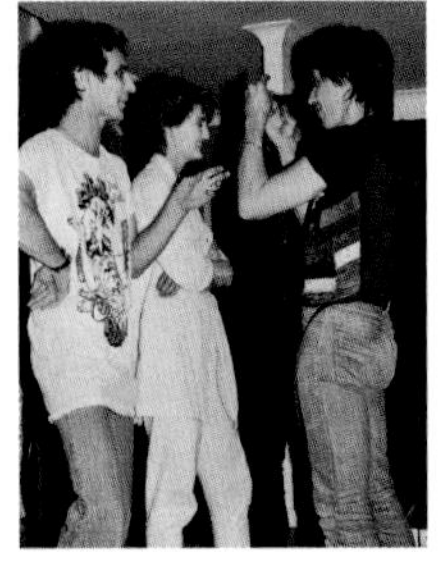

Iggy Pop & friends,
London, 1980

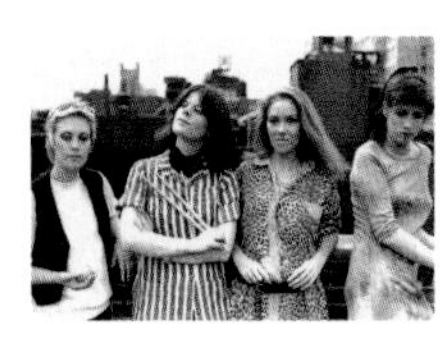

Crayola, New York,
1978

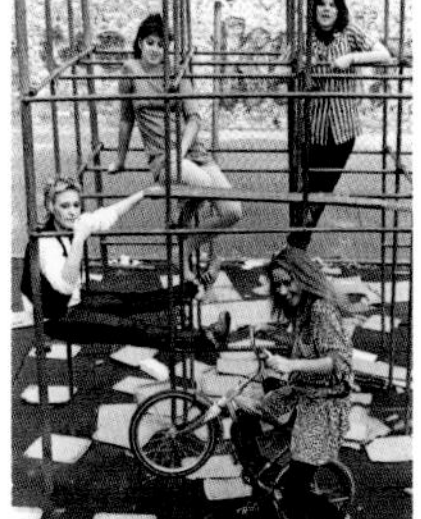

Crayola, New York,
1978

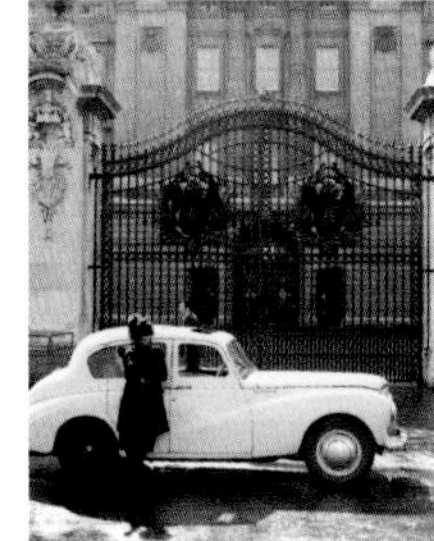

Patti Palladin,
London, 1980

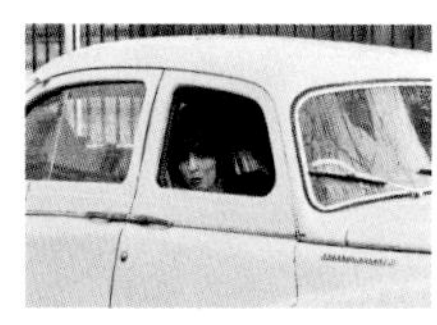

Patti Palladin,
London, 1980

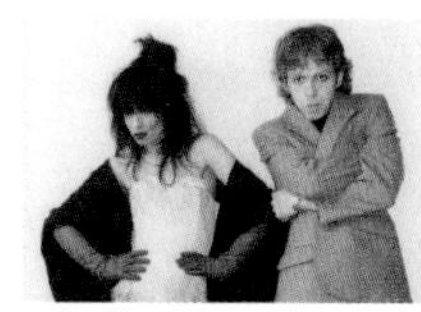

Flying Lizards,
London, 1980

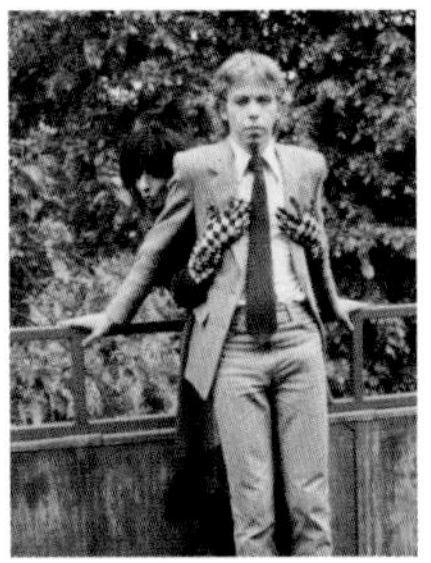

Flying Lizards,
London, 1980

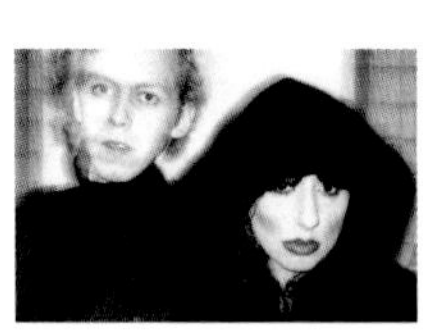

Flying Lizards,
London, 1980

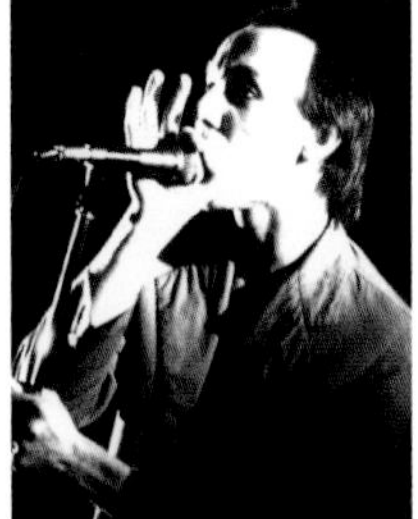

Howard Devoto:
Magazine,
The Roundhouse,
London, 1978

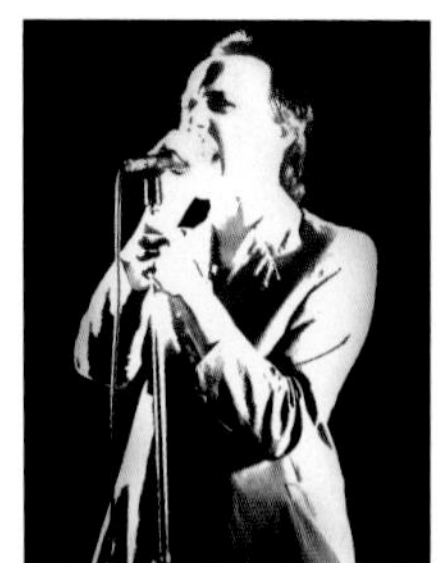

Howard Devoto:
Magazine,
The Roundhouse,
London, 1978

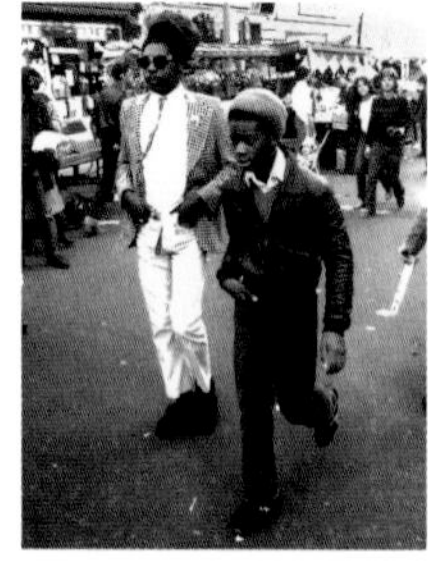

Portobello Road,
London, 1978

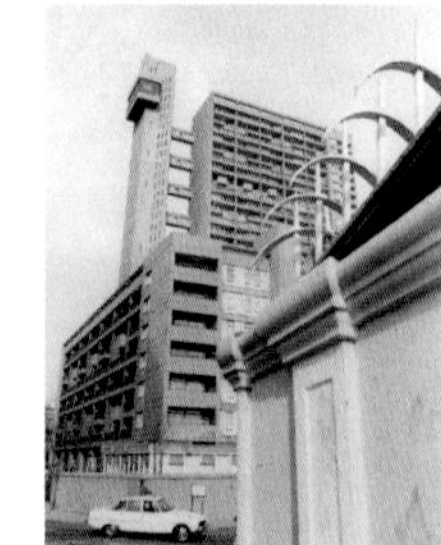

Trellick Tower,
London, 1977

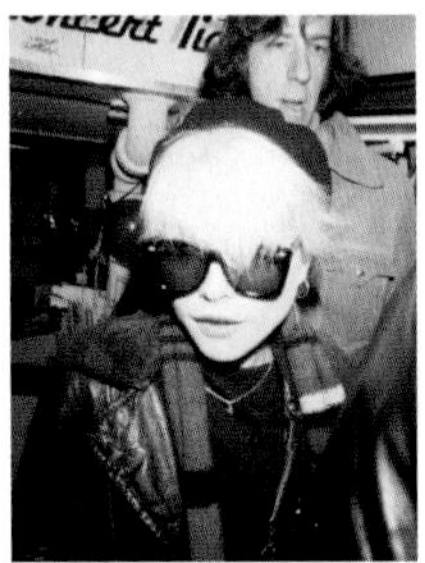

Debbie Harry,
London, 1978

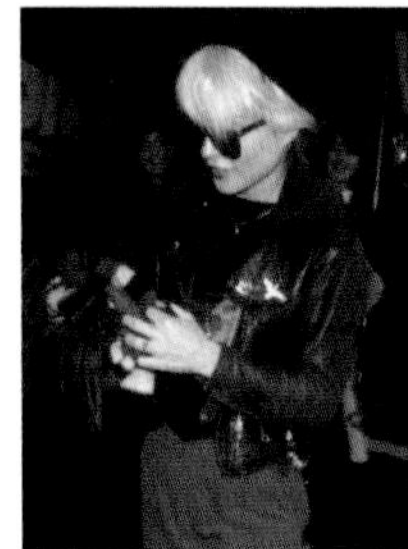

Debbie Harry,
London, 1978

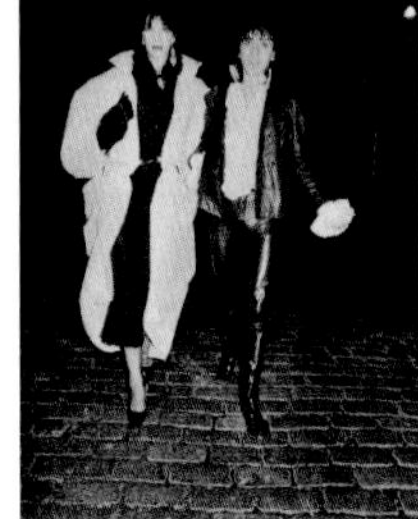

Magenta Devine &
Tony James,
London, 1981

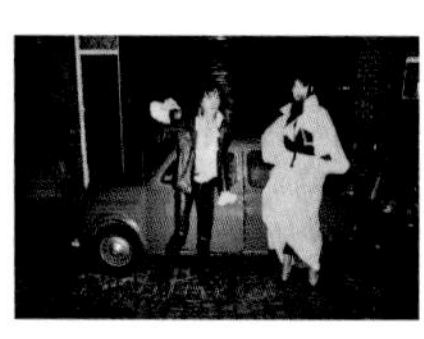

Magenta Devine &
Tony James,
London, 1981

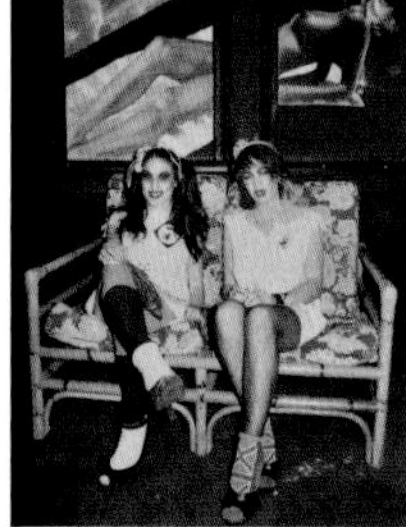

Halloween Party: The
Venue, London, 1980

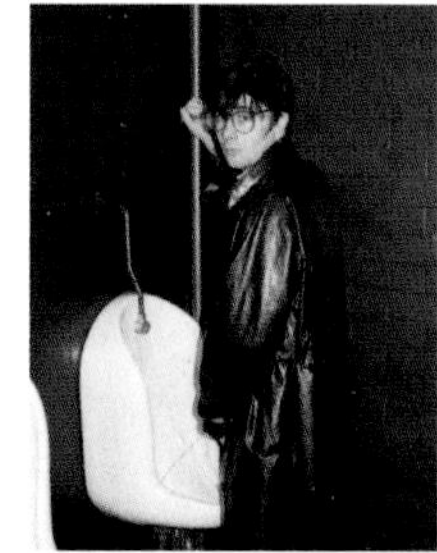

Glen Matlock,
London 1980

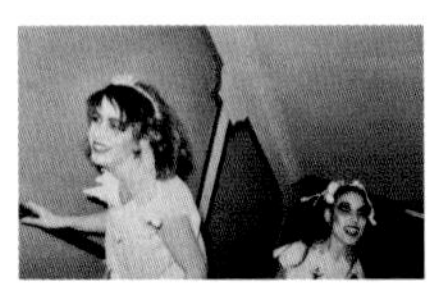

Halloween Party: The
Venue, London, 1980

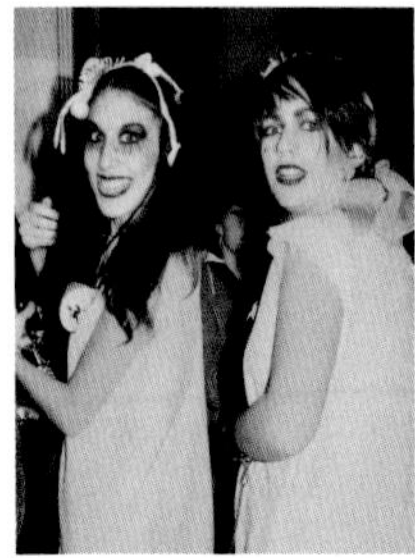

Halloween Party: The
Venue, London, 1980

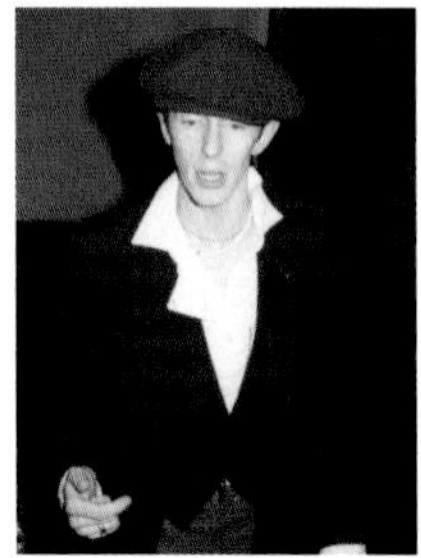

Topper Headon,
London, 1980

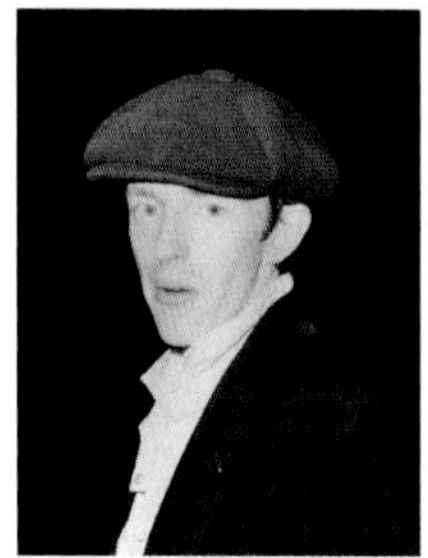

Topper Headon,
London, 1980

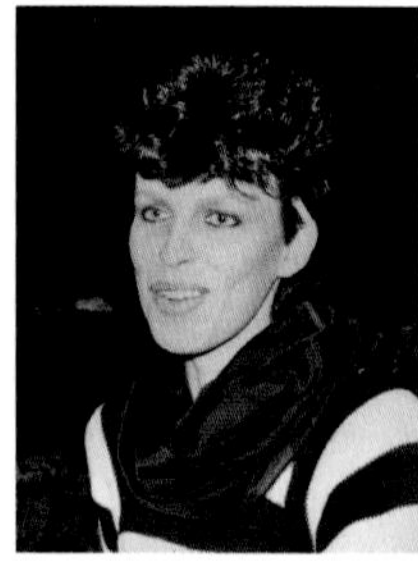

Judy Nylon, London,
1980

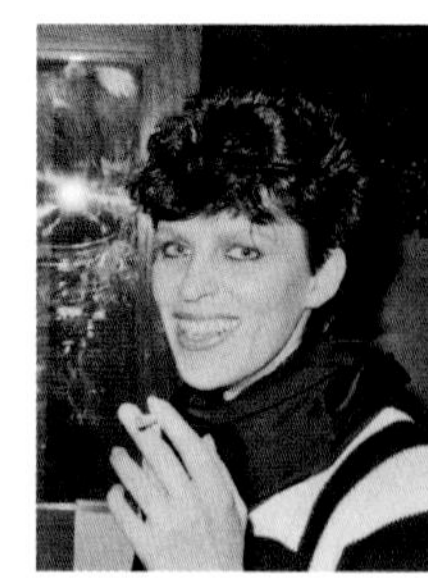

Judy Nylon, London,
1980

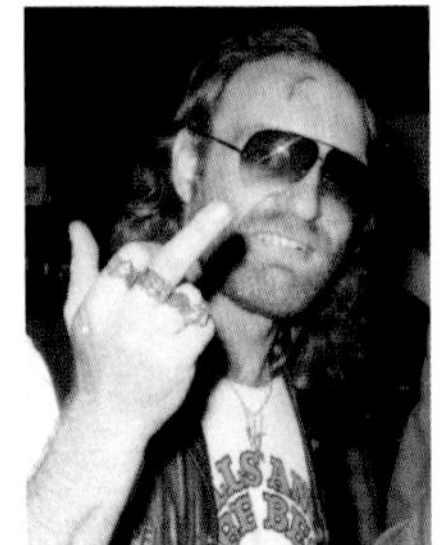

London, 1980

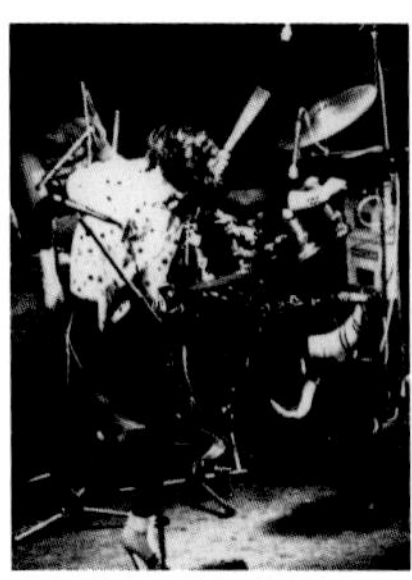

Siouxsie and the
Banshees, Music
Machine, London,
1980

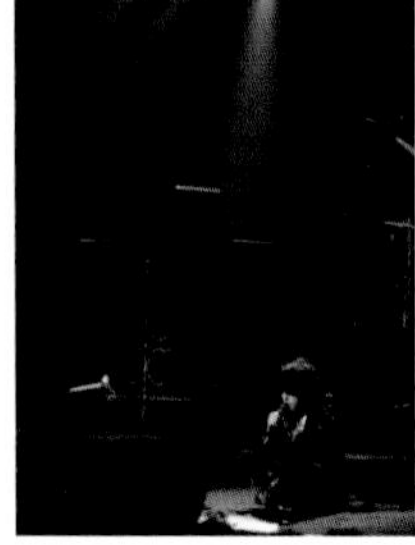

Siouxsie and the
Banshees, Music
Machine, London,
1980

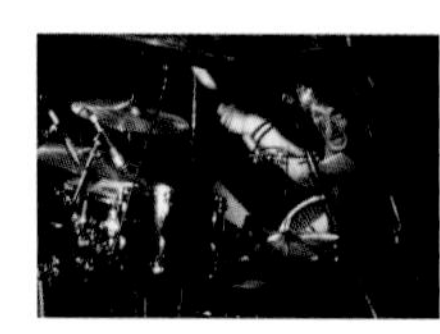

Siouxsie and the
Banshees, Music
Machine, London,
1980

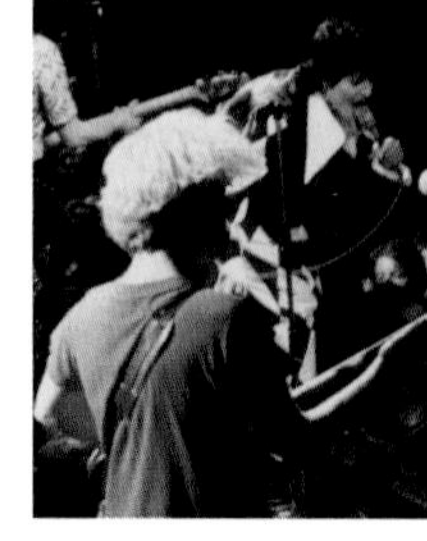

Siouxsie and the
Banshees, Music
Machine, London,
1980

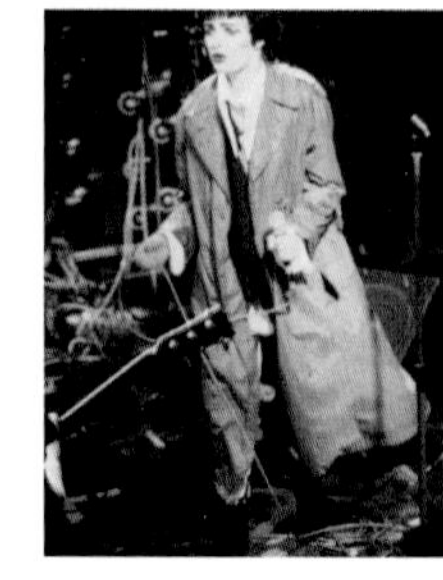

Siouxsie and the
Banshees, Music
Machine, London,
1980

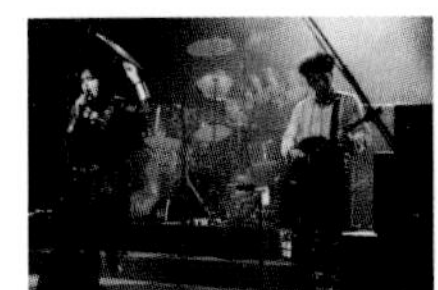

Siouxsie and the Banshees & Robert Smith, Music Machine, London, 1980

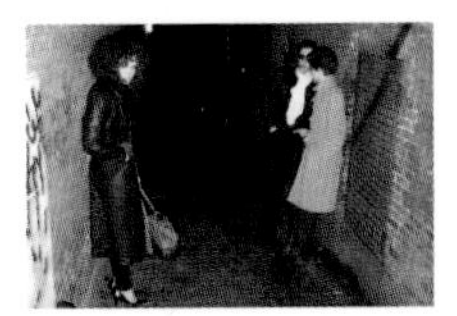

Sarah, New York, 1979

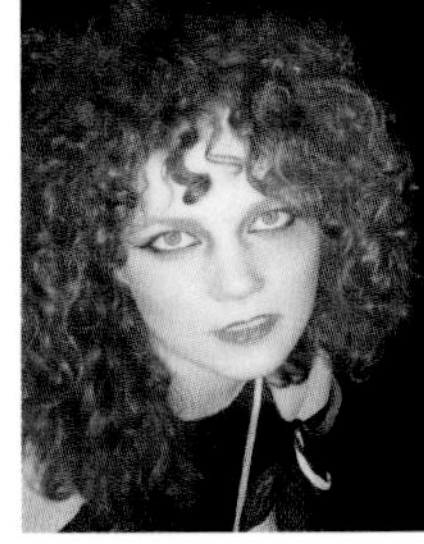

Sarah, New York, 1979

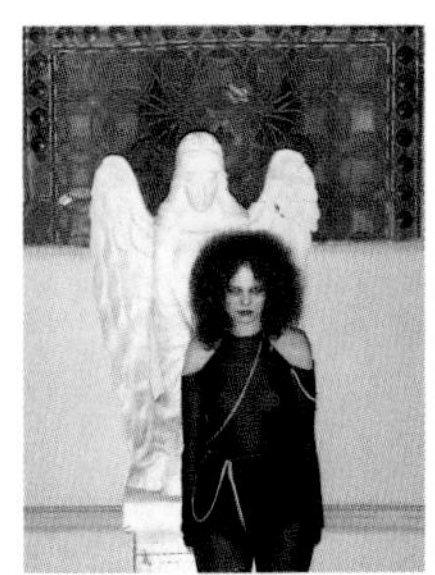

Sarah, New York, 1979

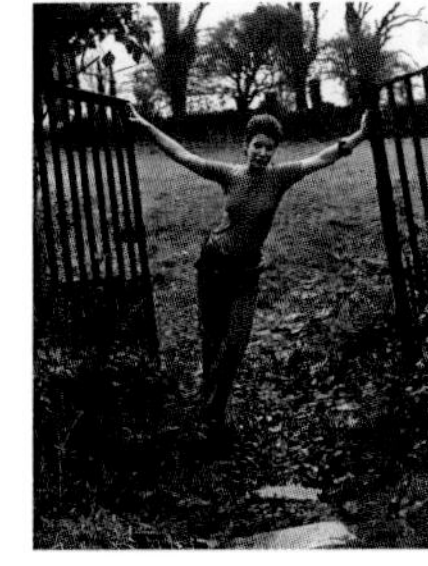

Laura, Kilworthy House, Devon, 1974

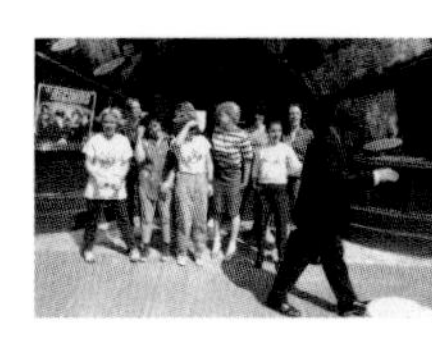

The Go-Go's Nashville Room, London, 1980

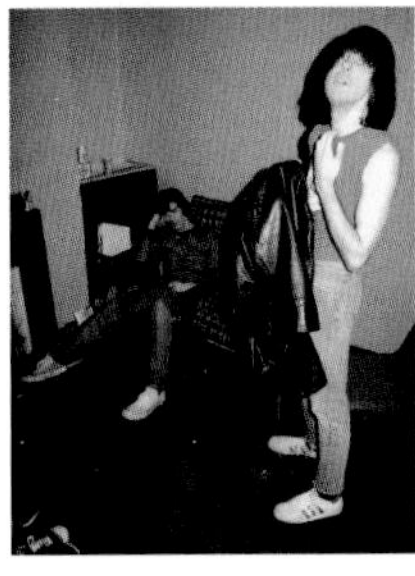

Dee Dee & Johnny Ramone, Electric Ballroom, London, 1980

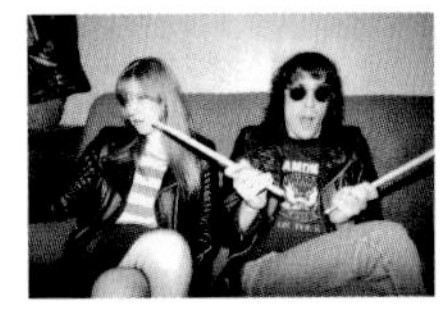

Marky Ramone & friend, Electric Ballroom, London, 1980

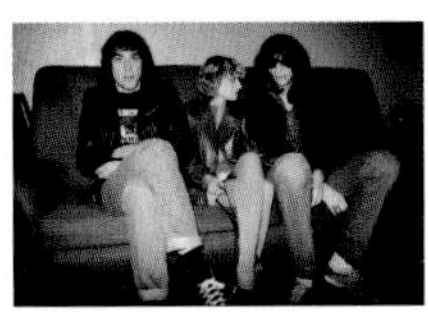

Marky, Linda & Joey Ramone, Electric Ballroom, London, 1980

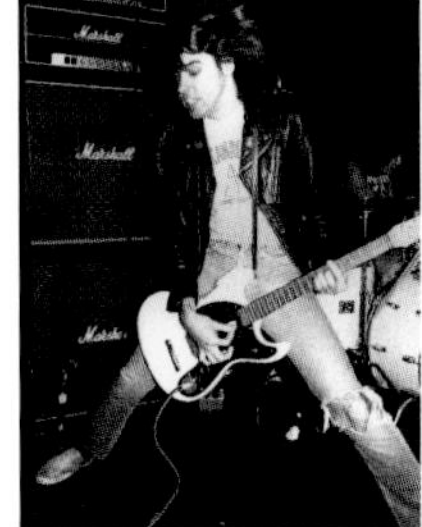

Johnny Ramone, Hurrah, New York, 1978

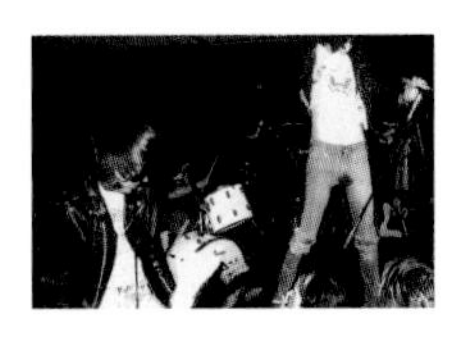

Johnny Ramone, Hurrah, New York, 1978

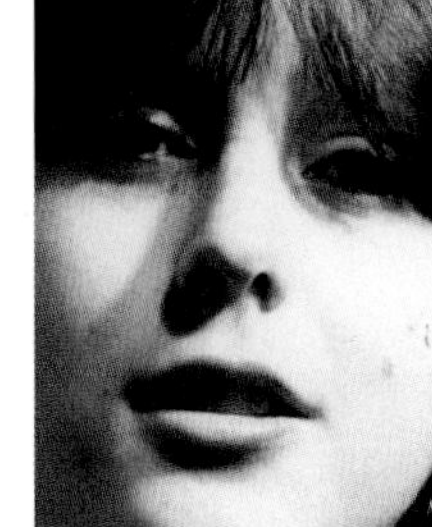

Lisa, London, 1976

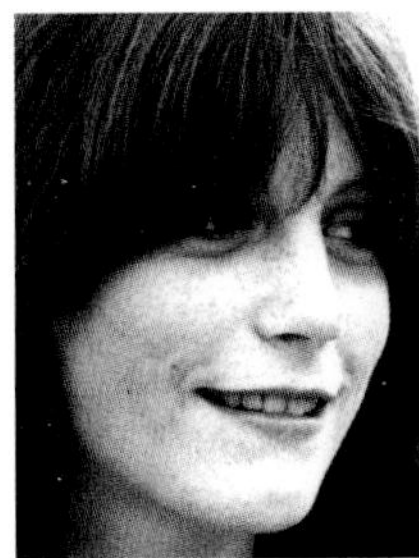

Kate, London, 1976

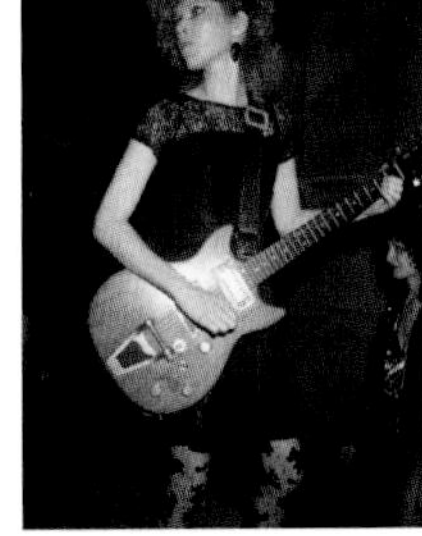

Poison Ivy: The Cramps, Hurrah, New York, 1978

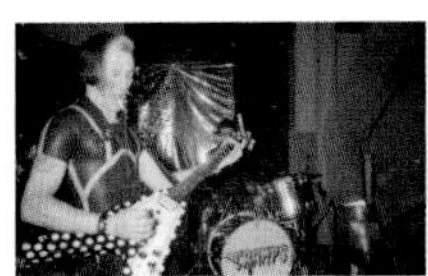

The Cramps, Hurrah, New York, 1978

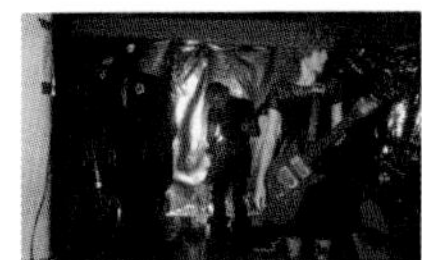

The Cramps, Hurrah, New York, 1978

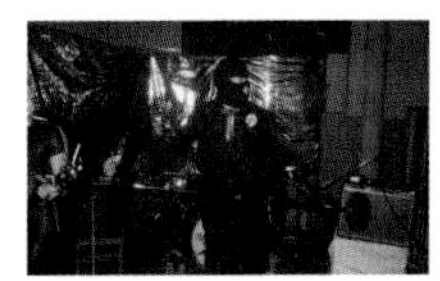

The Cramps, Hurrah, New York, 1978

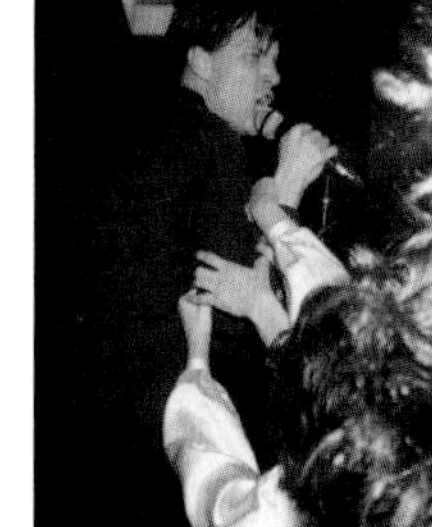

The Cramps, Hurrah, New York, 1978

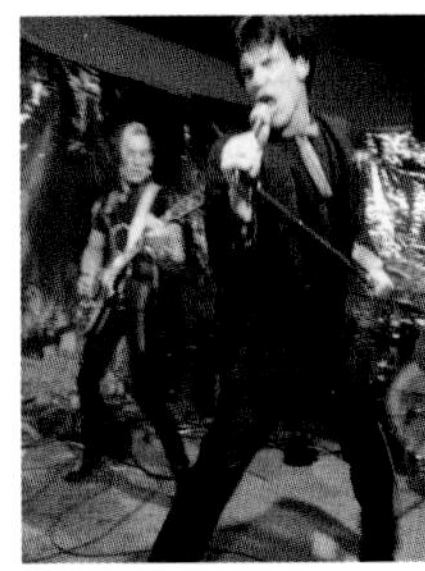

The Cramps, Hurrah, New York, 1978

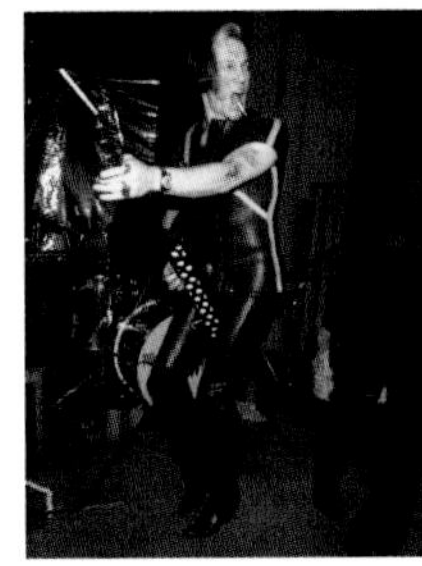

The Cramps, Hurrah, New York, 1978

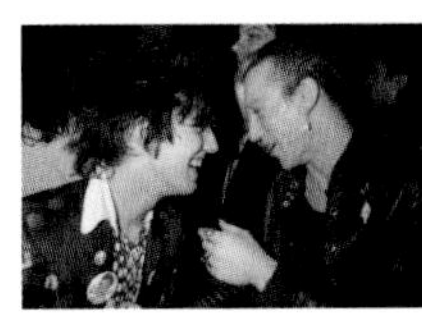

Howie Pyro & Bryan Gregory, New York, 1978

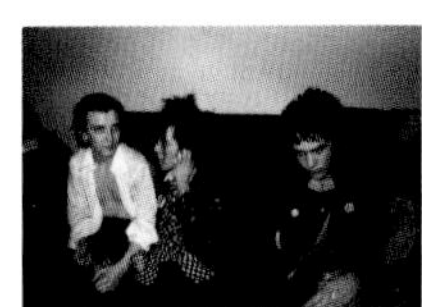

Nick Berlin, Howie Pyro & Rick, New York, 1978

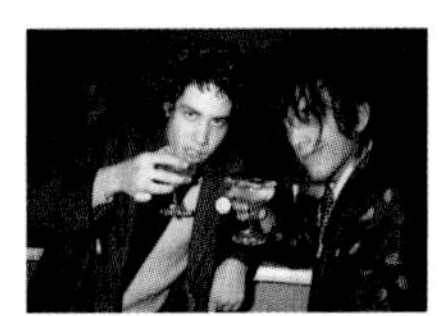

Rick & Howie Pyro, New York, 1978

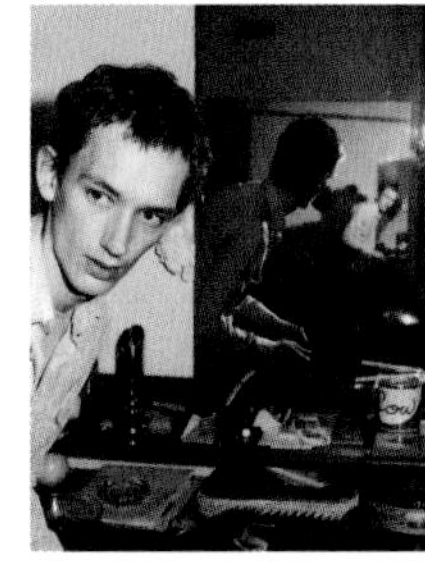

Keith Levene, London, 1981

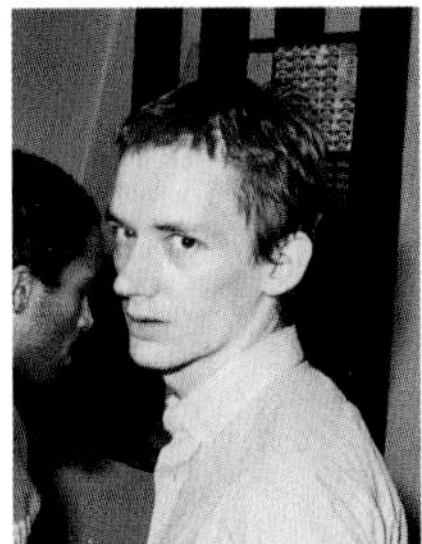

Keith Levene, London, 1981

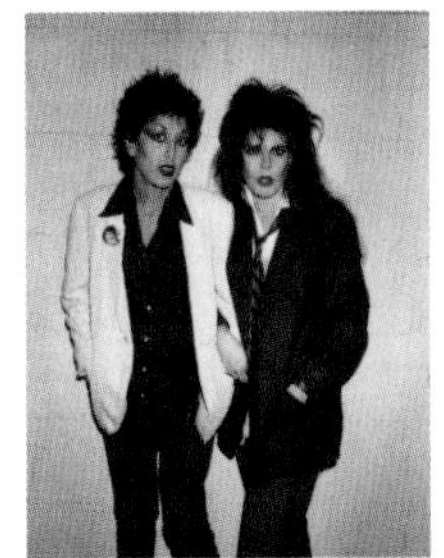

Alice Bag & Patricia Morrison, Los Angeles, 1978

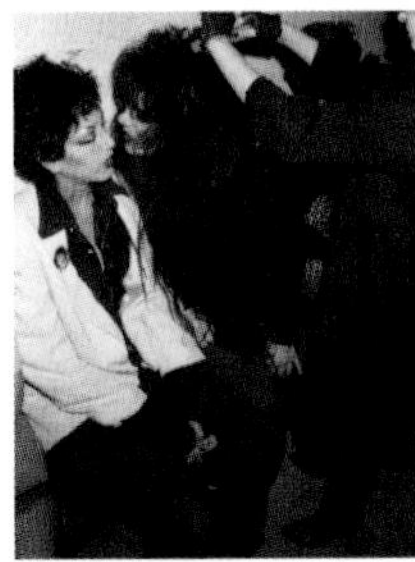

Alice Bag & Patricia Morrison, Los Angeles, 1978

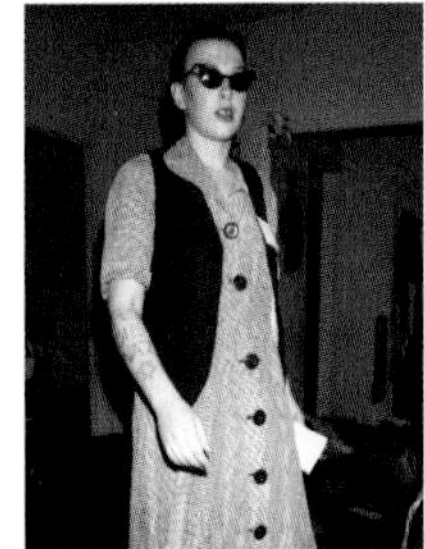

Sheila, Los Angeles, 1978

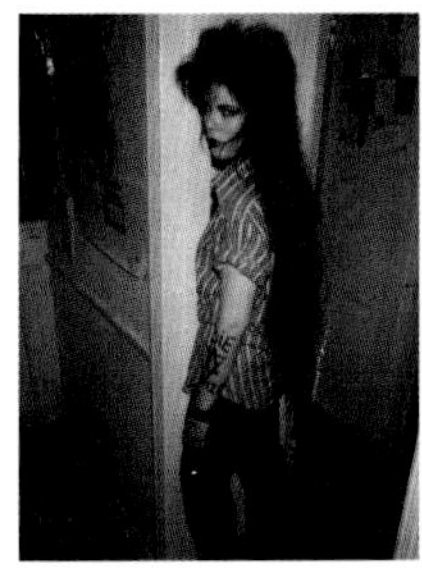

Patricia Morrison, Los Angeles, 1978

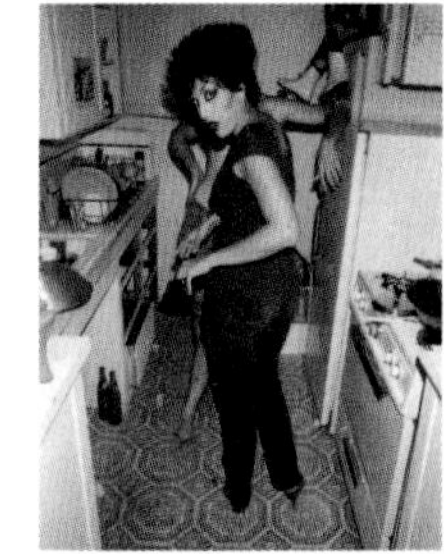

Alice Bag, Los Angeles, 1978

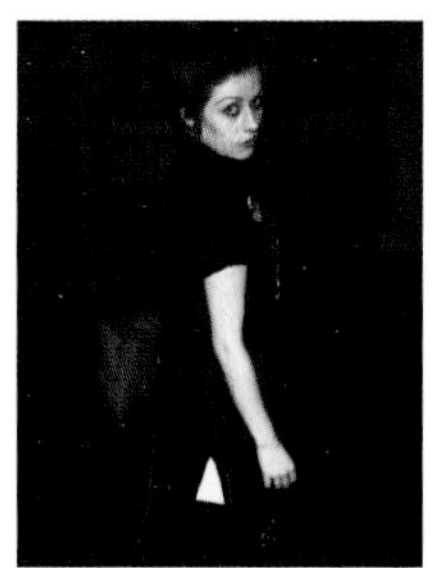

Shannon,
Los Angeles, 1978

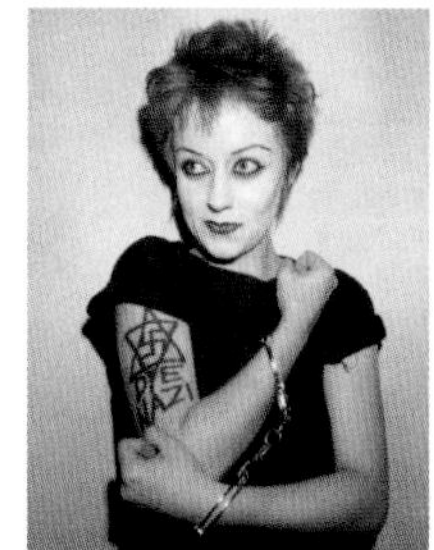

Shannon,
Los Angeles, 1978

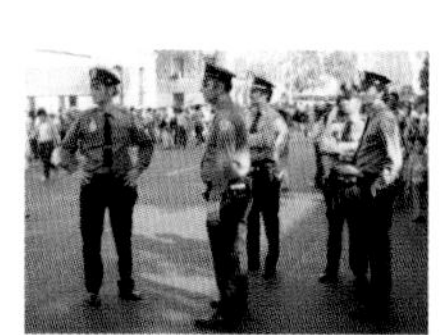

New York, 1978

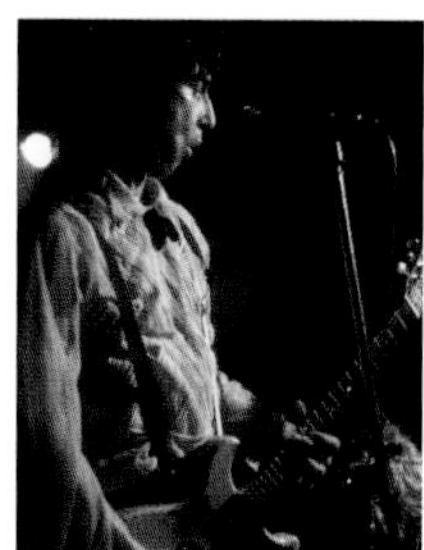

Johnny Thunders,
The Speakeasy,
London, 1977

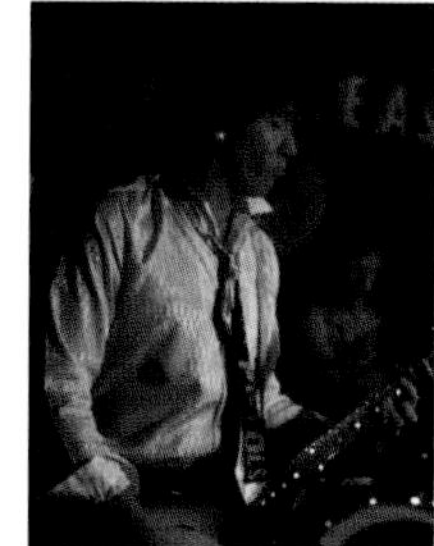

Steve Jones &
Paul Cook,
The Speakeasy,
London, 1977

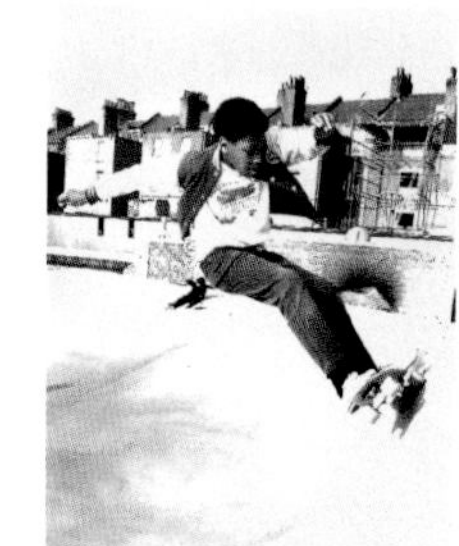

London, 1977

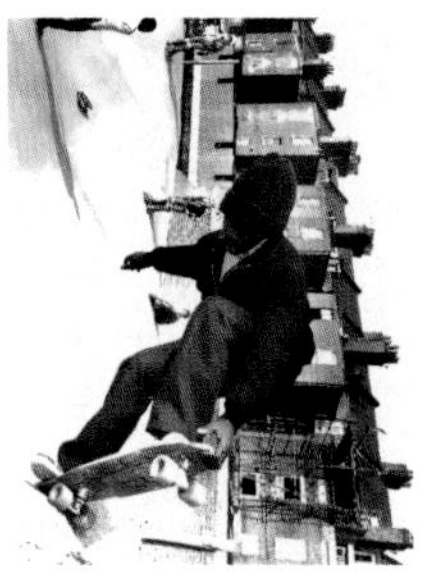

London, 1977

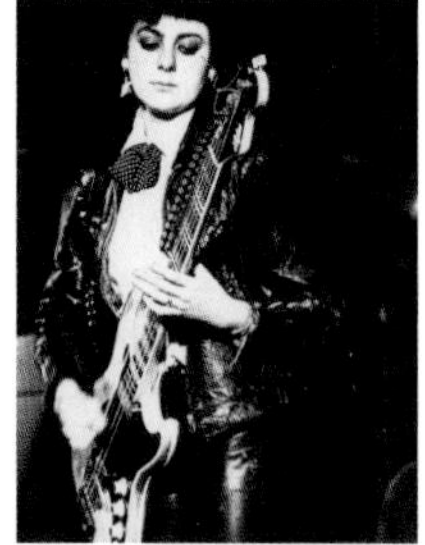

Tessa Pollitt: The
Slits, Acklam Hall,
London, 1978

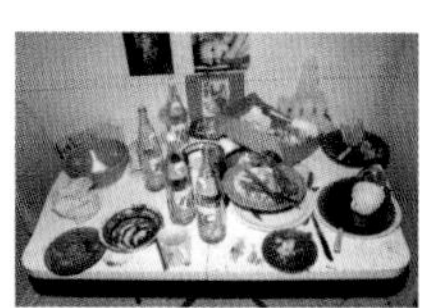

The Canterbury,
Los Angeles, 1978

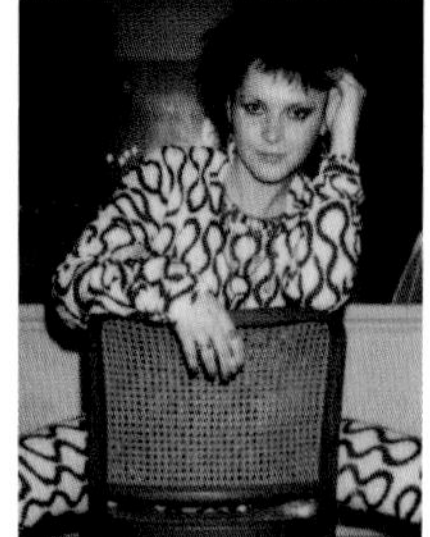

Sue, London, 1980

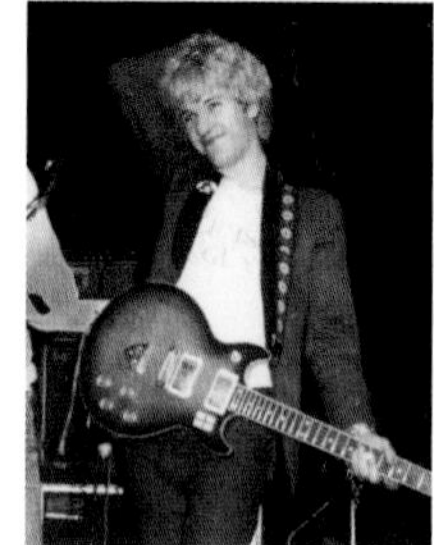

Captain Sensible:
The Damned,
The Roundhouse,
London, 1977

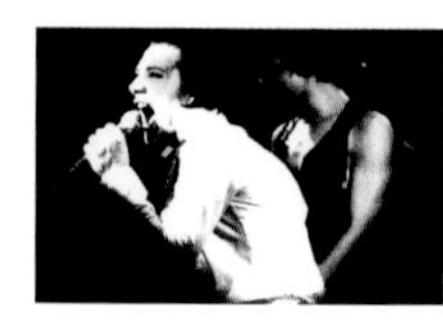

Dave Vanian & Brian
James: The Damned,
The Roundhouse,
London, 1977

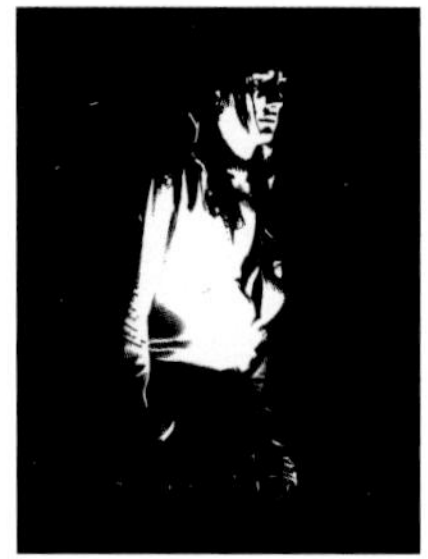

Dave Vanian:
The Damned,
The Roundhouse,
London, 1977

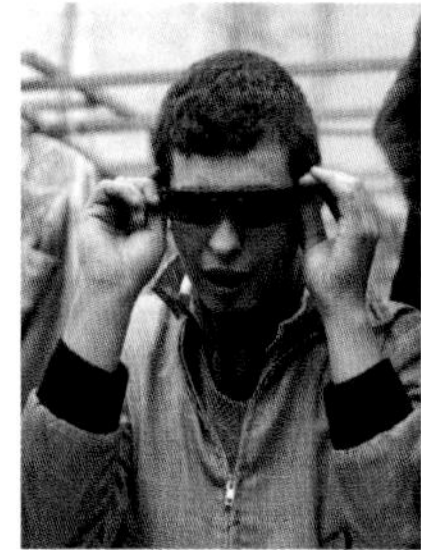

Portobello Road,
London, 1976

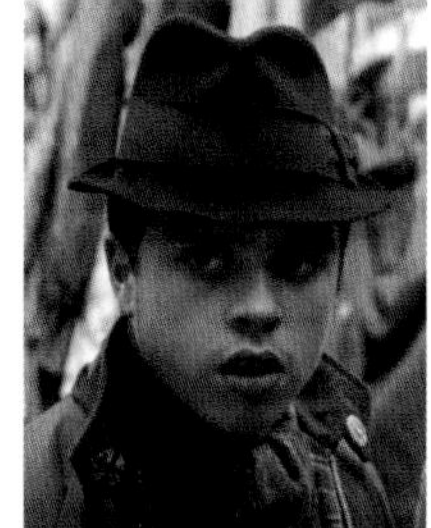

Portobello Road,
London, 1976

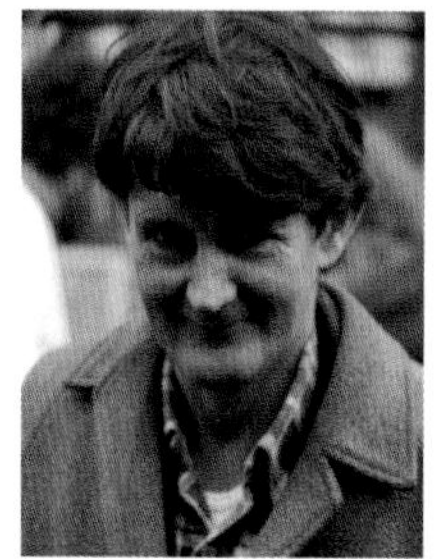

Portobello Road,
London, 1976

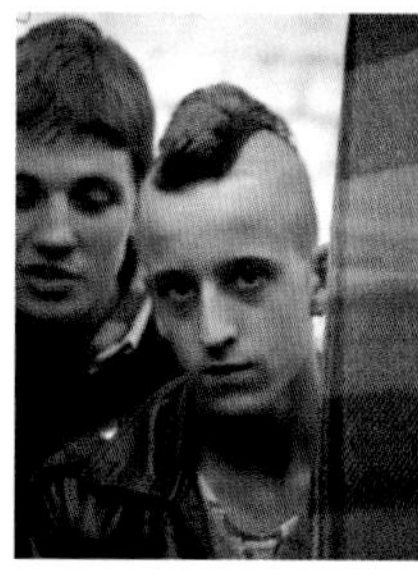

Portobello Road,
London, 1976

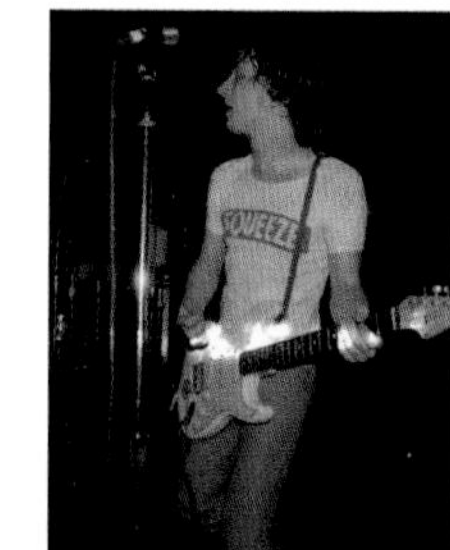

Glenn Tilbrook:
Squeeze,
The Starwood,
Los Angeles, 1978

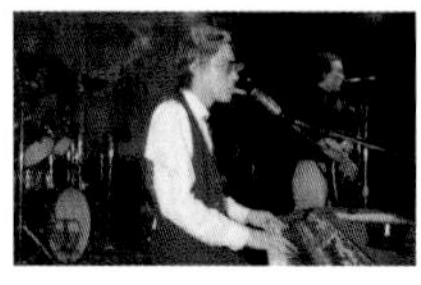

Jules Holland:
Squeeze,
The Starwood,
Los Angeles, 1978

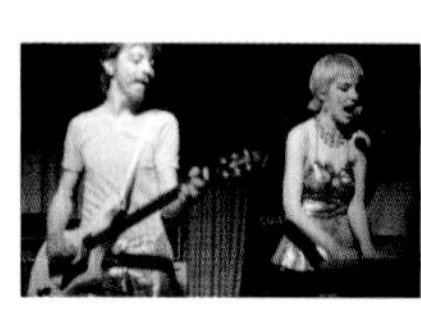

Dave Stewart &
Annie Lennox:
The Tourists,
London, 1976

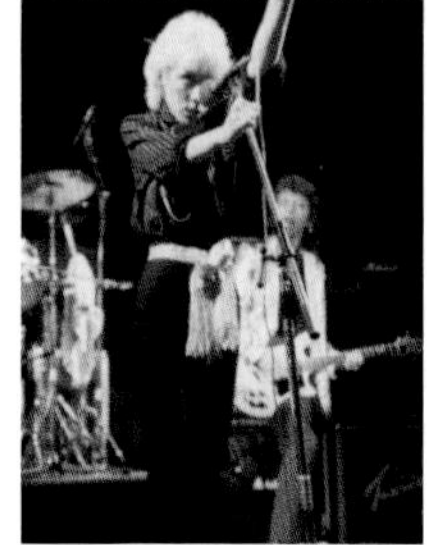

Annie Lennox &
Dave Stewart:
The Tourists,
London, 1977

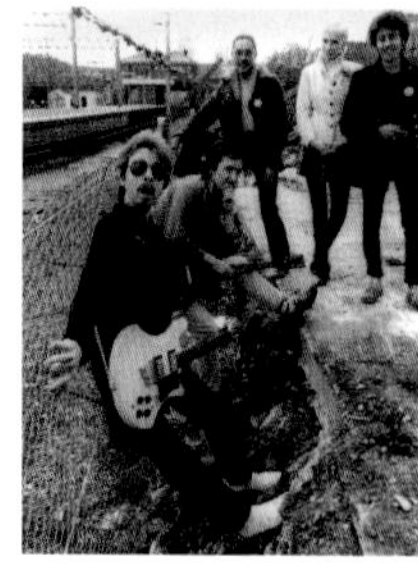

The Tourists, London,
1976

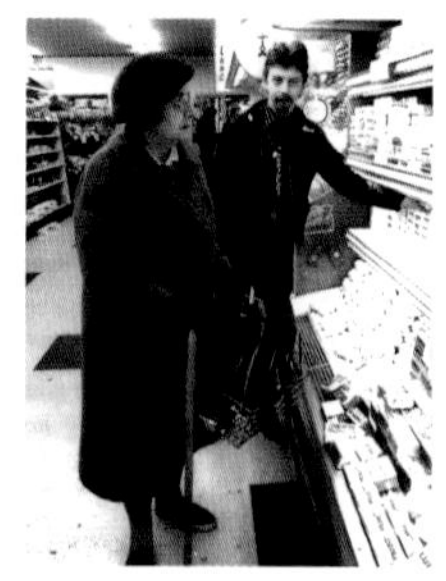

Dave Stewart,
London, 1976

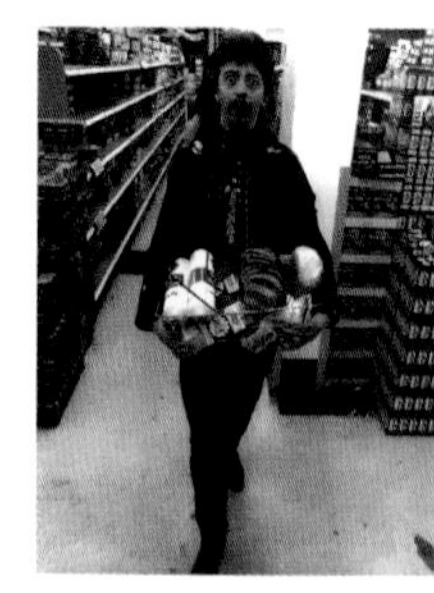

Dave Stewart,
London, 1976

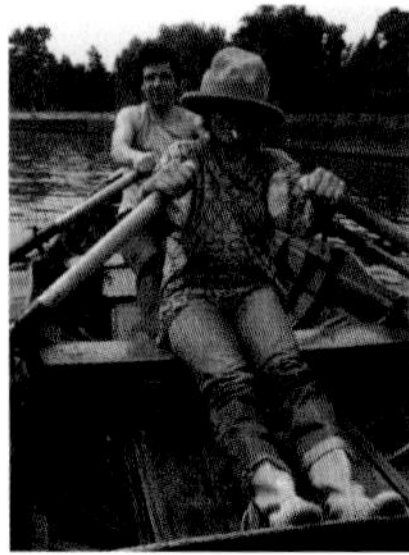

Anita Pallenberg,
London, 1982

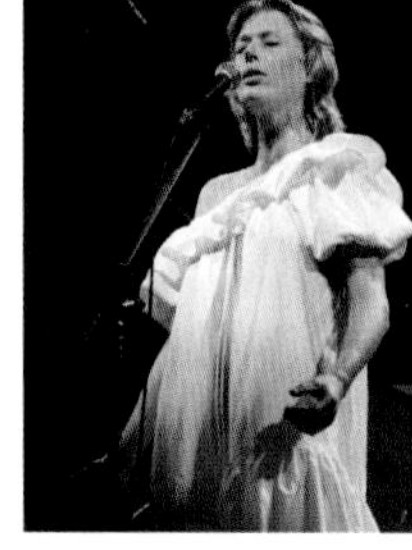

Marianne Faithfull,
L'Olympia, Paris,
1982

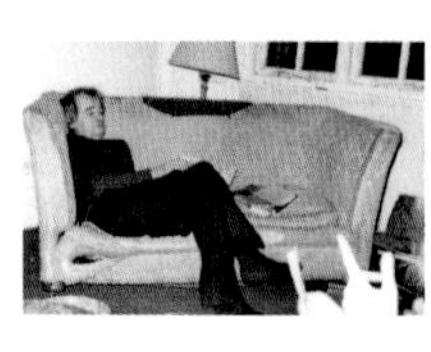

Kit Lambert, London,
1981

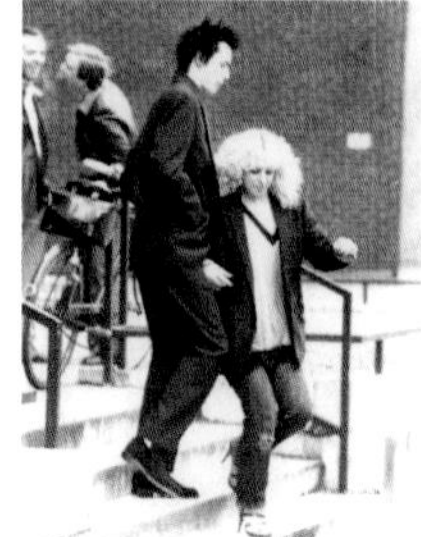

Sid & Nancy,
Marylebone
Magistrate Court,
London, 1977

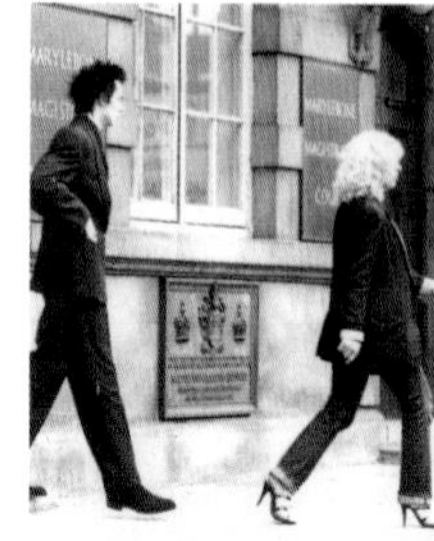

Sid & Nancy,
Marylebone
Magistrate Court,
London, 1977

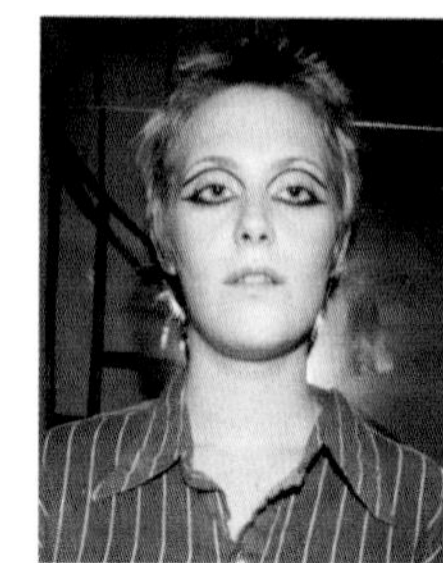

Janek Five: Crayola,
New York, 1978

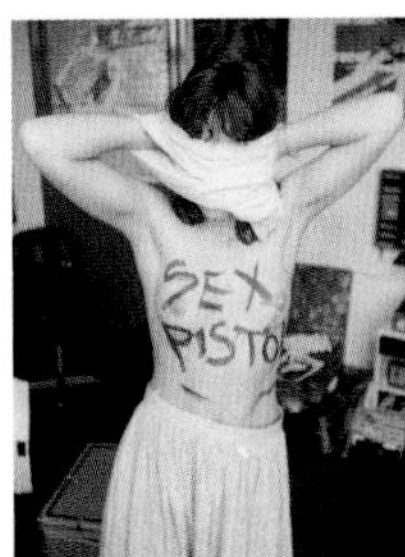

Kate, London, 1976

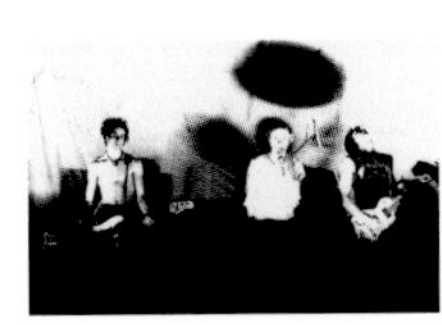

Sex Pistols, Brunel University, London, 1977

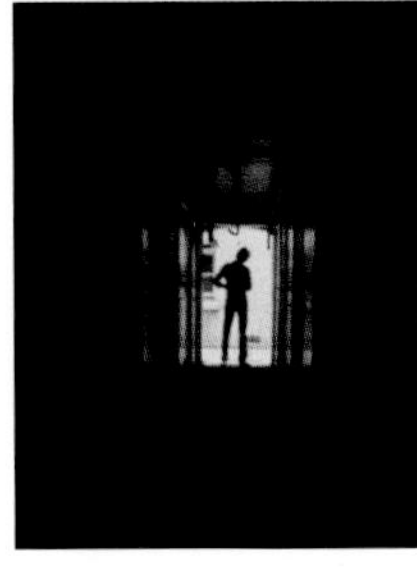

Self-portrait, London, 1976

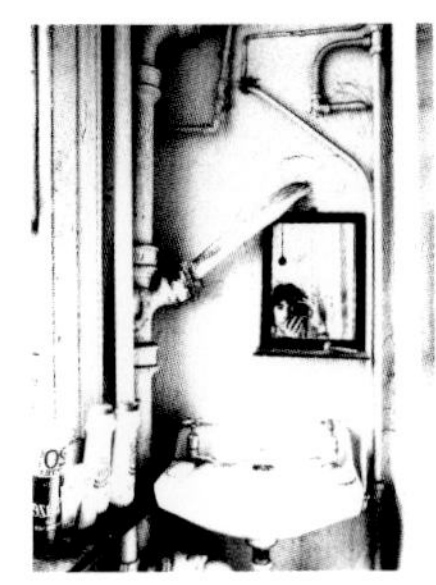

Self-portrait, London, 1976

A special thanks to,

Barry Jones, for many things but especially for coming up with the name, DB
Sammie Purulak
Lila Rogers
Aaron Pierce
Erik Foss, for pushing me to make this a book, rather than a zine.
Sean M. Johnson
Evan Gordon
Taschi Belt
Nar Wiryawan
Max Burkeman
Carlo McCormick
Paul Gorman
Glen Matlock
Patti Palladin
Michael Lorenzini
DJ Bunny Ears
Brie Burkeman
Kid Conga
Patty Powers
Justin Strauss
Alice Bag
Jane Wiedlin
Eileen Polk
Tiggy Burkeman
Kate & Matt Colleran
Nick Petti
Howie Pyro
Fat Tony
Anita Pallenberg
Marianne Faithfull
Keith Levene
Erin O' Brien
The Tourists
Bleecker Bob
Gyda Gash
Rusty Egan
Marilyn Cole
Toby Wynn
Jan Davies
Lisa Wison
My London bastards...
Jules, the bandit
Ash, the dark one
Mikey, the bastard
Most annoying Micky
Father Ben
David, the alien
The K.A.S. kids...
Mitch Brenard
Dave Lyttelton
Sue Knight
Pedro Santos
Dom Saville
Peter Saville
Dawson Wilson

And to all the bands for making the music that got me out of bed,
and for all the new ones that continue to do so.

Words & Photos
DB Burkeman

Design & Editing
Sammie Purulak

Project Management & Editing
Elliott Rogers

Logistics Management
Sean M. Johnson

First Edition

Printed in China

ISBN 978-1-7361562-6-1

Library of Congress Control Number
2023948200

blurringbooks.com